THE THRI
TRICK

edited by
John Murray

*an anthology
of modern
world writing*

PANURGE PUBLISHING
Brampton, Cumbria
1995

THE THREE-ROPE TRICK

first published 1995 by
Panurge Publishing
Crooked Holme Farm Cottage
Brampton, Cumbria CA8 2AT

EDITOR John Murray
ASSISTANT EDITORS   Jessie Anderson
Annie Molloy
PRODUCTION EDITOR Henry Swan
COVER DESIGN Andy Williams
EDITORIAL ASSISTANT Janet Bancroft
Typeset at Union Lane Telecentre, Brampton, Cumbria CA8 1BX
Tel. 016977 - 41014
Printed by Peterson's, 12 Laygate, South Shields, Tyne and Wear NE33 5RP
Tel. 0191-456-3493

ISBN 1 898984 15 8

Copyright this collection Panurge Publishing 1995
Copyright the authors 1995

**All fiction is unsolicited but must be accompanied by
SAE or IRCs or be a disposable photocopy. Work is considered all the year
round, and talented new writers are especially encouraged to submit.**

British Library Cataloguing in Publication Data.
A catalogue record for this book is available from
the British Library.

PANURGE PUBLISHING
Crooked Holme Farm Cottage,
Brampton,
Cumbria CA8 2AT
Tel. 016977-41087

Panurge Publishing gratefully acknowledges the assistance of the
PAUL HAMLYN FOUNDATION
1994-1995

P A N U R G E

Anthology Number 22

MARY MAHER	*A Just Belief*	5
JACK DEBNEY	*My Apprenticeship*	9
JONATHAN STEFFEN	*The Hanging Man*	32
SUSAN DAVIS	*Creative Spirit*	47
T.M. MERREMONT	*The Unexamined Life*	56
JEN WALDO	*The Ultimate Equality*	63
JOHN GOWER	*Home*	78
PETER SLATER	*Fires*	87
DOROTHY SCHWARZ	*Matriarch*	97
FREDERICK LIGHTFOOT	*Funny Things*	105
RICHARD BEARD	*The Three-Rope Trick*	120
PAUL LENEHAN	*Old Flames*	133
ALFRED NADIN	*God, Leonard And The Thin Man*	140
EDWARD E. STONELIGHT	*The Bus*	161
FREEDA FITZGERALD	*No, She* Never *Takes Sugar*	171
RICHARD C. ZIMLER	*The Pleasant Surface of Things*	176
KATHARINE HILL	*A Share For The Domovoi*	186
NICK PEMBERTON	*Truckstop*	194

Publishing Against The Grain

DICK McBRIDE	*Whizzkiddery*	37

First Person

KATHY PAGE	*Success*	155

Photographs

PHILIP WOLMUTH	11, 39, 61, 123, 165
Subscriptions, Back Issues, Quizzes	62, 8, 86, 104
Contributors, Letters, Competition	200, 139, 4

LANCASTER UNIVERSITY NEW SHORT STORY COMPETITION 1995

The Department of Creative Writing at Lancaster University invites entries for our new Short Story Competition. There will be a First Prize of £500, a Second Prize of £200, and a Third Prize of £100. The three winning stories will be published in Panurge, Britain's premier fiction magazine, in October 1995.

The judges will be David Craig, Linda Anderson, and Alan Burns. The finalists will be judged by Janice Galloway, acclaimed author of *The Trick Is To Keep Breathing*, *Blood*, and the recent *Foreign Parts*.

Conditions of Entry
1. Stories must be in English and must not have been previously published or broadcast.
2. There is no limitation on subject-matter or style. Stories must not exceed 5000 words.
3. The author's name should not appear on the manuscript but should be entered along with other details on the entry form below,
4. Each story must be accompanied by an entry fee of £3.00 sterling. Cheques should be made payable to *Lancaster University*.
5. Stories must be typed on one side of sheets of A4 paper.
6. No manuscripts will be returned.
7. No correspondence will be entered into over the decisions of the judges.
8. Copyright of all entries remains with the authors, but the Department reserves the right to publish the three winning stories in *Panurge*.
9. Authors who enclose a S.A.E. with their entries will be notified of the winners.
10. The closing date for receipt of entries is *15 April 1995*. The winners will be announced in July 1995

Entry Form

I enclose £   entrance fee(s) for   entry(ies).

Title(s): _____

Name (CAPITALS) _____

Address (CAPITALS) _____

_____

_____

(POSTCODE) _____

Please send entries to: Administrator, Short Story Competition, Dept. of Creative Writing, Lonsdale College, Lancaster University, LA1 4YN.

Photocopy this form if you don't wish to spoil your copy of Panurge.

Mary Maher
A Just Belief

Graham Watkins had a root in his toe. Under his big toenail. In spring he wove the shoots in and out between his toes and in autumn the shoots grew brittle and died.

At the nursery garden where he worked he was known for his attentiveness and quiet dignity. In winter he wore boots to work and in spring Meg his wife put away his socks and got out his sandals, and the elastoplast and sellotape he sometimes used to anchor the shoots. There were rarely more than two and they were thin and strong.

By the time he knew that it was he, who was different, he was used to it. He was chosen. Was special. And in that knowledge was a grain of humility that grew alongside the root.

Mrs Watkins hadn't been surprised that day when she propped her two year old son on the wooden draining board to give him a lick and a promise with the flannel and saw it for the first time. He was already special coming early at only three pounds. "It's unlikely he'll live Mrs Watkins. Pray but prepare yourself." The midwife had looked round at the jars and jars of flowers and leaves from the wood. And the dust.

The root was safe. Graham wasn't aware of it as he ran around the garden, his feet bare, just like he never noticed when his nose ran or his mouth was sticky with jam. MrsWatkins told the neighbours that every once in a while a child on her side of the family would be blessed and the neighbours were not sure what to think. They gossiped but it was in the days before the war when women used to look up to the skies over their back yards and gardens in case God who knew all the mysteries was listening. And then the planes took over the skies and the neighbours forgot Graham Watkins was special.

At school anyone who called Graham mucky got as good as they gave. He swallowed his cod liver oil, orange juice and milk as though he was drinking for two and he did his drill carefully in the playground and when the swimming pool came after the war Mrs Watkins said her son had a chest complaint. The swimming pool stank she said and it was never hot enough to get undressed like that in England.

Once Mrs Watkins was called up to school by the Welfare and when she was questioned she blessed the Welfare man 'and all your babies, sir.' She put a hand on his arm which made him decide to leave the matter well alone. In his report he said: 'Graham Watkins lives in a condemned cottage and is a strong and healthy boy which in the circumstances is a miracle.' No mention of the root in the boy's toe. The following month the Welfare man's wife fell pregnant and now that it was after the war he looked up to the sky for reassurance many times during the following nine months. When his daughter was born and she was beautiful the Welfare man took to prayer and lay preaching.

Meanwhile girls had begun to hum around Graham. He'd let it be known he had extra powers. He was big and swarthy with the best smile in the district. He soon settled for Meg because he could see she believed in him. She loved miracles and read all the books on them: Lourdes, relics, that sort of thing and she was sensible. Didn't believe in baths. All that soaking sapped away your strength unless it was immersion for the Lord of course. And she called him Graham in that same slow way like his mum. The two women loved one another and in spring he would bring them flowers for their yards from the nursery: lobelia, lupins, pansies, geraniums. One thing Meg wanted to say to Graham, she never got round to saying. She was too embarrassed. She wanted to wash his feet, gently with a bowl like Mary and the Lord. But she was too embarrassed and although the thought simmered near the surface of her life she never got round to saying it in all their married days. When each of their babies was born she and her mother-in-law looked at the babies' toes. They found no roots. "Sometimes it misses a generation," said Mrs Watkins. "Or two," she added when she couldn't quite recall the last person in her family to be born with the root.

The children grew up and away. They passed exams, wanted bathrooms and proper kitchens as well as flowers and woods in their lives. They loved their parents but found it easier from the distance of another county. "It was the exams," said Meg. She was proud but she missed them and grew closer to her mother-in-law. They grew to look like sisters and would shop together and stop for tea and doughnuts because their bags were heavy with potatoes, carrots, parsnips, swedes and meat. They liked to cook proper meals and the three of them were now quite strapping and trips out in Graham's van were bouncy affairs. When his mother died the outings in his van became more stately. Visits to the churchyard to tend her gave. The most beautiful for miles around guarded by a white marble angel.

A Just Belief

'Of course it's what you'd expect, him working down at the nursery,' people said. Meg missed her badly and took up books again, on faith healing and tales of the stigmata. She stared at the palms of her hands and wondered what it would be like to see them bleeding. Graham was understanding but said these things were rare and to divert her brought home postcards with flowers on them from the nursery. "Send them to the grandchildren," he said, "you're good at writing." And their children started to visit more often with their young families. It was grubbing round in the garden they liked and the peace and memories which came to them in the new deckchairs Graham had bought. Meg never asked about the new babies' toes. Not since that awful day of shouting and Graham shied away from discussions about the root. He believed he was different. In fact he didn't like it being made into a family concern.

When he retired he made a friend. They used to share a beer or two down at the pub. An educated man. A doctor, a therapist who liked Graham to talk. To talk about anything. He always sought him out in the pub and gradually got Graham to trust him enough to talk about the root. Graham could see a fond respect, an awe in the therapist's eyes. And he was puzzled because he himself could hardly read or write and he'd never met anyone who believed in him like his mother and Meg did. Not from the outside world as he called it. And yet he could see the therapist was happy and relaxed when they were talking together.

Once the therapist told a conference, "This man," (and he gave Graham a false name) "has such marvellous self-esteem because of a root in his toe. The sort of self-esteem clients come to me to help them restore."

Graham would have been amazed to hear him.

When Graham collapsed and they took him to hospital Meg panicked. Looking and nodding at his toe poking out beneath the short blanket and coverlet, she said to the nurses, "He's been blessed. And it must not be touched."

The two nurses attending to his admittance looked at the state of his toe and back at Meg with patient incredulity.

"And there's a curse with it." Meg was desperate and glad Graham was sleeping at the time.

The nurses withdrew into sister's office and shut the door and Meg went home and took down her books on the stigmata again. It was like a revelation. She could see now. She went back and told the doctor and the nurses, "It's a stigmata. It's a relic, a root from the same tree which grew the cross of Calvary." The doctor who had diagnosed Graham's condition told his busy staff, who were already in awe of Graham's inner strength, to comply and let the matter rest. "No one can be sure of anything these days." Meg relaxed and when Graham died she felt empowered to tell the undertaker the same thing. And then she remembered her old wish and asked to help wash and lay Graham out.

When the shoot broke through the burial mound the following spring Meg could hardly contain her pumping heart. It was greater than that first time in the grass with Graham. Greater than the births of her children. The shoot was strong and brilliant green. In three years it grew to the height of the headstone and its branches and leaves were like an umbrella or a parasol over the stone and jars of flowers Meg brought. Sometimes a grandchild would come and sit with her in its shade.

BACK ISSUES AT ROCK BOTTOM PRICES
Some of the Best New Fiction of the Last Eleven Years.

Panurge 2 - Christopher Burns, Michael Schmidt. Sixteen stories. £1	**Panurge 13** - Aisling Maguire, James Waddington. Eleven stories. £1.
Panurge 6 - David Holden, Dacia Maraini. Twelve stories. £1	**Panurge 15/16** -Twenty two stories! Dilys Rose, Michael Wilding. £1.50
Panurge 8 - David Holden, Serpent's Tail. Eleven stories. £1	**Panurge 20** - A great tenth birthday double issue. 17 stories plus Tale of Two Cities winners R.C. Zimler and Mairead Irish. Still selling full price £5.99.
Panurge 9 - Norah Hill, William Palmer. Ten stories. £1	
Panurge 10 - Kathy Page, Jonathan Treitel. Fourteen stories. £1	
Panurge 11 - Iftekhar Sayeed, John Rizkalla. Eleven stories. £1	**Panurge 21** - Nineteen stories plus Julia Darling and John Cunningham still selling full price at £5.99
Panurge 12 - Geraldeen Fitzgerald, William Bedford. Nine stories. £1	

(N.B. Panurges 1, 3, 4, 5, 7, 14, 17,18, 19 all out of print. All prices include postage. Cheques to Panurge, Crooked Holme Farm Cottage, Brampton, Cumbria UK. CA8 2AT. Overseas add £1 per book.
SPECIAL OFFER! All available back issues for only £20 incl. postage.

Jack Debney

My Apprenticeship

It was Marshall who showed me how the island looked like a theta, with its oval shape and the bar of mountains across the middle. As though consolidating the lesson, he paused on the signature he was writing at the foot of a business letter and then carefully drew a horizontal line through the O of Oliver.

"See?"

Imagine the route from Cyprus to Tobruk and then that from Crete to Alexandria; you'd find Efestia somewhere about the intersection. The country has an area of 1,472 square miles and a population of just over 300,000. Everybody's been there in their time - Greeks, Romans, Arabs, Crusaders, Turks, British - and that racial mix has done wonders for the genetic inheritance. Most of the population is concentrated in Balyabole, the capital and only real city, in the south-east corner of the island: "Looking towards Africa but forever dreaming of Europe," as my employer put it.

Of course he'd caught me drafting a poem the first week I was there, but he only nodded with heavy sagacity as though he'd been along that way too in his time.

"Young writers in England now," he pronounced, "make their parents the dominant cause of woe. In my day we were more generous. History, economics, Hitler, Stalin, they all took the brunt of it. Now, it seems, we're put in the world so that our children can judge us! No doubt you were writing balefully about your mother and father."

But when I told him I was writing most unbalefully about my girlfriend, he just let his open palm glide towards me as though he'd set the whole thing up for the pay-off line and was congratulating me for coming in on cue.

*

Cornflake City, skyscrapers and suburbs divided by the particular brand name. There was a run on such items in Efestia that year. In the great warehouse I watched the sweeper hanging over his broom, mesmerized by these stacks. The storeman, too apprehensive of rebuke to marvel at anything, scurried out of his glass cubicle at our approach, a sallow man in a spotlessly white overall. It was then it really came home to me that, through the grace of Oliver Marshall, I now belonged to the boss class.

After checking consignments and deliveries with the storeman,

Marshall guided me across the wide floor of the warehouse. He pointed to a row of freezers along one wall. "Haven't done much in perishables yet though. I'm not sure about the market there, Mac."

Inevitably, I was Mac. My grandfather was Scottish, but I'd never really known him as he'd died when I was small. At the age of eleven I'd had a brief flurry of interest in clans and tartans; little had stuck with me about our lot, the MacFarlanes, except that they claimed the moon as their particular lantern. Something got to me in that absurd, over-reaching boast.

But otherwise Caledonian romanticism was remote from my Midlands upbringing. And then there was the University of Lancaster where I became friendly with a research student from Efestia called Stavros Butters, whose family knew Oliver Marshall, Import and Export, 10 Aboukir Street, Balyabole. One day I mentioned to Stavros that I wanted to work abroad for a couple of years after getting my degree, widen my horizons - that sort of thing - before settling down to some sort of profession. And so here I was as Marshall's assistant, my medical over and pronounced satisfactory, an Efestian residence permit freshly stamped into my passport.

*

"I helped to liberate this island from the Germans in '43 and, after the war, I came back to help liberate it - much less bloodily, may I add - from my fellow-countrymen, as they still were then. Sometimes I wonder what it all signifies. Most of the E.N.P. leadership is of part-British descent, you know, but when we were struggling for freedom, what-have-you, that was kept under wraps. Now, twenty years later, it's a different story. Time to dust off the fair-skinned forbears, prink them up for show."

In Marshall's office the fan fluttered the papers on his desk beneath their marble weights and the Venetian blinds were drawn almost vertically against the sun. Marshall levered himself up from his chair and went to the cupboard where he kept bottles and glasses. I watched him pouring out generous measures for us both. He was a stocky man, on the edge of stoutness, with a high complexion and a shock of grey-black hair.

"Take the President, for example. The family name on his birth certificate is Sewter, not Sotiris. He re-identified himself just before the Occupation and the subsequent emergence of the Resistance. Timely, wasn't it? - especially as Sotiris means 'saviour' in Efestian."

"But he can't really change his name back to Sewter now, can

Harrow School *Philip Wolmuth*

he?"

"No one would expect him to do that. But recently he paid an English genealogist a small fortune to research his obscure Northumbrian ancestors. After he got the results, he commissioned a local painter, best known previously for producing icons of instant antiquity, to provide him with a series of 'genuine' ancestral portraits. They adorn the walls of the main reception room at the presidential palace and, in their way, they're very good."

"But how did they know what the Northumbrian ancestors looked like?"

"They didn't. But the artist endowed each one of those solid yeomen with something of our good Dr. Sotiris's face, the nose here, the mouth there. It's that backward sweep of the imagination, Mac, where poetry trounces history. My dear young man - what's the matter? You look as though you've just discovered that you've come to a very strange place."

*

Shortly after this, I was given my first real task, which was to accompany the driver of a van loaded with the precious cornflakes up the east coast of the island to a village called Ag'Ioannou. There I was to present the cargo and the invoice, and make sure I got the proper signature and the official chit guaranteeing payment.

"Be thoroughly English, fresh out from the old country. Civil - but if absolutely necessary introduce a strain of controlled hauteur."

I promised to do my best, but said that they didn't teach you much about hauteur where I came from, controlled or otherwise.

On arrival at Ag'Ioannou I duly met the officer in charge, heavily armed and in battle kit as though about to go up to a front I certainly knew nothing about. He wore a flash of gold-white-green, the national colours, across his cap and, beneath the dark glasses, his long fine nose led like a pointer to thin lips laid like one blade edge over another. This forbidding appearance increased the apprehensions Marshall had awoken but, in the event, the officer turned out to be perfectly friendly, asking rather wistful questions about England as we supervised the loading of the cornflakes onto the motor launch in the small harbour.

About a third of a mile offshore there was an islet called Little Patmos, which was the destination of the goods I'd brought. A local legend proclaimed this to be the real Patmos where St. John had written the Book of Revelation but, somewhere during my brief time

My Apprenticeship

on Efestia, I'd also heard the place mentioned in hushed, evasive tones. In my mind now I had the vague idea that Little Patmos was one of the Efestian National Party training centres, held in ambiguous respect, of which there were several dotted about the country.

Everything went smoothly with the transaction. Not a single hitch. I told Marshall this, rather pointedly, when I got back to Aboukir Street.

He smiled, nodding approval, and then his pale blue eyes gave me that over-sustained, candid look which I was beginning to recognize as something to beware of.

He suggested that we get a bite to eat at a restaurant nearby. Once we were settled there, he raised his glass to me.

"Well done, Mac."

"Thank you."

"Actually," Marshall said, when we'd finished our meal, "it's a first for the firm generally. We've never been asked to supply anything to Little Patmos before. A new heaven and a new earth!" Once he had registered my smile, he caught my eyes in his again. "I'm afraid this is part of Efestian life too."

"What do you mean?"

"Little Patmos is where people are sent when Dr. Sotiris deems them to be too naughty. You delivered cornflakes to a concentration camp today." He adopted a mask of mock-pensiveness. "Shouldn't think the inmates will get any though, would you?"

*

Six months later there was a clumsy attempt at a coup which was severely suppressed. Some of the plotters fled, some were executed, but the greater number found themselves bundled off to Little Patmos, whose 'facilities' were considerably expanded.

Our business with the place expanded too. Marshall, worried he'd hurt my feelings after that first time and yet strangely excited at having corrupted me in such a sly manner, took over the Little Patmos run himself for a few weeks. And then I discovered that my indignation had receded and I insisted on getting the job back. It helped to be a long way from England, I think - moral strictures were looser for me here. Besides, I wanted to prove something to Marshall: that the initiated not only survived the rite but rose above it.

Occasionally, though, my finer feelings did play up, especially if an incident occurred which personally affected me. When a friend of mine was arrested and sent to Little Patmos, I found it very hard to take the van up to Ag'Ioannou.

Later that evening, round at Marshall's, drinking the same expensive whisky that we were now supplying the interrogators and torturers at the camp with, I had an outburst. At the end of it I shouted: "How *can* you feel loyalty to such a place?"

Almost immediately I regretted my words. It was easy enough for me - I could pack my conscience on a plane tomorrow. But Marshall had been more than a quarter of a century on the island; he had changed nationality and faithfully served the E.N.P.

He began to pace up and down now, an anguished expression on his face. Then he sat down again and leaned towards me, as though worried we might be overheard. At his best Marshall was sensitive to atmospheres and clever with them - when he chose, a skilled smoother of ruffled feathers.

"Look here, Mac," he said. "I want to tell you a few things. But in strictest confidence, right?"

He informed me that he'd got to know one of the senior officers on Little Patmos, an honourable man who'd been reluctantly seconded to his jailer's post and who was appalled at what was happening. He was feeding Marshall with information about the prisoners and the treatment they were being subjected to. Marshall would pass the name of my friend on to him; we might hope for some easing-up on the worst excesses, nothing more in present conditions. Additionally, Marshall was fortunate in having gained the ear of one of the Vice-Presidents, whom he'd be meeting again shortly. He'd have to tread carefully, but ...

It seemed to go on for hours, this insistent whisper of reassurance, the seductive allure of practicalities. I had no way of knowing whether my curious mentor was telling the truth, yet when the evening ended I was still his henchman, still his accomplice in supplying the security thugs at Little Patmos with the best whiskies. There was a difference though. I was now also his accomplice in humanity; I would help him in this principled subterfuge as best I could. It was only later that Angelo's line from *Measure for Measure* rang through my head: "The tempter or the tempted, who sins most?"

*

Oliver Marshall lived on the western slopes of the city, in an outer suburb called Perivoli. The house was large; it had been built in the

My Apprenticeship

Twenties by a prospering White Russian and was called the Villa Dmitri. But after the collapse of his second marriage, Marshall had come to dread the spaces left by departing wife, children and servants and had moved up to the top floor, converting the lower two floors into flats which he rented out. Apart from the study Marshall's own flat was quite small, but it had a marvellous terrace that seemed as big as a tennis court when you first stepped onto it.

In the study there were books in their thousands, including a whole section, from ceiling to carpet, on things Efestian. If I hadn't heard Marshall reminisce so often, I might have thought he'd read his way into his adopted country.

One area, however, had been left free of books. Here, instead, were pictures of his family or, rather, both his families: two wives, two sets of children, everybody smiling and jolly. Painful estrangements didn't seem possible in the kind of world their images presented. I wondered about all that - to no avail, as Marshall had placed both marriages under conversational taboo.

Marshall was not completely alone at the Villa Dmitri. His servant-cum-cook, an Egyptian called Abdel Latif, lived in. This formidable person surveyed his employer with somewhat cynical affection, providing a regular commentary on issues both domestic and national in ripe soldier's English. Marshall had first come across Abdel Latif in the army in Alexandria during the war. The servant, dressed in a gallabeya with a red sash binding in his princely belly, occupied a little room next to the entrance of the flat. Once admitted, I passed down a short dark corridor towards the thick curtain drawn over the study doorway at the other end. It was like being blinded and then propelled along a tube, as neither Abdel Latif nor his master ever saw the need for a hall light.

Often when I was round there, Marshall would talk to me as though I were writing his biography. We covered his idyllic early childhood in Suffolk, followed by schooling at Christ's Hospital, then Cambridge, the war, Alexandria and Cairo and the exiled Efestians he'd got to know, missions to the island to help the Resistance, Liberation and, finally, his part - inadequately acknowledged - in the apotheosis of Dr. Sotiris.

What I didn't care for so much was the late, well-oiled stage of the evening when Marshall would feel the need to expatiate about England. He'd indulge in the smug gloom that only a wealthy transplanted Englishman could afford, although I scented guilt there

Jack Debney

too, the need to justify what might be seen as desertion.

For Marshall, decay hung over the mother country like a pall. Everything was cheapened and dehumanised; society was bereft of the regenerative impulse that had saved it so many times before. He gave me many examples, drawn from various trips back to England over the years, now all shaken up in the same bowl so that it seemed as though disaster had followed disaster on the same appalling journey.

I quickly realised that whatever I said in attempted protest or amelioration simply provided fuel for the flames, so I learned to shut up during such moods and just listened wearily to Marshall beating this crippled, modern England with the pure staff of the one he'd known of old: part Constable landscape, part radical but eminently civilized 1930s Cambridge, part Dunkirk spirit and, in its most distortedly partisan and truest sense, wholly myth.

*

I was standing at the seaward end of Hephaestion Square, watching a gulli-gulli man go through his paces. Instead of a pea or a shell he used a live chick which made his sleight-of-hand seem even more skilful. I never betted but the game rarely lacked a dupe, led on by the fake wins of the gulli-gulli man's assistant in the crowd. The dupe too would be allowed his wins but only small ones and only until the stakes were raised. Then the losing would begin and it was not the least part of the show to see the recklessness with which those who were truly hooked would bet, in an increasingly frantic attempt to recoup their money.

I felt a hand on my sleeve. Turning impatiently, I saw Abdel Latif.

"Ah, there you are, Mr. MacFarlane."

"What is it?"

"Mr. Marshall. He's in a bad way tonight."

"Gulli-gulli, one two three!" chanted the magician as he moved the big inverted metal cups at lightning speed. The customer considered, put down his money, made his choice. The magician lifted the selected cup to reveal emptiness and then upended its neighbour. There stood the docile chick, shivering a little in the breeze from the sea.

"But I have to see my family. And the wife's fucking poorly."

Abdel Latif's family lived in Goro Arabei behind the docks and he visited once a week, leaving Marshall's in the evening and staying overnight to return to the Villa Dmitri at breakfast time the next day.

My Apprenticeship

It was an arrangement of many years standing, a kind of mid-week sabbath. Now it seemed that Marshall couldn't be left alone and I was expected to fill the breach. This was also part of a young man's education.

"All right. I'll go up and see what I can do."

Abdel Latif gave me a broad smile and then, with an alacrity unusual in such a bulky man, disappeared into the crowd thronging the square.

I took a taxi to the Villa Dmitri and ran up the stairs to Marshall's flat. I rang the bell, but got no response. Then I tried the door. It was unlocked. Entering, I could see a glimmer of light at the end of the hall where a corner of the thick heavy curtain had rucked back a little. I called out Marshall's name and announced my own.

The first thing I saw in the study was Marshall himself slumped over the desk, an empty araq bottle beside him. The room stank with the cloying aniseed smell. The desk-top itself was in compelling disarray. Among some finely-bound but tumbled volumes of Henry James there was a pistol and an abundance of ammunition. Bullets studded open pages, lined the crevices between the finely-wrought tales of sensibility, even hid showily amongst pens and stationery. I doubted whether all this had been on display before Abdel Latif left to search for me but, remembering his curious smile, I couldn't even be sure of that.

I shook Marshall roughly by the shoulder. There was something about that blotted-out face and the pistol next to it that frightened me. It was too close a rehearsal for death.

When he surfaced, it was with a great shuddering and shaking, a bleary shock at seeing me there. I might have been an E.N.P. security man come to arrest him rather than his provincial English apprentice, and it set me to wondering whether that was what it was all about, this downward rush, the descent into punitive toping - some political dread. But it might just as well have been a private matter. And as for the gun, I had no way of knowing whether Marshall had been planning murder, suicide or just to drive a series of holes through the tortuous prose of *The Ambassadors*.

To begin with - the little restorative tasks, the easy ones: putting on a cup of strong coffee, bringing him his blood pressure tablets, promising him a couple of pick-me-up beers later. It was true - I was tonight's Abdel Latif. Marshall accepted my presence without query, as though it were simply my shift.

Then I commandeered the bullets, putting them meticulously into a paper bag like sweets. To remove the gun from Marshall's possession was a more difficult task. He arrested my hand in mid-air.

"Leave her with me, Mac. A Tokarev. Quite rare around here. She's a good little thing."

"Then it's only fair to give her a rest, Oliver."

Eventually, grudgingly, he was persuaded and, like a household vigilante, I toted the pistol into the kitchen when I went to fetch the second pot of coffee. There, as a present for Abdel Latif, I stuck the damn thing into the fridge amongst the lettuces and tomatoes, barrel facing outwards, an ambush in the salad.

I suggested to Marshall that we go out onto the terrace. I pulled up two chairs and we sat there gazing out over the city, the way it rose from the bay to the presidential palace and from there up to the illuminated ruins of the old Turkish fortress, the Yedi Kula. This panorama of Balyabole, by day or night, rarely failed to enthral me. I would never have said so, but I thought it the most beautiful sight I'd ever seen.

Marshall got the cold sweats and I brought him out a thick cardigan. His hands were shaking but not too badly. Slowly, his voice regained something of its clarity and decisiveness yet, for the first time in our relationship, he left most of the talking to me, and I realised it didn't matter what I came up with as long as it soothed him. I told him stories about my upbringing in Leicester, amazed that all that dreary business could produce so much narrative.

We were still on the terrace when the muezzin's first call of the day rose up from the big mosque on the edge of Goro Arabei. In the new-morning air it seemed fuller than ever of a sweet, elusive yearning. I asked Marshall if he understood what the muezzin was saying. He nodded, but I didn't ask him to translate because I thought that, however good the words, they would fail the music somehow.

Not long afterwards, I judged it safe to give Marshall his beer. I'd have one or two myself whilst waiting for Abdel Latif to turn up to relieve me.

*

Balyabole in my experience was always a city of wild rumours - jewelled fabrications, arrant fantasies peddled as truth - but somewhere history was showing its real face if one was sharp enough to spot it.

My Apprenticeship

There was a definite increase in public nervousness from the time of the Yom Kippur war onwards. Some people worried about that conflict as if it were happening just beyond the next hill rather than a couple of hundred miles away overseas. Others cast nervous or anticipatory eyes towards Damascus and Beirut, and there were calls from the more right-wing Christians in the E.N.P. for an alliance with the Lebanese Phalangists.

But, naturally, it was in domestic issues where anxiety was uppermost. By the following winter, 1974, the whole city, from sedate Kastali immediately below the palace to down-at-heel Ras Dragouti on the tip of the western arm of the bay, was alive with talk of plots and counter-plots, prophecies of the definitive coup which was always imminent and yet always, like the end of the world, mysteriously receding.

Cold, damp, blustery days, but to me oddly appealing and resonant. I sat in the cafes around Hephaestion Square, watching people talk to each other like excited ventriloquists, holding their mouths in strained smiles (spies and informers everywhere, it was said) whilst they swapped the latest political gossip. The official media remained determinedly bland and evasive.

By now I had a wide acquaintanceship in Balyabole but through Marshall I was also introduced to some of its luminaries, amongst whom were numbered Colonel Gordon Smalley of the Ethniki Filaki, the National Guard, Athanasios Smith-Tsaouissi, the ex-Minister for Religious Affairs, and Leon Burvis, a director of the Hamadan Publishing House and author of the official schools' biography of Dr. Sotiris. Mostly they met at the Villa Dmitri where Marshall seemed intent on chairmanning a kind of Efestian political brains trust. These distinguished figures went out of their way to be kind to me, only gently patronising in their efforts at correction when it was thought I'd erred in Efestian matters. Normally, of course, I took a back seat when the discussion got under way, just putting in the odd comment or respectful question here and there as every tyro should. But, discreetly, I was soaking everything up in my excellent sponge of a memory.

Marshall's wise men were firm Establishment figures and had no thought of turning against their party. The corruptions, the erosion of freedoms, must be reversed through subtle adjustments to the system, so that one day Dr. Sotiris would wake up and find it impossible not to be a democrat. Regeneration of the E.N.P. meant regeneration of the country.

They seemed wilfully ignorant of the growing strength of the clandestine political groupings - illegitimate relatives they haughtily refused to acknowledge - but, even so, I noticed that it was one of their chief pleasures at these gatherings to listen to the tidbits Oliver brought them. They could allow themselves that naughtiness occasionally. Their esteemed friend Marshall was also their political pimp.

At such moments I got to wondering how far he was hedging his bets. Was he simply an opportunist after all? In favour of his integrity, I had clear evidence that he had managed in his oblique way to help various prisoners on Little Patmos; also there was the report he and others had compiled and sent to Amnesty International and, anonymously, to various relevant embassies. Yet still I wasn't sure and that nagged at me, as though I were in danger of losing a faith I didn't even admit to.

When the sessions in Marshall's study were over and we were preparing to leave, the notabilities would warn me like slightly skittish uncles against the risk of surveillance. Pausing at the entrance of the house, one of them would be sure to say in a tone of mock-bravado: "Gentlemen, at this very moment we are being watched!" And we would laugh with merriment which was just a little strained, like late leavers from a party, but certainly my island uncles were right. We were being watched - and followed - though I could never make up my mind whether it was by E.N.P. security people or by plainclothes guards that Colonel Smalley had prudently brought along to protect us.

After the first few meetings I had no fears about the shadowy figure in my wake as I went home. In an odd sort of way I even found it flattering. I was living in a film or a book; I could write the end to my own advantage. Whatever happened in Efestia, whatever the turmoil, I never seriously believed I was in danger. It wasn't really that I had any residual belief in the protective power of my blue and gold passport; it was more something running perkily in the blood. Youth and hope protected me - that frequently preposterous but always invaluable duo.

*

Back in my flat after these meetings at the Villa Dmitri I wrote down everything I'd heard, however trivial. The next day, early, when I was fresh, I would try to put all this hurried mass of prose into some

My Apprenticeship

kind of order. What resulted were sketches - my sea-girt, Mediterranean Ruritania. I shifted the country somewhat towards Malta, retaining the British and Arab influences but downplaying the Greek in favour of a strong Italianate colouring. There was an old Italian couple living in my apartment block whose help I plundered mercilessly without their knowing why.

A friend of mine in England had become the editor of a little magazine - the circulation was up to two thousand, it was adequately financed and beginning to get respected. He liked what I was doing and so I became a regular contributor to his pages, gradually gaining a small but useful reputation for off-beat political satire in an exotic setting. It was my editor-friend who gave me the title for the series - 'Dwelling Carelessly on the Isle', a phrase from Ezekiel he'd slightly adapted.

Of course, there was local censorship of the mail but, perhaps as a gesture towards the old ties now so fervently being strengthened, little of the traffic between Britain and Efestia ever seemed to be tampered with. My sketches were peacefully sent away and, in due course, returned just as peacefully, embellished by print. I suppose I was taking a small risk, but even if the copies had been opened I doubted, remembering Swift's adage, that the Efestians would have recognized themselves.

You may wonder whether I felt any guilt about these rather sneaky caricatures of people who'd been kind to me and welcomed me into their confidence. But I can't shrive myself with hindsight and say that I did. Not then.

*

I became involved with Marshall's secretary. The whole business was messy from the beginning and demanded considerable secrecy and deception because the girl was also Marshall's mistress.

Angela Bavlidou was middle-sized, pretty, with a mouth that tended to open in a wondering expression which could entrance or exasperate, depending on the mood one was in. There was a small mole at the corner of her bottom lip and another on the side of her nose; they almost blended with the light-brown colour of her skin. Her hair was a darker brown but it turned fairish at the ends so that in some lights they looked as though they'd been dipped in gold. Angela was well-bred, spoke beautiful English with just a trace of the island lilt and pleasingly old-fashioned phrasing.

She came from a type of family not unusual in Balyabole, one

Jack Debney

which boasted an ancestral line back to the Macedonians who'd arrived with Hephaestus - Alexander the Great's friend and companion - after whom, so it was alleged, the island took its name. I never really grasped the complicated, mythifying genealogies of those far-off times. It was easier to cope with the admixtures of the nineteenth century; in Angela's case the inevitable transplanted British soldier, but also a Pole, an Austrian and a Christianized Turk. I'd never come across a people who treasured the ethnicity of their ancestry so greatly. Even after we'd just made love, Angela would sometimes scale a few branches of her family tree for me. At first I found this quirkily charming, but after a while it got on my nerves.

"Can't you see that all this bloody stuff means nothing, Angela? It's just a crutch for people who are afraid they might be inferior."

Angela turned angrily from me. I traced lines along her back, marvelling at the smoothness of her skin, growing tender at the sight of her shoulders hunched forward in pique. I played noughts and crosses between them and then my fingers turned into a busy parade of ants making the long trek from neck to rump. Soon afterwards, I proffered suitable apologies and we ended the afternoon as happily and busily as we'd begun it. Once, during our affair, I thought we might be contributing a little genealogy of our own but, mercifully, that was a false alarm.

I showed Angela the published sketches and, as she read them, watched her face carefully. Firstly, her expression showed puzzlement and then, when it dawned on her what I was really doing, anger. Secretary to the end, she put the magazines back in their folder neatly, placing it before me on the table like a file she would have preferred not to handle.

"I hope you're proud of what you're doing."

There were some kind comments about my overweening Englishness - a unique mode of treachery - which was followed by the magisterial remark that people from 'humble backgrounds' invariably made the biggest snobs. Laughing, but incensed in my turn, I replaced the file in the drawer. I tried to show Angela that the satirist was perhaps the only truly sane man and that, actually, I stood in a long line of honourable scoffers and, anyway, people of all countries, big or small, would benefit from tempering their solemnities with humour.

Angela remained unconvinced.

"Imagine if Oliver saw these silly articles you've written."

My Apprenticeship

"But he won't."

"He's so easily hurt, Mac. I have to protect him from so much." Whilst Angela enjoyed going to bed with me, Marshall was the person she worried about. His sexual demands were slight but his emotional demands more than made up for that. He had to be consoled and flattered, indulged and gently guided. There was the prospect of all that money and status too. How the whole complex of things charmed Angela's burgeoning hopes of becoming Mrs. Oliver Marshall III!

*

Sometimes our boss needed to double his audience and took both his mistress and the tricky apprentice out together. His favourite restaurant for these excursions was a place near the Yedi Kula. We would sit in a courtyard virtually covered over with vines. Just before moving out of Balyabole, the Germans had shot four members of the Resistance there, against the far wall, many coats of whitewash ago now. Marshall claimed to have known each of these men well and would deliver panegyrics on them all - clipped and military or fierce and lachrymose, depending on mood and the amount of drink he'd taken. Whatever his manner, I'd rarely end up without the feeling that these national martyrs were there in spirit, very tangible spirit you could say, so that a circus knife-thrower might have outlined their shapes on the wall they died against.

To tell the truth, I was in awe of Marshall's war-tales. I needed the gathering of the partisans at evening in the olive groves, the gun battles in the narrow streets of the old part of Balyabole and then, finally - to be down at the port with Marshall and the others, watching the ships bringing the Allied troops from Egypt as they came closer and closer.

I also needed to have been through it all so that I could sit here now in this restaurant, an honourable survivor, basking in the admiration of the pretty girl and the young man avid for heroic narrative.

Yet, increasingly, after these sessions, to break the dependence I felt, the abject desire to melt into someone else, I would go off and play my very private and spiteful game of iconoclasm. Then Marshall would become:-

The old Cambridge soak lost in the Mediterranean, playing with the bullets on his desk like a gangster in second childhood; the cornflakes emperor who quoted Yeats and Cavafy as he tallied his stock in the warehouse; the whisky-tickler of thuggish palates; the ageing roué who pressed imported British goodies on Angela as apology for his miserable, dribbling comes. So observe this great watchdog of Balyabole on his wide, lofty terrace, a space for dreams that captures and magnifies moons in its tiles and makes lunar paths along the parapet; switch then to the family man whose wives and children stand within the photo-frame on his wall, bagged, trophied, paid off ... And so on and so on.

In the small public garden of the square below my flat, the dusty neighbourhood peacock was screeching desolately, drawing as it always did the proprietorial mockery of the regulars at the pavement café. In my wiser moments I took the hint and turned to some absolutely non-Marshallian activity.

*

Understandably, Marshall was chary of being thrice burnt. And, equally as understandably, when her hopes of marriage began to dwindle, Angela resented with increasing bitterness the position she found herself in. But when the break between them finally did come, I didn't think I had cause to worry. It would make sense for Angela to conceal our affair, if only to guard her own back - because, surely, once things had calmed down a little, a man with somewhat old-fashioned notions of probity like Marshall would offer some settlement. It was then that Angela would need all the bargaining power that an aggrieved ex-mistress could summon.

But when we met in Hephaestion Square for a coffee, I soon realised that she had told Marshall everything, including the relevant details about my 'Dwelling Carelessly' sketches. She'd lose her job, her particular privileges, but it didn't matter. Angela was high on confession and bridge-burning.

It was curious what I felt on hearing her news. Amidst my anger at her display of foolish courage and my apprehension, I seemed to recognise the point we'd all reached, as though it had been planned a long time ago. There was a weariness in me, as if the island and those who held my life on it in thrall ought now, in all decency, to just dissolve. A flick of my fingers, say, and let it all be gone.

"How did Oliver take it?"

"He shouted a lot at first, called me ugly names. A few choice ones for you too. And then he fell into a dreadful brooding. You should have seen the colour of his face, Mac! Purple - on the edge of bursting apart!"

My Apprenticeship

"And the upshot?"

"Oh, he threw me out. What did you expect? He got Abdel Latif to escort me firmly from the building. It was the moment that grinning ape had been waiting for."

She was slightly pale but withal attractively composed, that fine hopeful mouth as ever a touch out of true.

"And where do you think this puts *me* with Oliver, Angela?"

"You?" She hesitated, then did her best to adopt a manner of cynical shrewdness. "You've no need to worry. It will be a bit hard at the beginning perhaps. Let Oliver bawl you out to his satisfaction, and ... and grovel a bit. Then you'll both join in saying what a whore I was and end up weeping on each other's shoulders!"

"I bet!"

But, even so, I couldn't help laughing at the idea with her, and that's the note I left Angela on. I had no real desire to see her again and I think it was a mutual feeling, though neither of us said as much. I glanced back at her once. She was looking around, enjoying the bright chatterers of the cafe. It wouldn't be long before she started searching for another gallant, preferably someone younger and healthier than Marshall but older than me and, naturally, considerably richer. With a bit of luck she would find what she wanted.

*

I was hardly surprised when Marshall rang me that evening and said he'd like to see me about 'a certain delicate matter'. He considered it rather urgent. He was working late at Aboukir Street. Would I mind coming round about nine? He sounded calm, if rather deliberately so. I promised him that I'd be punctual. He assured me he wouldn't keep me long.

Rather too eagerly, I took my cue from this tone of courteous restraint. Our encounter was going to be terribly civilized, it seemed. I would get a severe wigging, certainly, but it would be something out of the senior common room which would allow a decent, not undignified contrition. Buoyed up by this quick hope, even Angela's version of my punishment to come appeared extreme.

*

When I got to Aboukir Street that evening, I didn't find Marshall in the office as I'd expected, but in the warehouse. The lights at the far end of the vast space were turned on and he was bent over, apparently checking something. There was no sign of the ghaffir, but then he often sloped off to his hut beyond our parking lot when he should have been patrolling the building.

"Oliver?"

"Ah, there you are, Mac."

He straightened up over the edge of a wall of cartons. It took me a moment to register how slowly and unsteadily he did this, somewhat longer to register that the Tokarev was pointing straight at me. The face behind the barrel was roughly the colour Angela had described it. Oliver Marshall had been preparing an ambush for me. So much for the senior common room.

"Do you like her?"

On the cardboard surface next to him, I now noticed, there was a thickly-stuffed envelope and a bottle of araq, about a quarter full.

"I said, do you like her?" Testily, he tapped the barrel of the pistol with his other hand.

"Oh, sorry. Yes. We're old friends. Acquaintances anyway."

"Part of a consignment the Russians sent to Egypt, a few years back now. I acquired her on the rebound, as it were. Businessmen get rewarded in curious ways sometimes. Come closer, Mac, do! I've been making up your wages. Shall we include a bonus for those of sin? Oh, laugh, laugh for God's sake! Can't there be decencies in entrapment?"

Marshall reached for his bottle.

"Drink?"

"No thanks."

He leant his head back and took a long draught, then sighed with a sybaritic gusto. The sickly aniseed smell flew straight towards me as though to reclaim a backslider.

"How do you like my little empire here, Mac?"

He walked a couple of paces and struck at a battery of switches. Now the whole place was pitilessly lit.

"I've liked it a lot, Oliver."

He turned his bogusly frank look on me.

"Service de guerre - is that what we'll call your time in Efestia? Three years. Longer than national service used to be, but shorter than many wars." He paused. "Still we became your material, didn't we? Ah well. Incidentally, there's your envelope."

"What?"

"It contains the salary you would have earned for the next month, plus enough to pay for your journey home. I've also included a testimonial, the usual glowing stuff, in case you should need it some

My Apprenticeship

time. You are leaving my employ forthwith. And the island."

"Look, I know I've hurt you, Oliver, but I honestly didn't ..."

"Honestly!" He mimicked my tones. "Now take your envelope, you prick, and go!"

"You must have had some inkling about Angela and me," I trailed off miserably.

"Perhaps you could say that I had one shred of naivety left, Mac, or that the blind eye doesn't like being made to see. And about the other matter, your satires, those humorous little corruptions, I had no inkling at all." The muzzle of the Tokarev moved from me to the envelope. "Your due. Take it."

Someone finer, more courageous than I was would have turned on his heel there and then, disdaining haste in his step as he'd disdained to take the money. But I wasn't made that way and told myself all too easily that I couldn't afford to be. In abject submission, the pistol virtually nosing the back of my hand, I grasped the envelope and put it into my pocket.

"You have no loyalty to people or place, Mac. Absolutely none. You've been educated into nothing."

"None of that's true!"

The bottle was listing badly on its cardboard counter. With surprising dexterity Marshall caught it just in time and took a prolonged swig. He regarded the sunken level sadly, then hurled the bottle to the side where it shattered on the floor.

"I made my choice. I have my country. I'd recognized it, you see, all those times in the mountains and in the city, skulking about with Sotiris and the others."

He looked beyond me dreamily. Before his eyes fixed on me again, I took a surreptitious step backwards and then another.

"Both my marriages were difficult, troubled ones. My children are reluctant even to speak to me these days unless the rotten little bastards want some cash. But none of them, Mac, ever demeaned me the way you did. None of them!"

The grossness of his assumption granted me a brief burst of defiance.

"I'm not your child, though, and I wouldn't care to be."

He drew breath in a bolt-eyed, shuddering sort of way, as though determined to blow out in one go all the candles on an old man's birthday cake.

"Get out this minute! Now, damn you, now!"

Jack Debney

Over the long, endless floor of the warehouse I ran, my footsteps echoing off the ceiling in a percussion of pure panic. Behind me I heard confused noises - curses, stumbling, cartons being thrown aside - and then the first shot came, pinging off a metal beam somewhere. My instinct was to put as much distance between Marshall and myself in the shortest time possible, but some remnant of cunning told me to adopt a zig-zag motion to confuse his aim. Were his intentions murderous, intimidatory or didn't he know? I wasn't planning to stay around long enough to open a public enquiry on it.

"How would you rate my empire at this particular moment, Mac?"

As he sent along the second shot, he was laughing - a sort of strangulated howling. Whatever his intention, the bullet was uncomfortably close, splintering the wood of a pallet a few feet away. I imagined him now aiming the Tokarev at the door, knowing even in his befuddled state that I must be heading there. It would be a wise move in any case to distract his attention and before me now I saw the means of doing so.

In the far corner, opposite the entrance, was the shelf reserved for the very best and most expensive malt whiskies, connoisseur's stuff that was dispatched to wherever there was wealth and power on the island. Abruptly, I changed direction, dashed along the wall, crouching low, and then leapt at the shelf, sweeping as many of the precious bottles to the ground as I could. Amidst the sounds of breaking glass and splashing liquid, I could hear Marshall's roar of anguish and rage. I ran back, crouching even lower, and whilst Marshall was smacking off bullets at the whisky shelf, as though my jumping shadow were pinned there, I reached the metal door and tugged it open.

Through the hallway to the outer door - I locked it behind me and then flung my warehouse keys on the ground. I breathed in and out deeply; it was something like freedom. Then I started the second stage of my flight like a sprinter from the running block, but almost immediately I was brought up sharp by the sudden apparition of Abdel Latif. He held me by the shoulders.

"Easy, Mr. MacFarlane."

He gave off a pungent smell, the sweat not simply of unwonted hurry but also alarm. For a while we stood in that tableau, listening for sounds from within. But the walls of the warehouse were thick and, besides, there was a gust blowing up from the sea. Abdel Latif's

My Apprenticeship

hands tightened on my shoulders, putting them into a vice of his own anxious strength. Sweat puddled his brow and his eyes searched the darkness ceaselessly as though it were hiding pointers for sound.

"No more shots," he said finally. It sounded curious, an expression of hope couched in a tone of command, yet for all I knew it was simply an observation from a man sharper-eared than I was.

He released me and, with a heavy dropping forward of his belly as if it contained a boulder, bent down to search for the keys I'd thrown away. He found them quickly and raised himself laboriously to his full height. I noticed then that he was wearing the red sash which he normally only donned when he was stewarding for Marshall at the Villa Dmitri. It had almost worked loose.

"I can manage the boss now, Mr. MacFarlane. You'd better go."

But before we shook hands and parted for good, he gave me a brief harangue on the evils of 'that fucking bint'. Poor Angela! In Abdel Latif's version of things, or at least the one he delivered to me, she was to be held responsible for the state Marshall was in. We were back in the comforting world where women could be blamed for everything. At that instant, I wasn't going to argue the point. The truth seemed a small sacrifice to make.

*

Expulsion takes time to organise, however, and it wasn't until the following evening that, laden with baggage, I was able to leave Efestia on the shambling Greek ferry en route from Alexandria to Piraeus.

Not long after I'd started my packing the previous night, the peacock in our square had had an attack of dementia which sent it screeching and tottering along the dusty pathways like an old courtesan in search of her vanished protectors.

I broke off what I was doing and went down into the centre of the city, mainly Hephaestion Square. I mooched around for a couple of hours, saying goodbye to places I'd come to know so well. I was something like a one-man debating society then: I should cling to what I had, I should renounce it; Marshall was right, Marshall was totally wrong.

At one point, I remember standing across from the Pella Hotel at the top of the square, beneath one of the new lamp-posts the municipality had installed. It was like a long stalk with something resembling a broken, gleaming rose on top. An aesthetic disaster let alone a practical one, much the butt of local satirists, but at that moment, looking up, I was very much drawn to it. Perfection of form only excluded you - you weren't needed - but this giraffed, illuminated cripple pointed to dreams that aimed high with absolutely no expertise whatsoever, the caught-out, if-onlys of art.

I stood at that exact spot ages later when I finally returned to Efestia, long after Marshall had died, allegedly of a heart attack, whilst being interrogated by the police over what they said were minor infringements of import regulations; long after Dr. Sotiris had been overthrown too, perishing by insurgent gunfire in the burning wreckage of the palace. But standing beneath the gawky lamp-post wasn't the same and I could only remember the intensity of my earlier love, rather than feel it again.

In the intervening years I had become a professional humorist and I was back on the island gathering material for a skittish travel book about the eastern Mediterranean for the summer trade. The public liked what I did and I was well paid for it, but I never wrote a thing that really touched people, not the way a real comedian would have done.

*

It's my last night in Balyabole again, after my flight from Aboukir Street. I'm listening to the peacock and then I'm clattering down the stairs and through the foyer into the open air as though I'm an intruder alarmed by discovery.

But this time I don't wander about Hephaestion Square. Instead I find myself going along the Corniche, up the eastern side of the bay, in the direction I took when I delivered the cornflakes to Little Patmos. I go past an Orthodox church, past the American Library, then blocks of fine, white, expensive buildings with silent balconies until I come to the old harbour at Liman. From here the houses and apartment blocks become noticeably shabbier, less metropolitan.

And then, further out, near the edge of the city, still keeping close to the sea-wall, I come across something weird - a floor of marble sloping gently into the water. I know that, objectively speaking, it doesn't exist and for that reason it exists all the more. There's a bright moon that focuses on the marble and tracks it, the moon of the MacFarlanes, their personal lantern that I read about so long ago.

Gingerly, I ease myself over the sea-wall and step carefully down onto the marble causeway. Soon the water is up to my knees. I hear a short laugh behind me and, glancing round, see that Marshall is with me now, sitting cross-legged on the parapet of the wall.

My Apprenticeship

He's playing a gulli-gulli man but, instead of the three metal cups, he has three of the ludicrously extravagant shakoes that the Ethniki Filaki use for ceremonial occasions. And instead of the shivering chick there's the Tokarev. With many flamboyant gestures and warm smiles, Marshall is urging me back, to the game.

I stand below him. The moon flickers like an uncertain bulb and Marshall glances angrily at it before directing his gaze down at me again. "Play, Mac," he says gently. Somehow I know he's not planning a sucker-gambit to set me up for the fall. This will be for real. I have to make a choice.

Marshall shows me the pistol with the flourish of a conjuror, then places it beneath one of the helmets and passes his hands over the three of them, his movements getting ever faster. All the time he's looking at me and smiling, that old, familiar, brightly dubious look I recognise from a thousand memories. When he stops and invites me to choose, my hand goes out with a determination that surprises me, my index finger extended. "Ah, you intend to win this time, do you?" Marshall says approvingly.

But it's always here that the MacFarlane moon comes rushing down the sky like an angry zip letting in the blackness, as though I've offended something basic in the universe, committed some transgression I can't even imagine except in strictly local terms. The whiteness of the moon has gone. It's now the colour of Marshall's drinking-face, purple-scarlet; it's sped right down, an expiring match-end tossed into water, the dodgy lamp of a fishing-boat on the horizon.

"Oh, play, play," says Marshall wearily, and if I can't shut it off there, I have to go back to the beginning and I'm walking out of the city again, towards this point, always hoping that this time I'll be granted the grace to push the whole thing further and then further still, until finally I'll be able to cancel out the blackness which would tug Marshall from the parapet - Tokarev and all - down into its relentless depths, the lair of cancellation.

Jonathan Steffen

The Hanging Man

Some time between the invention of the six-gun and the invention of the skyscraper there lived a gambler, Memphis-born, whose name need not concern us and whose nickname changed with every hotel. He wore a fancy waistcoat and a shoestring tie, a silk shirt and a shiny top-hat; he slicked his hair with bear-grease and his smile flashed gold. The picture of his profession from the tilt of his top-hat to the tip of his polished shoe, his appearance was contrived with such nice sterility as to seem more abstract than apish; and in the lamplit fog of innumerable back rooms, whilst inferior players spat tobacco-quids upon the floor and let down their suspenders, this gambler wore his top-hat on his forehead, chewed a cheroot, smiled his golden smile. Last onto the table, he would always leave it last, his fine hands fisted round chips which he would cash or dollars he would bite - 'And that's how I got this tooth,' he'd say to the preening crinolines who waited for him at the bar, all eyes to catch his winning smile and win the night with him.

From New Orleans to St. Louis, in the towns and on the riverboats, his world was harlequinned with colour: the red and blue and yellow of the court cards, the black black of the ace of spades; the silver shimmer of the dollar which sang when he flipped it, caught it, flipped it; the unreal emerald of the baize, a green which always seemed astonishing, and would admit no second vivid aberration. These were his sightlines and his compass-points, a world of fixed migration so alive it could be nothing else but artificial, utterly clearer, impossibly better than the mist which clung around the edges of the tables, the four sides of his real, cardbright life.

At the table he sat like a ramrod, drank like a lady, smiled like a mandarin, his whole being, or half-being, simplified into the pure attempt to teach patterns more exquisite patterns. He had no system and no tricks; his game was finely wrought of experience, concentration, and flexibility. His major wins were born of minor gains, his losses never more than temporary, a calculated sidestep in an intricately improvised pavan of the imagination. He played with his gold-plated gambling-pistol by his right hand, and he never used it. He never argued, and he never cheated: a real gambler, he staked his life on play alone.

Some people, misled by his success, his smile, his exact dandyism, mistakenly credited him with the American innovation of the Joker,

The Hanging Man

but at this his face grew serious: he played a fifty-two card game, he said. The Joker was a visitor, and always welcome, but it was not his card. He knew his own card.

Away from the table, he lived as if through someone else's afterthoughts: the regular failure of things to connect was at worst untroublesome, at best, relaxing. Once he told a girl he loved her: the consequences were so slight that he repeated this idea to almost every girl he hired, in every rented bed. This one had red hair, and that one had black eyes: the uniform softness of their breasts reminded him that daylife was a thing devoid of shape, of edges, of significance. Time passed as on an actor's Sunday: a not unpleasant shade of grey which other people coloured for themselves, somehow. He wasn't sure how. The idea didn't interest him: his colours were ordained.

He saw his poker-life in terms of a simple narrative image which his mind gradually purified until it could repeat itself in all its details like a looped-up clip of cinematic film. He stood beside a row of foursquare gaming-tables, set so close together that there was no gap or chink between each one: the row ran with the authority of railroad across desert, to disappear over an inconceivably distant, possibly only theoretical, horizon. What he sought was the final table of the sequence; for the final table, he knew, would not be green but some other, undreamt-of colour which he would at once recognize as miraculously correct and utterly astonishing. It might be patterned like a card itself, it might be plain: it would explain everything. In his hand he held a virgin deck of cards, its edges crisp and cool, a double set of sweetly sliding parallelograms: easing and teasing the unbroken card pack, he would walk along the line of tables, his step like an Indian's and his head on fire, his manhood raised before him like a lance.

For years the gambler stalked the road to paradise.

Until the nightmare came and at one stroke demolished the neat walls of his mental haven, laying bare the furthest corners of his mind. The gambler dreamt that he was playing a game in which the stakes were dangerously high, even for him, and that the cards had run against him. He knew full well that cards are simply dealt and played, but in this dream they ran as if directed by an intelligence whose like he had never encountered before. The situation had reached the point at which he realized he would have to cheat or be ruined. Here lay an irritating warp of logic, a double bias; for though

Jonathan Steffen

the gambler never cheated (hence his continuous success), yet in the dream he took the decision to cheat with utter calm and on the basis of a straightforward calculation - just as in an ordinary game he would decide to raise the stakes by a precisely necessary amount. As soon as he made the decision, he became aware that there was an ace up his sleeve, an ace of spades, fixed to the inside of his lower forearm. He took his time, picked his moment and, throwing in his last chip, played the ace of spades. The sensation as he snapped the lacquered card onto the slightly yielding baize was prolonged, intensely pleasurable, and entirely exact. He took his hand away, already envisioning the look on his opponent's face, and as his fingers left the card, the image changed into a picture of a man hanging by the neck from a gallows. The legs swung very slightly.

An answer which refused to answer. The final table - did it bear the death-card? Did it? Did he then already know its colours and its pattern? Would the surprise be simply in its sudden, stunning position - the end of the row is *here* - as he looked down one day in a lifetime's second to see the magnified image, bright but felt-furred, gently moving, its legs slowly swaying, swaying, a pictorial miracle achieved with all the mocking effortlessness of dreams? And so the question was, the question simply was: At which green table in which smoky room?

He scripted possibilities: His opponent would see the card, lean back in his chair and fire - the gambler could feel the bullet pushing its way into his chest, taking as long to penetrate the flesh as it had taken him to lay the false ace on the baize. Or he would see the death-card and his heart would freeze - then start to pump, and pump, and rock his wriggling body till he saw his eyeballs pop out one by one and roll across the table, gathering fur. Or a noose would take his neck and lift him to the ceiling: was it the room moving down there, or was he moving? His tongue shot out and danced before his eyes: Why can't I die, why aren't I dying...? Hanged men ejaculate; and at this point in his thought he would see himself not walking along the row of tables but jerking like a puppet through the air above them, the noose around his neck, his thick seed spilling on the brightly lit baize.

And so the gambler smiled when he played poker.

From time to time he tried to tell his fear, not to the girls who moved their limbs between his sheets but to a whore's child or a favourite and sexless Madam; but the words stuck to the inside of his

The Hanging Man

mouth, the air grew thicker as he tried to say them, impenetrable with the threat of comprehension. Instead, he smiled, and was adored and hated.

He attempted to fight his way out of the half-locked logic of his visions: imitating recklessness, he tried to tempt death, to entice it, persuade it away to another place. Leaving his gambling-haunts, he broke horses, swam rapids, crossed deserts. When death would not be beckoned, he began to seek it openly: in avalanches and in burning buildings, his immortality laughed at him. Death sat at a poker-table, simply: at a certain poker-table.

Returning to his game, he now played with a hermetic ferocity, his lip stuck to his golden tooth. The particulars of the rooms he played in, the names of towns and faces of opponents now faded from their prior misty significance to none at all: even as he sat, he walked beside the tables, always walked beside the tables.

One night in Memphis, towards the end of a century which had not existed for him, he came out from the back room to find the saloon girls gathered round a lamplit table in the corner: the rest of the room was empty, and in darkness. He paused for a second, expecting the group to break up and come towards him with their usual frills and imprecations; when they stayed, he moved across the room towards them.

Silent, the girls sat in a circle, watching one of their group laying cards out on the table. As he approached, the gambler could see that the cards were not of the standard English design but of a different pattern. At first he took them for a particularly ornate transformation-pack of the type then much in vogue, but coming closer he realized he had never seen their kind before. He asked the woman who dealt them what they were.

- Not your kind of cards, I think. She spoke with a pronounced French accent.

He asked again.

- You cannot make money with these cards, she said, you cannot win. You would become so poor. She laughed.
- What are they?
- *Le tarot.*
- What are you doing with them?
- Making time pass. What do you do with your cards?
- Get rid of these girls.
- Monsieur!

Jonathan Steffen

- Get rid of them.

He took a handful of dollars and threw them into the corner of the room. The group exploded, hissed and scrabbled in the darkness, thinned out into individual giggles which shutting doors truncated. The gambler sat down opposite the Frenchwoman: half-hidden by the lamp, her face was carved in stone, older than it had first appeared. He told her that he wanted her to explain something to him; he offered money.

- You cannot make money with the tarot, she replied, picking the cards up from the table and slowly squeezing the pack into shape. But I will tell you what you want to know.

With utter clarity, lucidly and simply, he explained his vision of the tables, his journey towards the final table, his nightmare of the hanging man. She listened like a mask.

- The tarot, you have not seen it before?
- Never. I don't know what it is.
- Few know it in America. They will. In France we have known it for a long time.

She tapped the table with the card-pack, once, and disappeared into the contemplation of this gesture. When she resurfaced, she said:

- What you have seen is *Le Pendu*. Your own *Pendu*.
- Pendu?
- *Le Pendu, L'Appeso*, the Hanging Man. I will show you.

With a single movement she took the card from the pack in her hand and laid it face down on the table.

- Turn.

The gambler flipped the card.

It was extraordinarily beautiful. It depicted, as it always does in tarot packs, a man strung upside down, suspended by one leg from a gibbet, a smile upon his face. He clutched a large money-bag in either hand.

- *Le Pendu*, she said.

And then, as his smile began to waver:

- Do not worry. It does not mean death. She laughed. Not death as you imagine it. You see - and here she paused - they cannot die, the dead.

PUBLISHING AGAINST THE GRAIN

Dick McBride
Whizzkiddery

So, you want to get into publishing/distribution? Encouraging to know there are still some of you guys left (you tender genders), although rather sad to contemplate the heartaches (joy-accompanied) you're going to have if you take the plunge.

*

When it was suggested I might have a thing or two to say on the subject I remembered a conversation with my son, Sean, who was then about twenty-one, in his final year at the University of Essex, majoring in, of all things, American literature. As a matter of fact his final paper was on Jack Kerouac. I was still in business at the time, McBride Brothers & Broadley, International Book Distributors, operating out of an old chapel (Methodist denomination, I think), in Great Horwood, Bucks.

It was a cold day, and we were wrapping books for the culture-starved masses in England and on the Continent. There we were in the bombed-out chamber (pigeon shit), surrounded by rising damp and about 30,000 books. We were both wearing fingerless gloves, standing as close as possible to the calor gas heater, but not that close because then we would have been too far from the Tilly lamp to see to put the labels on. This was the chapel's only light as the winter evenings drew in.

"Sean," I said, "what are you going to do when you get the degree?"

Hoping, possibly, he wanted to help me sell books, play his sax on weekends maybe. Something like that ...

"I don't know."

"Give it some thought," I said.

He gave it some thought.

"All I know is, whatever I do, it won't be selling books."

Surprise, surprise!

Dick McBride

(Brennan, my youngest son, got his degree - in science - at Bristol University, and is now doing things with computers back in California.)
After that if you are still interested, here we go.

*

There are basically two types of publishing/distribution: (1) Establishment; (2) Anti-establishment. Although I prefer to call number two alternative.

Establishment publishing brings out books that will not disturb the waters of commerce; will not change the way things are; mollification, panaceatic pap, valium books; a world where the chief motivation is greed, the bottom line - profit. If that is what you want (to compete in) - in the consumer society - to preserve, bolster up, spread the manure, there are just a few things to remember as you prepare to enter the fast lane. First, you must learn the rules of the game; then play it as hard as you can. After consideration, though, I can honestly say that as far as the establishment goes, there is just one rule, and that is bugger your neighbour, screw the competition; if you break any rules try not to get caught. In the consumer world that is the only crime - getting caught.

Go to university (although this is not absolutely necessary), take courses in economics, computer sciences, political science, political correctness, practical psychology (euphemism for pornography), market psychology (if there is such a course), craft-design-technology; above all, learn how to establish, interpret and earn by the bottom line.

It is absolutely unnecessary to study or even be concerned with literature, art, culture; a waste of time to even consider morals, the rights and wrong, dreams. Waste of time.

If you haven't already done so then, before you go any further into the jungle of hypocrisy and greed, you must join the nearest branch of the BTB (Brown Tongue Brigade). Otherwise, keep your nose clean.

Easy, eh?

*

If by establishment we mean the way things are (the winners, the losers, the drudges in-between who live and die to keep it all going and are paid just enough to make what they are doing seem worthwhile), then what does anti-establishment mean? Anti - against, opposed to... Ah, but wait, that's no good, because this

Royal Ascot

Philip Wolmuth

Dick McBride

really means replacement, not change; it means that the still greedy although unsuccessful competitors want to be on top. Anti-establishment is merely the flip-side of establishment; it just hasn't come up yet. There should be another way of living until we die and, dying, stop the only ballgame in town. That's why I prefer to call the other publisher 'alternative' - choice between two (or more) things, either one of which might or might not be the answer. Confusing? My head spins.

This confusion leads me to a memory of the 1993 Cheltenham Literary Festival.

*

I went one day to hear Allen Ginsberg (the Big-Daddy of the dot-dot-dot school of writing, only Allen always filled in the dots), an old friend I hadn't seen in about ten years. Allen was to give a matinee and an evening performance. The latter was to be a reading of old and new poetry; the afternoon job (when it finally got off the ground) was an interview conducted by that stalwart publisher, John Calder, another old friend (despite the fact that he has never published me). Due to diluvial weather conditions and the perpetually swamped British Rail, Allen was more than an hour late arriving from London. The big tent was packed with propers (blue blazers, blue rinse) and impropers (beads, beards and friendship bracelets). When the meeting began to get restless PJKavanagh introduced John Calder, who proceeded to extemporize a reminiscence of Allen and the 60s. He was starting to run out of steamy memories when someone in the audience wanted to know what John was going to ask Allen, if the poet ever arrived. Calder said that, among other things, he would ask Ginsberg how he felt about drugs today, when they were such a danger to young people, especially since so many of Allen's friends had died of drug abuse. At this a moist Birmingham busker (how did he get in?), shouted "Why don't you ask him about his friends who took drugs and are still alive today, even though they're fucking pensioners?" This was more like it! Memories of 60s' poetry readings flooded back. (Once at a poetry reading in Fugazi Hall, San Francisco, Robert Duncan, looking like Dracula in a floppy hat, walked out on Allen.) But back to Cheltenham... Suddenly, Martin Wheeler, a Cockermouth publisher, stood up, white beard quivering with indignation, and, looking like Moses or the Wrath of God, blasted the loud-mouth offender with a magisterial tirade, ending with, "How dare you insult a great poet and his friends, one of

Whizzkiddery

whom, Richard McBride, is sitting right here beside me, and I can assure you he is very much alive and still writing and publishing!" Nice going, Martin! And, thinking that, I turned and shouted my own two-pence worth: "Yeah, and I'm a fucking pensioner, too!"

*

What has this got to do with publishing/distribution? Nothing, or perhaps everything, for before you can become an anti-establishmentarian you have to have something alternative, perhaps even politically incorrect to say, the desire or need to say it, and above all the courage to say it. In other words before you even get started you have to be in love with life, the creation, men, women, children, birth, death. You must have a dream, and strength to make it work, make it real, even if you eventually discover that this reality is simply another dream, the pretended ignorance of God. But the search is fun, and more meaningful than greed.

How do I know this? Because it's right (as opposed to wrong). It's as simple as that, Junior. And before we get involved in definitions - what is right? what is wrong? - let me remind you of what Satchmo Armstrong told an inquiring reporter, who had asked him what jazz was. "If you have to ask you never know, man."

Where does a moral sense come from? Heredity, early years, parents, training, experience? Religion? Who knows? I certainly don't.

Don't laugh, but I suspect it has something to do with instinct.

But whatever it is, wherever it comes from, hold on to it, you'll need it. Even if you eventually fail, it will help soften the blow, perhaps give you strength to try again. This belief - and anger - has sustained me.

If you are in the second category and also a writer, artist or composer, you will have no choice, you will have to write or paint or sculpt or compose; it goes with life, the love of life, hopes, dreams, and the need to express yourself, tell others how good it all is, the evolution, dissolution, the absorption into what possibly is just a dream, energy, as yet unborn and, therefore, incapable of ever disappearing. What is not, always is.

A creative person needs to learn how to use the tools of his calling. If you are a writer all you really need (apart from the ability to read and write) is paper and pencil. And a dictionary... A more advanced way of putting words down on paper is the typewriter - in order of preference: manual (although these are being phased out by

Dick McBride

technology), electronic and, as a last resort, a word processor. I prefer pencil or pen, always for the first draft, a portable electric job for the 2nd, 3rd and 4th drafts. I consider the word processor an abomination, the lazy writer's way of cheating. I won't listen to the feeble excuse that the W-P saves time, time is precious etc. If you are a writer time shouldn't concern you; you can always make time. As a matter of fact, time is expendable. How anyone can possibly think that putting a poem, story or book onto a floppy disk then reading it on a wavery little screen (which possibly is brain as well as soul-destroying) can replace the fun of seeing pages pile up (or be thrown away) and then to look forward to the fun of proofing mistakes and scribbling comments and corrections, how anyone can think that is beyond me.

(Take a break from planning your future, close your eyes, try to understand solitude. Think of elite-ism for a moment; that's something you'll have to get used to when the new dark ages complete their descent. The only people who will be able to read, let alone write or illuminate manuscripts, will be locked away in a monastery. Although they will probably be called book depositories...)

On the other hand, I'm a poor example to follow, perhaps; three of the five bookshops I have worked for are now gone and one is in the land of the living dead, having been swallowed up by the W H Smith monster. And after fifteen years my own company (started with brother Bob and our friend, Martin) went into voluntary liquidation. But it was a hell of a lot of fun while it lasted.

(Fun comes up a lot, you will have noticed, and that's a lesson. When something is no longer fun then stop it. There are enough things we don't like to do but have to.)

*

More than thirty years ago when I was working for City Lights, after the notorious fame of HOWL, young writers and their lovers, or just disaffiliated youth, rebels with or without a cause, used to come by City Lights with their dreams and aspirations. Kids from Pocatello, Idaho, Omaha, Nebraska, Paducah, Kentucky, sometimes even from California, all wanting something, to see Ginsberg or Kerouac or Corso, to lay a manuscript on Ferlinghetti, convinced their poem was better than HOWL. Most of them just wanted a piece of the action, which probably meant that greed, not need, was motivating them. If Ferlinghetti wasn't there, or was hiding out in the basement, Shig or I usually took on the Guru-role. After the *Howl* trial, subsequent financial success and media-manipulated fame, more and more Beats wanted to know how they could start a bookshop like City Lights, how they too could become a daring publisher. How, how, how? I didn't know then, and I haven't come up with a satisfactory answer even now. But knowing something of the cost of running a bookshop, and how much printing bills might come to, my first question, in reply, was: "How much money do you have?" After they told me (and many times it was obvious they had nowhere near the amount they said they had), my usual advice was "forget it". I think I was more cautious than necessary, for if you are determined enough you can manage to at least start something on a shoestring. If you're young enough.

The two most important items for success are luck and being in the right place at the right time. Ferlinghetti was and probably still is an astute businessman, showman, poet. He was also lucky, and definitely in the right place at the right time. San Francisco (then the Paris of the Pacific) was as ready for Ferlinghetti as he was for it.

*

Let's concentrate on publishing for a moment. Have a clear picture of the kind of book you want to publish, then try to decide how many readers such a book might attract. Remember it is always better to underprint than overprint (one way of saving trees. Also it is better to leave the audience asking for more than to be booed off stage); if you think a book might sell 500 copies, print 400 not 600. If it goes out of print you still have 400 people who know of you and what you are doing. To know (or feel sure) there are 400 people out there who have actually read you, and formed some kind of opinion about you, is infinitely more satisfying than the information that 40,000 customers have bought your book. Most establishment books at best are merely alternatives to television; if they are really crap you can always use them for propping up the idiot box or coffee table, or for throwing through windows. Why help W H Smith pay its bills when you're behind with your own mortgage payments?

Next make some enquiries; find out how much it will cost to publish the cheapest edition possible of the book you want to bring out.

Learn the rudiments of printing/binding in order to do as much as possible yourself. Don't try to compete with the big boys; don't try to make your book look like theirs. I suppose you will have to learn

Dick McBride

a little about word processors, computers, that kind of junk. I don't know if it's even still possible to do it without all the damned technology, but if it isn't then there's another joy down the drain. I will never forget the excitement generated by the Bread & Wine Mission when it first began putting out *Beatitude*. The first editions were run off on an old mimeograph machine, collated and then bound with a staple gun. Hot off the press! Pierre de Lattre and his disciples used to run down the hill to City Lights with the latest edition, dropping off bundles along the way for footsore, wandering poets to hawk on North Beach streetcorners, while keeping a lookout for Bigarani, the Beat-hating cop. A few years (or possibly only months) later, the Bread & Wine Mission acquired an old-fashioned handpress and brought out a few small editions of poetry, "Hand-set and printed at the Bread & Wine Press, San Francisco, California by Wilder Bentley". Those days are now possibly gone forever, but, gosh, it was fun for awhile! So, learn something about the machines, as little as possible, because if we wait long enough the pendulum will come back our way.

I was first made aware of the nightmare coming (now here) one day over lunch in the New Pisa, with Claude Pelieu and Mary Beach. We were bitching and complaining about various things, including rejected manuscripts, when Mary informed me that there was an increasing number of New York publishers who wouldn't even look at a manuscript unless it was on a floppy disk. I wonder what chance William Burroughs would have today if he sent out THE NAKED LUNCH on scruffy, scribbled-on pages like the ones we read at City Lights.

*

Next comes the hard part, selling the books. Forget advertising (I feel the same way about these buggers as I do about the conglomerates and the VAT boys). Word-of-mouth is still the best way to sell books (and by books I do not mean products). When we started McBride Bros & Broadley in 1967, we were like return journey-pilgrims landing at Virgin Rock, England. Bob and Martin spent a lot of time that first year visiting many bookshops, contacting friends and libraries, writing letters, managing to get interviewed by the *Bookseller*. Many people had heard of what was being written and published in San Francisco, but until we got here about the only way of getting a City Lights book was to have a friend bring one over. Again it was a case of being in the right place at the right time.

Whizzkiddery

If you are a distributor of small press books, and giving good service, the word soon gets around. When McBride & Broadley started we had six publishers on our list, when we went bust in 1983 we had, as I recall, thirty publishers, the best sellers being New Directions and City Lights. Why did we go under then? Success in every area but the bottom line, i.e., profit. It takes money to make money. We had started the business with very little money and ran with it as far as we could. It was like the last big pot in a poker game we had a chance of winning, but we couldn't find anyone to take our markers. To be honest, I was getting tired, and the alarm-clock didn't work anymore.

So, find yourself a distributor - read the trade magazines, ask at your friendly neighbourhood bookstore, if you can find one - and, once found, stick with them as long as they move your books. Buy a mailing list, get in touch with libraries, send out letters. When you print the first book also run off a brief promotional fact sheet, price, size, author, a little about the book, plans for future publications. To cut expenses type the poop-sheet yourself and use a photocopier. Send out as many as your postage allowance will permit. Invest some money in packaging material, but don't spend too much; save cardboard and padded envelopes; learn how to wrap packages yourself; don't worry if it takes time. McBride & Broadley packages were easily recognisable (unprofessional-looking), but our customers rarely had to return damaged books. Pound the pavements, take samples around bookshops, become a door-to-door salesman, attend the markets, even become a book-busker. When I was still distributing books, on my monthly trips to London, Compendium bookshop in Camden Town was always my first stop. I would arrive at the red door at least an hour before the shop was to open, often catching Nick and Diana still in bed. I always arrived with a case full of new titles and a bag of donuts. It was a most pleasant way to sell books, and besides I could catch up on the latest gossip over the second cup of coffee. Nick, in those days, made quick decisions. I liked his philosophy. He bought books he would like to read. He liked a lot of books.

*

In the early days City Lights did its own distribution. Then, as time went by, and more publishers started to spring up in San Francisco and the Bay Area we began to get requests to distribute other publishers as well. This was good, but it meant more paperwork,

Dick McBride

more attention to accounting details. Before long City Lights turned all distribution over to the Subterranean Co, McBride & Broadley, Wild & Woolley and others. So, all said and done, perhaps it is not such a good idea to get too heavily involved in distribution, not if your main interest is publishing.

Never forget the dream, hard work, luck, being in the right place at the right time.

*

Unfortunately, money is also necessary, but keep it in its place, don't create a monster. Don't let need become greed. If money becomes too important then your little anti-establishment vision becomes just another establishment publishing house, and the next phase is conglomeration. You should have (or be able to get your hands on) just enough money to bring a book out, and sell it. If you are unlucky, don't worry about it. As my now dead friend, Jack Trevor Storey, told me when McBride & Broadley went bye-bye, "The first bankruptcy is the worst. Have another drink." On the other hand, if you are lucky and manage to sell the entire edition, or enough to pay the printer, you're home and dry. Who knows you might even make enough money to start thinking about volume two. Without a doubt - unless you are lucky enough to marry someone with money - it will be necessary to hold a regular job. Try to find something far removed from reading, writing, printing - dig ditches, stock shelves. If you have to teach, don't teach literature or creative writing; try physical education, or maths or science. Nothing is more deadly (for a writer) than grading English papers, essays, stories, whatever. Try to watch as little television as possible. (Dirty videos okay).

*

After thirty years in the book trade (wholesale, retail, publishing, distribution), I still get the itch. Can't enter a bookshop without rearranging books that careless customers or bored clerks have put in the wrong alphabetical order or on the wrong shelf. And there are still a few books (including a couple of my own) that I would like to see published. Michael Wilding and I have an idea about this, but, being paranoid, I will say no more. But if I could find £1,000 over and above the amount necessary to keep alive I'd show you kids how to do it. And I'm a fucking pensioner too!

Susan Davis
Creative Spirit

Some people will do anything in public. They spit on the pavement, shriek at their children; even take their clothes off. Wesley would not have dreamed of disgracing himself in this way. What Wesley did in public was to pray; in the street, the supermarket, whenever he felt the need; standing with his eyes screwed tightly closed, hands clasped in supplication.

Like now for instance; Saturday morning in the middle of the Chapel Craft Centre, buffeted by handbags and elbows; his feet trodden on by small children. He might have been a scrawny bird, dozing in some uncongenial place; resolute against the world. He was a tall, spindly man with a beard that sprang from his chin like the root of a giant leek. And his habit of standing before the stalls, communing with the Almighty, was guaranteed to scare the customers away. It was no use the stall-holders complaining though. The converted Chapel was Wesley's house and a man could do what he pleased in his own home.

Today, Wesley had come to stand by the stall of a woman who made ornamental frogs from sea-shells. She tried to look appreciative. People seemed to have gone off her frogs lately and Wesley often prayed for better sales. She was not to know that this time, his prayers were entirely selfish and that Wesley was praying for himself and his wife Hortense. Hortense, who had gone astray. And all thanks to the Poets. The poets had been a big mistake; he knew that now. Wesley opened his eyes and glared at the frogs. If only he had stuck to good honest craftsmen, like those who now surrounded him.

The Craft Centre had all begun from what Hortense called one of his 'funny turns'. And the 'funny turns' were all the fault of his aunt. Great-Aunt Gertrude had left him a lot of money. An obscene amount of money. Enough money to buy a villa in the South of France and live like a lotus-eater for the rest of his life. But Wesley was not that kind of man. He had set the money aside, using just enough to convert the Chapel into a home for himself and Hortense.

Since the Church had seen fit to deny his real vocation, living in the Chapel seemed like the next best thing. He never could figure out why the Church had turned him down. At least in the army, as he said to Hortense; at least they gave you a reason, like flat feet or knock knees. But the Church had turned its back on him and he was left to prowl the Chapel, cursing Great-Aunt Gertie's money, obsessed by 'the eye of the needle'. On really bad nights, he would tear the books and papers from his shelves, searching for answers while Hortense fluttered about, picking up the discarded wisdom of the ages.

Hortense would say sensibly:

"You just sit and do your breathing exercises dear, while I make cocoa."

His wife, who, to an outsider, might not have amounted to much, was indispensable to him at these times. She was a shy, self-effacing woman; small and rustling. She had a habit of blinking anxiously, as though she couldn't believe her eyes. Her hair was prematurely grey. She was well-used to Wesley's 'funny turns'. Once, she had sat up all night with him, reading aloud from *The Light of Asia*, while he rocked back and forth, knees drawn up to his chin, moaning softly. Her tones were so comforting, she might have been reading 'The Three Bears', but it did the trick. It was his wife's voice which calmed him; not the Buddhism which made him feel small and alone, with all the universe swimming around him. Usually, he finished up clutching the Bible, watching the dawn break, while Hortense went about with a dustpan and brush, sweeping up the confetti of his madness.

But, the dawn brought with it, inspiration. It was at one of these times that he convinced Hortense, that they should, once a week, open their home to struggling craftsmen. When she seemed a touch reluctant, he reminded her that Christ himself had been a carpenter.

"To foster the creative spirit my dear," Wesley said. "Could there be a nobler cause?"

Hortense agreed he was probably right. And so the Chapel Craft Centre was born.

If only he could have been content with that. But the craftsmen were a hum-drum lot. When he tried talking to them about the meaning of life, they would shuffle their feet and look at their watches.

"What we need my dear," Wesley told Hortense, "is a Poetry Circle. To make things with one's own hands is a fine thing; but poetry brings us closer to the gods."

Hortense agreed he was probably right. And so the Poetry Circle was born.

The poets gathered at the Chapel on Wednesday evenings. A

Creative Spirit

brash and arrogant lot, they seemed to Hortense, who scuttled in and out of the kitchen, bearing trays of her own home-made Millet Slices. She had to scuttle quietly of course, so as not to disturb their readings and the poets hardly looked at her as they plucked the biscuits from the plate. They dropped cigarette ash on the polished floor and often, she caught them smirking behind Wesley's back, especially when he prayed in front of them. What was more, their poems were rubbish! Hortense was sure she could do better herself.

Wesley could not have foreseen the effect the poetry circle would have upon his wife. He began to come upon her, scribbling away on scraps of paper.

"Ah!" he would pause, hovering in the doorway, waiting for her to notice him. "Ah! I thought it might be getting on for tea time."

"Hmmmmmmmm?" The pen moved at great speed across the paper. He watched it jealously.

"Doing a bit of scratching then are we?"

Hortense murmured absently. She didn't seem to hear his stomach rumbling. He was the sort of person who needed regular meals, had, in fact been known to faint if he had to wait too long. Now, it was necessary to cough a little to jog her memory.

"Is something the matter?" She looked up, startled, as if she'd only just noticed him.

He looked ostentatiously at his watch:

"Matter? No, no ... just wondered what you were up to my dear ..."

The stomach rumbled again and this time she heard it and laid down the pen.

"Good gracious! I didn't realize the time." She was blinking furiously. "I'll get something to eat, won't be a jiffy."

When she went hurrying off to the kitchen, he stole a quick look at the paper on the desk. A poem. Mostly about the glories of nature. He smiled to himself. Credit where credit was due. His wife was an excellent cook; a good little home-maker. But she had no literary talent and just as well. He had a sudden impulse to tear the poem up, but managed to restrain himself. Hunger brought out the worst in him. Never mind, just listening to the clink of crockery from the kitchen began to calm him. He sat down at the table and unfolded his napkin.

But, over the next few weeks, irregular meal times became all too common. Hortense had what he could only describe as 'writing

Susan Davis

fever'. Her scratching pen and the grey, skull-cap of hair bent across the page, began to irritate him. Now, when he spoke to her, there was a wild look in her eyes; as if she wasn't quite there. Sometimes, he thought she might be suffering some form of demonic possession. The kitchen was tidy but there were no savoury smells wafting from the oven, no comforting clatter or tinkling of tea cups. It was all wrong, he thought to himself. And playing havoc with his stomach. Soon he would have an ulcer.

Left to himself, he began to fidget. Dipping into his books, flicking pages, phrases drifting in and out of his brain. His usual practice of stroking the leather-bound volumes of his library; sniffing the clean scent of printed paper, had lost its magic. Meanwhile, the reams of paper on Hortense's desk began to fill satisfyingly with ink. Wherever he went, Wesley would find screwed up balls of paper and empty biros stuffed down the sides of chairs. The cat played with the balls of paper and Wesley clicked his tongue, as he burned them on the fire.

He began to find little ways to interrupt her. Wasn't it about time they had new curtains for the Chapel Hall, she was so good with her needle. He wanted her advice on the purchase of a range of travel diaries and...where were his clean woolly socks? He thought they might still be in the washing basket.

"Do hope I haven't interrupted your flow dear," he would chuckle, "but you wouldn't want me going about with smelly feet would you?"

Wesley had a desk diary, beautifully bound in faded green leather. The paper was pine-scented and the pages rustled like leaves as he turned them. For this book, he reserved his finest-nibbed pen; dipping in into the emerald ink before writing in his elaborate hand. The trouble was, since his wife's new-found hobby, he barely got beyond the date; staring at his spidery 'Friday 6th November', with an empty mind. It was very depressing. Eventually he wrote:

'I have been thinking... Hortense and I have been leading too secluded a life here. We will open our home to the poor and needy. Hortense may satisfy their physical hunger. I will care for their spiritual needs. It will be a small thing to do.' Actually it was a very big thing to do, at least Hortense thought so.

"I'm not sure I understand," she gazed at him as if she had suddenly become short-sighted. "You mean you want to turn our home into a soup kitchen?"

Creative Spirit

"No... not a soup kitchen."

Having succeeded at last, in halting her pen, he felt a sense of triumph. Better not to show it though.

"What then?" Hortense said. "You mean tea and biscuits..."

"Well, I was thinking of something a little more filling than tea and biscuits..."

He was a bit uncertain about Hortense suddenly. She looked brisk and stern, peering at him from beneath the grey cap of hair.

"I was thinking of something wholesome ... some warming stew perhaps; one of your marvellous casseroles. We could combine it with our poetry circle, a sort of Potage, Poetry and Prayer... Of course, people will be attracted by the free meal to start with, that and the entertainment..."

"Entertainment?" Hortense laid down her pen. Her eyes focused on some far distant point.

"The poetry readings I mean," warming to his theme, he began to gabble; "Then I could lead them in some prayers, or hymns even. People like that love a good sing-song don't they."

Hortense was silent. She had a vision of their home transformed into some kind of hostel, crammed with narrow beds and terrible old men, urinating on Aunt Gertrude's Turkish carpets.

Wesley patted her shoulders.

"I can't help noticing my dear, that this poetry circle of mine leaves you a bit... out of things. And this is something we can do together; helping these poor unfortunates..."

Hortense closed her book. She took a deep breath.

"If you think it's for the best," she said.

Wesley rewarded her with a kiss.

The posters went up in the Craft Centre and he warned Hortense to make enough food. He anticipated a crowd. Then, on the eve of the Big Day, he came home with two black bin-liners of old clothes scoured from a jumble sale. There was a rather fine tweed overcoat among the clothes with shoulder-flaps, of the kind Sherlock Holmes might have worn. Far from being impressed, Hortense seemed horrified when he showed it to her.

"It may be old-fashioned," he said, slightly offended; "But it's serviceable, that's what counts."

"I know you mean well Wesley," Hortense said. "But these people do have some pride. I mean the meal is one thing, but some folk are funny about wearing things from jumble sales."

Susan Davis

Wesley clapped an arm around her. She was such a nervous little thing, bless her!

"That's easily solved," he chortled. "You can have them cleaned up in no time dear. And if you get your sewing basket out, they'll soon be as good as new. I know what a clever girl you are!" And so, Hortense washed and sorted clothes. She sat up under her writing lamp, darning tears and sewing on buttons. The romance she had been writing was stuffed away in a drawer, and she thought of it now, with longing.

"Wonderful!" Her husband held up the re-furbished tweed overcoat. "I wouldn't be ashamed to wear that myself!"

*

The kitchen of the Chapel had not been designed for catering for large numbers and Hortense grappled with pots and pans with a kind of desperate efficiency. The potatoes were the trickiest. She had never before cooked such a huge quantity of mashed potato and was obsessive about eradicating every lump. It would not do to serve up lumpy mash, she thought, just because the meal was free. She felt Wesley's presence behind her in the doorway and was suddenly irritated, the skin on the back of her neck prickling.

"Are there many out there?" she asked, not daring to look herself. She could hear the murmur of voices and the chairs shuffling across the wooden floor. "Do they look hungry?"

"Well..." Wesley rubbed his eyes as he always did when nervous, "Well, they don't look as though they are starving exactly but I expect..."

"Well, how many are there? Will there be enough mashed potato do you think?"

He peered in the pot. "Oh, surely... yes I think so. It smells delicious!" He took an exaggerated breath as though transported by smell of her quite ordinary lamb casserole. "I hope we are getting some," he said.

"We will have ours this evening," Hortense said, although she couldn't imagine ever eating again at that moment. Her own appetite had vanished. She began to wonder how people who worked in restaurants ever managed to feel hungry.

Wesley disappeared to welcome the visitors and from the kitchen, she heard voices and laughter which seemed familiar. The poets must have arrived. Somehow she had not expected them to be included in the meal but peering from the kitchen, she saw that nearly

Creative Spirit

all the tables were in fact, taken up by the poetry circle. They were in a rowdy mood and she saw that bottles were being passed among them as they waited. Someone called for an ash-tray. Hortense standing in the doorway, still holding her potato masher in her hand felt herself go very hot. She beckoned to Wesley, who was hovering over the poets with a tea-cloth folded over his arm and the obsequious smile of a waiter.

"Where are these lost and lonely souls you were talking about? I thought we were meant to be feeding the hungry!"

Wesley pointed out the far table. "Over there my dear. They seem very nice, very appreciative."

Hortense looked up and saw three people; an elderly lady dressed in her Sunday best, a shaven-headed girl with a ring in her nose and a rather sinister looking fellow in a black overcoat and tilted trilby. He looked like a character out of a gangster film. She swallowed, feeling the onset of palpitations.

"Is that it?"

"Well it seems... for the moment..." Wesley stammered. Hortense fought hard to control herself. She had a sudden urge to hit him with the potato masher.

"So all this, all this work and effort," she indicated the steamy kitchen, "is for the poetry circle, people who are quite capable of feeding themselves, Wesley, I just... I just..." She found she was speechless with rage.

Wesley was suddenly at a loss. He had never really seen his wife in a temper before.

"Now, now, dear," he said, his voice rising with nerves. "We can't exclude them can we? After all, they are singing for their supper so to speak."

"Singing!" Hortense began gathering up saucepans and crashing them into the sink. Her spoon scraped the sides of the saucepan with a grating sound which made his toes curl. Wesley took up a tray but she snatched it from him. "I'll take it, I cooked it after all!"

The dining-hall had become quite silent as Hortense stormed about banging plates onto the tables. The poets watched her warily. They had never really considered Wesley's wife before, she was to them a little grey-haired, shy, scurrying creature. Now they made a lot of appreciative noises as she slapped the food before them. Only one, a girl with lank hair and a limp smile, had the temerity to ask if vegetarians were catered for.

Susan Davis

Hortense stared at her. She wanted very much to recommend the health food restaurant down the road but managed just to say 'No', and returned to the kitchen.

When Wesley went to find her, she had gone, leaving behind her the unwashed pots and pans. The vegetable peelings were spread like a collage on the table and the cat had found itself some gristly meat to play with. It was left to him to clear the tables and to serve the apple pie himself. The poets had good appetites and he found himself rushing back and forth to the kitchen for seconds.

He was worried about Hortense. Where was she? It was so unlike her to be difficult, to desert him in his hour of need. It crossed his mind that this idea of his had not been so good after all; even his attempt at a friendly chat with the strangers at the far table had met with monosyllabic replies.

His original plan had been to round the meal off with a little sermon on the nature of giving and receiving but now, with his arms piled high with dishes, he would have to scrap it. In any event, the poets had taken matters into their own hands. Already, a young man called Tristram, whose speciality was the heroic epic, had stood up and was beginning to read. Wesley knew from past experience that his poems or ballads as he preferred to call them, had been known to go on for half an hour.

He began to feel a little hurt as he put the two enormous kettles on for coffee, that they would start without him, with no consideration for their host and benefactor. He was looking very piqued when the elderly lady appeared in the doorway and introduced herself as Freda.

"You could do with some help," she said, shrugging off her coat and rolling up her sleeves. She quickly brushed off his polite denial, saying that she would rather wash the dishes than listen to 'all that rubbish out there'.

"Oh, in that case... it's most kind of you," Wesley said.

"Go on luv, give me that," she whisked the apron from around his waist, "I can't bear to see a grown man in a pinny. It goes against nature if you ask me."

"Well... my wife usually... yes... my wife..."

"Tired out after all that cooking I expect," Freda said kindly. "Crept off to bed I shouldn't wonder."

Wesley nodded. He excused himself saying he would go and make sure she was alright.

Creative Spirit

Hortense had not gone to bed. Far from it. As Wesley blundered into the hall; into the deep, candle-lit hush; the audience turned and frowned, held fingers to their lips.

His wife's voice carried well, he had to admit. The acoustics were good. And this was not the cosy murmur which saw him safely through his 'funny turns'. In fact, he thought he might have a 'funny turn' at any minute. His wife Hortense... but not his wife; somehow beyond him, above him, as she stood on the raised dais of the altar, transfigured by candlelight, reading from her little red note book. If only it had been the nature poem; then he might have been indulgent. But the words which rang out so clearly, which stunned even the jostling poets into silence, were sublime. Impossible. That all that frantic 'scratching' should come to this; that Hortense should be possessed not by demons but by angels. As she lifted her head, to deliver her final line; there was a glow about her blunt features, the grey halo of hair, which sickened him.

Wesley tugged at his beard. He had even lost the urge to pray. And he could feel it now, a 'funny turn', like an approaching train in the distance.

"Well then?" Hortense came over to him, her eyes bright, somehow, challenging. "Tell me what you think Wesley?"

"I think... I think..." he found himself at a loss; his stomach churned with resentment. "I think you ought to help Freda with the washing up. She is meant to be our guest after all."

"Yes, of course," her voice was brisk as she rolled up her sleeves, but her smile was serene. "But I'm afraid I won't have time for any more of these meals in the future. You see I shall be joining the poetry circle myself."

As Wesley went forward to lead the prayers, he felt as though his limbs had stiffened. He knew that he could not, this time, give thanks to the creative spirit, the spirit which had robbed him of his wife.

Bending his head, he clasped his hands together and cleared his throat.

"Let us give thanks..." he began but there was a feeling in his throat like broken glass. Someone in the audience sniggered but he pretended not to hear.

"Let us give thanks," he said again. Then, he closed his eyes very tightly, so that there was nothing but darkness, and then he began to pray with all his heart.

T.M. Merremont

The Unexamined Life

SOMEONE
No scholarly proof exists that Henry James had sexual intercourse with a woman. This information should only be taken at its face value. Nothing else is implied. We are always safer with literal meanings; don't you think?
    Poetry best exemplifies the communicative power of metaphor. A poet must choose illustrations that convey the temper of his age. In these illogical times, unusual metaphor is called for; don't you think?
    I have metaphors within that sing like salt on the moon.

THE CRACK-UP
I'll lock my own door,
and keep my own key.
I care for no inquiries
upon this shelf of me.

    I am much better now. The Doctor has explained that I have the mind of a poet. Fragile as grass.

ENTRE
The Doctor says that I must enter the professional world. At first, I am fearful, hesitant. I will be armed only with my talent.
The Doctor reminds me that I am young. Urban.
I counter that I lack sufficient credentials.
The Doctor writes me another prescription.
I stand corrected.
She does not enter his mind...

AT THE OFFICE
It is hard to enter the world without starving. I started my job at the 'NATIONAL SUN', where the money is very good. I bought two sharkskin suits.
    "Do not fall prey to hubris," the editor told me. "Hubris is our secret and our scar." A no nonsense type.
    Above his desk. On the wall behind his desk I notice an ear framed in a bed of jimson weed labelled 'Art'.
    Much doodling at the desk. A pride of diplomats - a graze of cattle - a haggle of politicians - a slobber of drunks - a query of

The Unexamined Life

scientists - a cheer of salesmen - a prattle of clerics - a stand of philosophers - a grovel of doctoral candidates.

CROSS COUNTRY (1)

Stumbling about in the abandoned house in Denver we stumbled across each other. As they made love she kept squinting at their coupling naked in the mirror. He assumed then that she was extremely sensuous. It took him far too long to realize that she was looking at herself.
  I do not mean that.

CROSS COUNTRY (2)

I approach you sunning yourself at the apartment complex pool. Phoenix was warm last spring. He does not recall the sun, only the heart shaped hole cut in the ass of her bikini bottom.
  "I want you," she said.
  "I could use a drink," he replied.
  "I want *you*." This firm, sincere.
  "I want you, too."
  "But I don't want to hurt Him," she said, drawing away.

STRANGERS

I know a woman now. I know a woman now with an inoperably tilted cervix. Insides jammed as the New York City phone system. We talk, take long walks in Central Park (daylight); cigarette smoke spiralling into the sun-spotted clouds. Hands brushed together lightly, lightly as if clasping a wounded bird.
  When we make love it hurts her - not so much then as the next day. In the morning she is gruff, bitchy. It is extremely odd, and also typical that our lovemaking should harbor pain. Such are the times.

THE CONTEST

At the 'NATIONAL SUN' we are sponsoring a contest. Name our mascot. Our mascot is a dog with no hind legs. Our readers send in their pennies to keep him in tires.
  Whoever names the dog (what will it be: Imhotep? Mahler? Saint Genet?) wins a free trip to Lourdes.
  This job is only temporary, until I finish my Epic. The metaphors are sleeping now. Incubating. They need the rest.
  Northrup Frye at the hunt; Hemingway at the tea table.

T.M. Merremont

THE THEORY OF LOGICAL TYPES
Books lie. People lie. All books are people.
Why will you only leave him when he is gone?

SUCCESS
They have promoted me to the book review position at the 'NATIONAL SUN'. Promoted me. Position.
My intent is to wean our readers away from trashy self-help books. The public deserves quality. I have editorialized about the vital need for a diet book by Kazantzakis, an exercise manual by Garcia Marquez.
He is much better now.

THE SCAR
It was then that he noticed the scar on his palm. Shiny, and pink as grapefruit.

CROSS COUNTRY (3a)
The next morning the sun chipped across the abandoned rug betraying the curtains.
She turned her back to him on the bed. The covers pulled tightly across her shoulders indicated desolation. Don't you think? The arched fingernail bones of her shoulders said, "I hate you for not helping me in my helplessness."
Is this a proper accusation?

MY FILES
In my files are kept used paper plates. Research materials on the gastronomy of success. With a leaf of my fingers I can tell what I ate on any given day, and how it affected my thoughts. From aardvark steak to zucchini polonaise. Flipping through, sniffing, licking here and there: ham 'n eggs, kim chee, borscht, abalone con naroz, peacock tongues, Livornese scampi. Quiche Lorraine!
Some days my thoughts were filling; on others they burned like gas. One Martinmas I was hungry again in an hour.
Sometimes he arranges the plates like a fan, and thinks of her. Earlobes budding like escargots; mouth lush as Alfredo sauce. The fan is coy by his face, then rustling with impatience. Then a flick of dismissal.

The Unexamined Life

CROSS COUNTRY (3b)

In Denver. Did she recall when he first found out about the two of them? Did she recall how gracious he was, and how wounded were his eyes? He felt like fondling his eyes then. She had told him that her man was evil, and was using her lovely mind as a crutch. Later, in bed, she was Teresa of the Flowers, and he the Devil's Advocate. Ixxxxxxxxx

HE	HE	HEHEHEHEHE
HE	HE	HE
HE	HE	HE
HE	HE	HE
HEHEHEHEHE		HEHEHEHEHE
HE	HE	HE
HE	HE	HE
HE	HE	HE
HE	HE	HEHEHEHEHE

Nothing can deceive him.

BECAUSE IT IS THERE

Inside this great machine. Inside this great machine in the middle of the tapping office. Inside. There is surety within. Here he can plot the patterns. Here the data does not conflict once he has learned to differentiate.

The rest of the staff here at the 'NATIONAL SUN' consists of McTank weighing in as religious editor; Angelico is Military Affairs; Warner holds down the National Desk, and Thompson covers Hollywood.

Each of them is a hard bitten professional. Angelico (rumor has it) was once seen pressing toothlike indentations into his leg with a fork. Each of us is hungry. We see things as adults. We seek to consolidate gains in position, power. Loyalties change each day.

We are all searching for the perfect pattern, so we affect alliances: combinations against the one. Such as:
    Myself, McTank, Angelico, Warner *vs* Thompson
    Myself, McTank, Angelico, Thompson *vs* Warner
    Myself, McTank, Thompson, Warner *vs* Angelico
    Myself, Thompson, Warner, Angelico *vs* McTank
    Thompson, Warner, Angelico, McTank *vs* He

SHE (EXCERPTS)

T.M. Merremont

"When I first met you I knew you were a poet just by your eloquence. You talked *con*stantly, darling. Not that it wasn't cute, of course, but it *was* a bit foolish. Will you please zip me up, dearest?... Oooo, you pinched my skin, damn you... oh, come here, my closeness, and give mama a hug. I forgive you. Come on now, don't sulk...there... Oooo, bloody fool, now you've smeared my make-up. You're always pawing me... What? Now, you don't *really* mean to say that. You know that I don't like to be hugged when I'm all made up. How silly of you. I don't know *what* ever put the idea in your head... Come closer, my hero, you just made a silly mistake, that's all. I forgive you. Will you hand me my wrap please?... Now you've mussed my hair, dammit. I spent an hour at Antoine's getting it just right for you, and now you've ruined it... There, there, don't sulk, my love. Ah, if I didn't already know as much I'd swear you were a poet just by the way you're so quiet; taking everything in...."

ESSAY QUESTION

Why did James Joyce, his eyesight rapidly fading, spend the last precious hours of his light reading and re-reading Anita Loos' *Gentlemen Prefer Blonds*?

EL CONQUISTADOR

Today at the 'NATIONAL SUN' I wore both my suits. I strode confidently to the editor's desk intent upon receiving a raise. Circulation has doubled since the appearance of my prize winning review of the book *Jivaro Cookery*.

Upon reaching his desk I noticed that the editor was not himself. That is, sitting behind the editor's desk - that is, the *former* editor's desk that now belongs to the new editor who is not the same man as the old editor who once sat before me.

"Yes?" her query is gruff, bitchy.

I inform her of the circulation rise, and my corresponding expectations. She shakes her head sadly. Tears plop on the pages as she shows me the red company books. They speak of Armageddon. She reminds me of the energy crisis, the starving millions in Africa, the rising cost of a decent patè. She exhorts me to sacrifice. I stand corrected.

Above her desk. On the wall behind her desk is a framed embryo labelled 'My Son, By Lanvin'.

New York Museum of Modern Art   *Philip Wolmuth*

T.M. Merremont

On the way back to my desk McTank, Thompson, and Warner surround me apprehensively. At first they shuffle about like expectant schoolboys, but soon, because we are all adults here, they approach me for dances. A waltz, a rhumba, a minuet, a clog. Soon my card is filled.

The tapping music begins to rise like aromas from my files.

All of them are straining for a dance with me now.

All but Angelico. Ah, but today, not Angelico. For today, poor Angelico does not exist.

Subscriptions and Resubscriptions

If you need to resubscribe there will be an appropriate reminder in this issue you have just received. **Please resubscribe as promptly as possible. Subscription revenue is literally our lifeblood.**

Standard Subscription / Resubscription (two issues)
Panurge anthologies come out every April and October promptly. Panurge 23 appears October 95. ***It will be 240 pages long and hence the increase in the subscription rate***

☐ £12 UK   ☐ IR£15   ☐ £15/$18 Overseas   ☐ £20/$30 Air Mail

All cheques to **Panurge, Crooked Holme Farm Cottage, Brampton, Cumbria CA8 2AT UK. Tel 016977 - 41087**

Jen Waldo

The Ultimate Equality

My daughter Sandra is marrying a white boy.
   My daughter Sandra is marrying a white boy and every morning the hall is filled with black women's faces so sad I feel like the history of pain is written on them. It's only the women who come. They come whining money, whining help. For their babies.
   The men, now. The men are gone or looking for work or hiding their heads in shame because they got people they can't provide for - or don't. Sometimes the women wear their men's shame on their faces - more of them have purpled eyes and clipped lips than not.
   Sandra's young man is quiet; he seems content to sit in a corner and watch her gush and bubble. He's intelligent but doesn't volunteer anything of himself. I don't know if he's shy or arrogant or maybe obtuse; either way he's one of those people who'll take time to get to know.
   He and Sandra have only visited me a couple of times since they announced their plans to marry and I resent it that he is so reticent; he might make more of an effort is what I think. He and my daughter will be married soon - married and off and I would at least like to have more of an idea of him.
   His eyes, which are a muddy blue, offer no expression that I am familiar with; I try to meet his eye, to glimpse his thoughts, but he's not sharing. He's thin all over, his face, his body, his hands, all of him long and bony, giving the impression that he's wasting away in pursuit of some ethereal ideal. In reality, he's very literal-minded, a scientist.
   This must be the only thing that he and my daughter have in common - their science backgrounds. Because I can find nothing else that would have attracted them to one another.
   Sandra is round-faced with laughing, reaching eyes. She is tall - five feet, ten inches - and there's a healthy layer of flesh covering her bones. Sandra tells her life story to complete strangers; she sings in the shower; she coos to plants; she looks people in the eye as she walks down the street. She has never made an enemy that I know of. Sandra is the product, the result of all my focused molding. She's everything I ever wanted her to be; being her mother makes me proud and humble at the same time.
   Sandra and Bill. Opposite in every way.

Jen Waldo

Will he always want to sit while she dances, to stagnate as she effervesces? He's so quiet; I worry that he'll sink into judgement, that one day his silent inflexibility will want to dominate Sandra's vocal buoyancy.

One woman, she gets her welfare money and goes to buy food for her children and three times now she's had her groceries stolen from her before she could complete the one block walk to her home. Home. That's what she calls it. ''Fore I can get to my home,' she says.

Home - a rat and cockroach convention in a tenement that should be burned and disinfected and left to clear for five years before anyone is allowed to walk within breathing distance of it and this woman calls it her home. A home with no groceries.

She's taken to feeding her children at the market. When her money hasn't been stolen. That's okay, she says. This way she doesn't have to cook; she only had the one pan anyway, she says, and that got stolen some while ago.

Starting at nine o'clock the clients line up in front of the caseworkers' stations. The lines soon combine into one thick pushing group that braids itself through the door and then spreads on outside and down the street a ways.

All the faces, all the stories, the same. It's no wonder welfare workers don't last long. The caseworkers, you see, they come in here with their new college degrees; they're fresh and all a-fervor with wanting to change the world but it only takes a month or so before their eyes begin to dim from the loss of those shining ideals.

Sometimes all this misery still touches me. I did my time on a desk and now I'm in charge of it all. Not because I did anything right but because I'm the only one who didn't run away after a while. I stuck it out and look where it got me. Me. The Queen of Deprivation.

Now I'm the right color to where I can go take a walk through the inner city and see what it's like and believe me, it's as bad as you hear. They got seven year-old gang members down here. And incest - brothers going after their sisters, fathers wanting on their daughters - it happens and you don't want to hear it because it's not pretty but it happens whether you want it to or not. And that brings on the babies and thirteen-year-olds having babies that're both niece and daughter, nephew and son and it's all pretty sick, wouldn't you say?

Like I said. It happens.

The Ultimate Equality

They got women carrying guns to protect themselves as they go their own way and they got people at night cuddling up four deep in the recesses of the doorways, keeping warm and trying to sleep. They got women who moan for their fixes and boys who steal from their mothers; they got men who'll kill for any reason and men who'll kill for no reason at all.

They got shelters, too. Only the shelters, they're full up and you got to think, these shelters, who pays for them? Good people, people with educations and fine homes and a bedroom for every person in the family and a car for every adult and enough food to get fat on. 'How much do those people need down there?' somebody might ask; and they also might say, 'They're bleedin' us empty.'

And that's so. Indeed. That is so.

Another thing somebody might say is, 'Something ought to be done.' I've heard that one plenty.

Yeah. Like I said. I been here a long time and if there's one thing I learned, it's this place, these people - their needs go on and on and on and there's no end to it. The misery down here, it's like something science fiction, the way it keeps growing and feeding on itself until it can't be controlled.

A black boy, say he's ten, and he's not a member of a gang, he's dead before he's eleven. That's the way it is. So he carries a weapon, he looks tough, he struts and talks dirty. Oh, he probably doesn't see action until he's twelve but he wants it. He wants it.

Does he go to school? Why? Who's going to make him? People like me? This boy can't read. He can't write. He can count money enough to know that he's never going to have enough to get out.

His life is without hope. He's seen the emptiness of his mother's eyes. When he was younger he came to the welfare office with her and saw the emptiness of the other mothers' eyes; he sees lack of hope everywhere he looks.

He steals and feels no qualms; as he grows, he rapes his neighbor or his sister. He kills and knows no anguish. Only anger, anger. He will not live to see eighteen years and no one cares when he dies.

This is despair.

And ignorance?

I have seen girls - children - holding their babies, saying, 'Where did it come from?' 'What caused this?' Yes. I have seen it.

And I have known young girls to lie with strangers because there is nothing else to do. For them, there is nothing else. They are no

Jen Waldo

more than the hole between their legs. They are told this on the streets, by their parents, by their friends. They feel nothing; they know nothing. They are nothing.

Enough.

Since Sandra told me she was marrying Bill suddenly I'm seeing couples of mixed race everywhere I look.

I don't know how I feel about his. A white boy. Isn't that something, now? Indeed. I remember the first time I saw her with a white boy. She was fourteen at the time. I'd come in from work and there she was, hunched over some studying at the table, her tamed black nap close to his sleek blonde one. I asked myself, What's wrong with these fools, they don't teach their kids prejudice anymore? This keeps up, they'll wish they had.

That's what I thought.

The next weekend, I had the kids start in an Afro-American extension program over at the college. I thought to teach them about being black; I thought there was something they should understand.

Sandra, at the age of twenty-four, has her Masters in Botany. She's old enough to have things in perspective, old enough to see things as they are. But here she's got me addressing invitations; she expects me to feel all squishy inside at the thought of bridesmaids' dresses and grown men wearing boutonnieres. She goes on and on about her 'fiance' - what he says, what he does, how he feels, what he eats. That's what she calls him, her fiance. Me, I had a boyfriend, then I had a husband; I had no fancy fiance in between.

Bill and Sandra. The two of them met last year at Yale while they were tutoring undergraduates. Next year, it's on to Stanford, where they will be junior professors while they're getting their doctorates. Bill's education is in genetics. There's an irony there somewhere.

They're no slouches, these two.

My daughter, though; she's caught herself a white boy. I keep my fierce, triumphant pride in this fact tucked away; it would not do, to be proud.

I have a culinary vision of myself slowly diluting; my coffee skin turns to chocolate, from chocolate to caramel, from caramel to butterscotch, from butterscotch to smooth cream. I change from a bitter flavor to a benign one. I go from being strong and hot and thin to being full fat, cool, and slow to run.

Will our noses and lips thin with the passing generations until we are no more?

The Ultimate Equality

There was a time when such a marriage would not be considered. There just was no such thing.

Last year there was an incident. I was walking behind the stations, going from the coffee machine to my office. Office - a cubicle, more like. The glass walls don't even go up to the ceiling. There is a wooden door; if I want privacy I have to stand behind it.

The welfare clients' black faces followed my progress hungrily as I walked through. A successful black woman. A black woman with power. They wonder how did I become what I am. I am so remote from them I might as well be God.

There are so many of them, so many.

I am used to it.

Like I was saying, my workers were busily interviewing and calculating and cajoling. They were an officious bunch, good at filling out forms and giving advice that would never be taken; their clients put obstacles before every goal, no matter how small. Excuses don't cost money so there are plenty of them around.

As I was walking through the area behind the desks, I heard one woman's voice above all the others. I looked at her. Skinny, she was, and tall. Her knees, at angles from the seat of her chair, looked boney through her jeans. Her teeth were large and yellow and one of her front ones was missing. Her eyes were not focusing properly. Right away I categorized her. Junkie-addict. Uneducated. Hooker on the downhill. She was like a thousand other women. There was a boy standing next to her who was like any other boy with his runny wide nose and his curly eyelashes.

"You got to help my boy," she slurred at the caseworker. I'd heard that one before and so, I'm sure, had the caseworker. "You got to help him." She pushed him forward slightly and I caught a glimpse of a bruised eye, a skinned cheek. Her tone was desperate. I'd heard desperation before, too.

I walked on.

I went back to the office, closed the door. I had a meeting later that morning with the City Council. I knew that before the council met with me, they would be meeting with the Hopskon County Medical Facility. County Medical would be asking for money. And then I would be asking for money. Medical needed more staff. I needed more staff. We all needed more, more, more. Medical always got to go before me because they are doctors and doctors are God's representatives here on earth and nobody keeps God waiting.

Jen Waldo

I had long ago resigned myself to the politics of it all. County Medical never got their money any more than I did anyway.

I wanted to work on my presentation. Every month I got a little bit more. A little bit more for the people. The month before I'd gotten a meat allowance for the shelters. No mean accomplishment, I tell you.

I glanced through the glass wall of my office and saw the woman still clutching her battered son, still pleading at her caseworker.

For some reason, I put aside the idea to work on my petition. I stuck my head out the door and called to the caseworker, "Bring her and her boy on in here, Gemma."

This was no surprise. I occasionally did this. It kept me close to the everyday. I couldn't distance myself or I'd forget. I've seen it happen. I've seen things you'd think a person would never forget but memories fade or soften and soon it's as though they'd happened to another person. I go to the people so I can be passionate for them.

The woman and her child were ushered in. The woman's face was wet and shiny with tears but I wasn't impressed. People down here, they're crying every day, all the time. Tears mean nothing. Nothing.

She shoved her boy at me. "You got to help me. You got to do something about my boy."

"I'm Ms. Murphy." I stuck out my hand so she had to shake it. There was no excess flesh to cushion her palms and her hand had a tremor to it. I held it until she met my eye. I raised an eyebrow, letting her know I was waiting for something.

She searched her mind for what it could be. She found it. "Nicoletta Louise."

"Well Nicoletta Louise, why don't you have a seat?"

She moved to the straight-backed chair I kept in front of my desk, putting the boy first in front then beside her, bending to prop her purse beside a chair leg. Her shoulder blades, I could see while she was hunched over, were like jagged mountains beneath the fabric of her T-shirt. Once again she said, "You got to do something about my boy."

I looked at the child as he stared at the top of my desk. "What seems to be the problem?"

The woman reached to the floor beside her, put her hand into her purse and pulled out a gun. A gun.

She put it to the boy's head. "You don't do something for this

The Ultimate Equality

child, lady, I might as well pull the trigger right now." Her eyes were wild, her whole body shaking with shock at what she was doing.
"Nicoletta. Why don't you put that away? There's no need to harm the child."
The boy was maybe four years old. Without asking, I knew his history. He had occasional meals - never nutritious; he'd never seen a piece of fresh fruit in his life. More than likely, he could not make a complete sentence. His mother left him alone for long periods of time. He had no toys. Lots of men slept in his mother's bed; this boy didn't have a bed at all. He'd never seen a playground, though by law in the inner city there was a recreation area within every six block radius.
He stood with the gun to his temple, not even realizing what it meant.
"I mean it! You got to help me!" She was shouting now.
Peripherally, I could see the heads of the caseworkers turning toward my office; I saw their shocked expressions as they saw the gun. I saw one of them reach for the phone on her desk and I knew that she was summoning the police. A waste of time. I'd have this woman calmed down and out of here in less than five minutes; the police wouldn't get here for twenty. And what would be the point? We'd take the child away from her, sure - but only for a while. He'd be back with her in maybe a month; he was hers and the law says a child belongs with his mother. All we'd have gotten out of it would have been the ink on our hands from the paper work. Some downtown counsellor would see the mother a couple of times then sign a sheet that said she was over her period of trauma. The mother, now, she wouldn't have changed - how could she change? And the child would be more confused than ever.
The woman's hand was weak and the gun was heavy. The barrel end began to drop.
"Nicoletta." I kept my voice calm. "I'll help you with the boy. I'll do something for him. Take away the gun from your baby's head."
She took it away. She took it away all right. She took it away and put it to her own temple and pulled the trigger before I even had a chance to sigh with relief over the saved boy.
The noise and the mess exploded at the same time. That woman's head went everywhere. Her body slumped sideways and fell off the

Jen Waldo

chair. The boy jumped and fell to the floor on the other side of my desk; he curled there in shock. The gun's report echoed for a few seconds, growing bigger before it fell to cold silence.

Then the caseworkers were frantically screaming and rushing toward the windowed walls of my office. They stood outside, looking in.

They couldn't enter. The mess of the woman's brains was splattered all over the place. I met eyes, reassuring them that I was all right. I hollered, "The police?"

"On their way," one of them hollered back.

I pushed my chair back and crouched down to the floor beneath my desk. I looked toward the boy; his face was pressed against the floor and I knew that he was feeling the cold of the gray tile. That's what children can become - animals that enjoy sensations like the cold of a floor or the flavor of salt or the texture of fabrics; sometimes that's all they live for.

I met his eyes. Out of habit, he looked away. He was calm, non-comprehending. The noise had frightened him, that was all. I crawled further under the desk, moving in closer. The smell of him was so strong that I wished I didn't have to breathe.

"Boy?" I said to him. "You all right?"

He didn't respond. Probably no one had ever spoken directly to him before.

"What's your name, boy?"

He didn't answer.

"Evelyn?" I heard Barb call. "Evelyn? You all right?"

I wiggled my backside out from behind the desk and stood up, shouting back, "Yeah. What do you think? Maybe I should be upset by this?"

There were brains and bone and bloody hair on my desk.

Theoretically, I was supposed to remain in place until the police came. I didn't have the stomach for it. I walked around the desk and stooped to pick up the boy. I lifted him - he wasn't heavy - and, trying to keep his head turned away from his mother's body, carried him to the door. The child was limp on my breast. I slipped once in the blood but luckily remained upright.

Someone opened the door for me and we stepped out.

Quite a story to tell, isn't it? Quite a memory to store.

It never once gave me nightmares. I've had people tell me I'm tough.

The Ultimate Equality

The boy's name was Boris. At the time of his mother's death Boris did not know how to go to the toilet. He could not speak except in grunts and signs. He had never used silverware or had a story read to him.

Now he lives in a foster home - a home away from the city. He knows his letters and goes to school and though he is behind other children his age, he will catch up. He will catch up.

My son. Mark. He's twenty-two and I wonder how he feels about his sister marrying a white boy. Does it please him? Does he ponder life's mutability? No of course not; Mark ponders nothing. He wears tennis shoes that cost as much as a good second hand car did when I was his age. When I look at my son I see a white boy in black boy skin. Is this a bad thing?

All my life I have wanted equality, have campaigned and strived toward equality every day.

But equality is not sameness.

Mark is artistic. He's studying film-making at UCLA. Now what mother would not be proud of such a thing?

I remember picking up Mark's socks from his bedroom floor. Rolled tight as condoms, they were. And smelly of a stink sweet like nothing else. At night after he was asleep, I would go in to kiss him goodnight and there I'd see these tight-rolled circles on the floor, resting in the slanted moonlight like sleeping donuts. And I would think, If I've told him once I've told him a thousand times to unroll these socks and put them in the dirty clothes. Then I'd pick them up, unroll them, and put them in the dirty clothes.

But God, what a happy child, what a loveable, smiling, intelligent boy he was.

Mark has no woman yet. When he decides to marry, will he go black or white?

My father was a janitor for the postal service in Arizona. I was raised far from here. It was a good life, out in Arizona. In our small town there were maybe only twenty black families. We stuck to ourselves; our mothers cleaned the banks and offices during the night-time hours and our fathers swept the sidewalks during the day.

I wonder what my father would have thought about his granddaughter marrying herself to Bill the white geneticist. I wonder.

The children's father and I are divorced; have been for ten years. He teaches history at a private college in the south. We believe in

Jen Waldo

education.
    Sometimes Stanley, my ex-husband, comes to visit. When he comes he sleeps in the same bed as me and we make love all night long. He'll say, 'Why won't you move to where I am?' During college breaks, he stays a long time and it's pure heaven.
    But I won't go. He knows why I won't go and he thinks I'm crazy. "You've done enough for those people," he says. "You've given twenty years of your life to the ghetto. Nothing's gotten better. Only worse and worse and still you go down there day after day and I want to know why!"
    But I don't answer because I've answered before. I think how the month before I gave CPR to a rancid drunk on the street just outside the office. I think how many children I've gotten out of there - children like Boris who are doing fine now. I think how school attendance has doubled since professional basketball players have been dropping by at odd times to do basketball clinics; though education is none of my domain, the project was instigated at my suggestion and it took off like a shot and I take pride in that.
    Stanley says, "Let someone else do the worrying and the coming up with new ideas. There're plenty people qualified for your job."
    He's mistaken but I don't say so. He works in a college and students write down everything he says. What does he know about reality? He doesn't know how few people there are who are willing to do my job. Who would do it if they didn't have to?
    Maybe he's right and I am crazy.
    I wonder if Stanley has ever made love with a white woman.
    Yesterday a man came in to the office and went after Bob Palley with a knife. Apparently Bob had told the man's wife about the new Elride Shelter for Women. So the husband had come looking for the one who'd helped her leave him.
    All the caseworkers circled around the two men, watching wide-eyed as the knife moved in toward Bob. One of the workers screamed. As a matter of routine, Cynthia moved to her desk and phoned the police. I came out of my office and watched, as helpless against that blade as everybody else.
    The clients just stood, arms wrapped across their breasts, their expressions smug and tight. The angry man laughed at the fear on Bob's face and he made little teasing slashes with his knife, slicing open Bob's cheek, his arm, his side.
    When Bob was down on the ground, his arms up to protect his

The Ultimate Equality

face, his backside exposed, the man with the knife kicked him and said, "Doan you be messin' in my biness again."

Bob lay on the floor and cried. Blood ran from his three nasty gashes. We had to get him up, get him to the clinic that was across the street and down a ways. But he wouldn't move. All he did was cry about how he knew that woman would be back living with her husband in less than a week and what was it all for anyway? What was it all for? Poor Bob. I've been cut some and I know it's a pretty scary thing to see that knife waving at you like that.

That was Sandra on the phone.

"Momma?" she asked. Her voice was so cute, so giddy, that I wanted to choke some depth into it. "What do you think? Should there be a groom's cake? Is that still a thing people do?"

"Honey? What do I know about grooms' cakes? Call the editor of *Bride's*. Write to Dear Abby." Outside my office door, I saw a uniform enter the bureau. Then another. And another. They travel in packs, these cops. They have to, I guess, but their numbers make me feel invaded.

"But Momma," Sandra was saying. "You have to help me out with this. I don't know any of this stuff. And anyway, did you know there's a problem with Bill's family? His aunt won't come to the wedding because I'm black. The woman hasn't even met me!" Her tone was indignant. She was going to take on the whole WASP population of the western United States.

I didn't say anything. What did she want me to say? Did she expect me to be surprised? Did she want me to get indignant with her? She didn't want to hear the truth - which was that people like Bill's aunt would be judging her by the color of her skin until she died. People like Bill's aunt.

"Honey, I got to go."

"But Momma?"

"Tonight, Sandra. We'll talk about it tonight."

Sandra was planning this wedding from home. I wondered what Bill's people would think of our church, our black minister, our all-black choir. Would they expect alien rituals? Or slick gospel singers? Or our eyes rolling back in our heads, the whites big and scary as we said our 'Hallelujah'-s? Had they heard rumors of us prostrating ourselves in the aisles and wrestling with snakes on the altar?

I almost laughed aloud as I fantasized on their doughball

Jen Waldo

expressions; frightened they'd be, or stiff with disapproval or big-eyed from their imaginings.
 How fraught. How potentially fraught.
 I did laugh.
 We are all the same in the eyes of God.
 I've spent some time with Bill's mother. I met her for lunch downtown one day. I met her expecting not to like her. What did she want - for me to apologize that my daughter is so vivacious, so beautiful and intelligent that she could attract and hold the attention of a white woman's precious son?
 She looked like I thought she'd look. Dressed real well and wearing heels. Frosted hair and eyelids that sagged just like Bill's. A blue dress that she probably kept filed under 'L' in her closet for 'Lunch dress'. Her skin was so dry it looked painful - too much sun, too many cigarettes.
 She was unhealthy and frail and though I arrived pettish and ready to bite, in the end I just felt sorry for that sad, sad woman who didn't know the politically correct way to handle this particular situation. She hid her disappointment deep inside to where I couldn't see it if I didn't look too closely. And I didn't.
 "Sandra seems like a very nice girl," she'd said.
 Indeed.
 As the uniforms move in, some of the women slowly sidle toward the door and disappear like they think they're invisible. One cop signals to another by raising his eyebrows and jerking his head and the women are followed and herded back into the building. The cop who ushers them in closes the door behind him as he re-enters. He turns the key in the lock and flips the 'open' sign to 'closed'.
 This means that we are, in effect, closed by the police until further notice.
 An identification check. These checks infuriate me. The police act official and my clients get intimidated. Now I'd like to know - if my clients aren't allowed to be free from intimidation at the welfare office, then where the hell can they be free from it? And these people here, they all have something to hide, every last one of them.
 Oh, it's all very respectful, very polite. Lots of 'ma'am'-s and 'please'-es. But those uniforms. You put a guppy in a shark uniform and he becomes a shark. That's all.
 One of the invaders comes to my cubicle to pay his respects. He holds his riot helmet in his hands and hangs his head. As though I'm

The Ultimate Equality

the one in authority. "Sorry, Ms Murphy. Sorry. Story's out that one of 'em's dealing drugs right here on the premises."

"Yeah right. Bought some myself just yesterday." I sniff at him. Blushing white boy.

"Sorry." He turns away.

"You got a warrant?" I ask his back. He just waves his hand over his head as he walks to join his colleagues in the i.d. check. That's no answer; a waving hand could mean anything. But he can't open their bags without any warrant. I won't stand still for that.

I see my caseworkers throw up their hands. They stack their papers on the corners of their desks and retreat to the break room. There they will drink diet caffeine-free soft drinks and wish they smoked cigarettes.

Then one of the cops brings in the dog. This one's just what you'd expect, a German shepherd. I hate dogs. And from the look of things, there's not another black face in the room that's fond of them either. I'm angry now and go huffing out there to the cop that just left my office. I'm a powerful engine but I'm under control.

"You have paperwork says you can bring that animal in here?" I make my voice demanding. I'm a demanding woman so it's a tone convenient for me to access.

"Ma'am?"

"Let me see the paperwork for the dog."

"We don't need such a thing."

I speak to the man with the dog - without going too near. I raise an eyebrow at him to tell him I mean what I say. "You get that thing out of here before I call the authorities." The dog's good; he sits, mouth closed, teeth politely concealed, and waits. He, too, is a powerful engine that's under control.

"Ma'am?" the officer says, just like the first one.

"You heard me. Its license. Its papers. I want to see it written where it says that thing's had its shots."

The black women's eyes are big with terror and they for all the world look like they're escaped slaves that've been treed. They've moved away, away from the dog and are huddled up along one wall.

"Ms Murphy," says the first cop. "This is a sniffing dog. Now I've already told you why we're here. This dog'll just help us do our job faster. Then we'll be on our way and you can get back to work."

"You get that dog out of here or I'm calling the authorities." I step toward the phone. Everybody in the vast room stares at me as I

Jen Waldo

look up the number for the animal control people. When somebody answers the other end of the line I say, "Hello? Animal Control? I got me an unidentified dog on the premises. Maybe a diseased one."

I'm put on hold and things on the floor begin to move. The one cop signals to the dog cop to begin the search. The dog is lead forward and the women shudder and pull back further into themselves as they clutch their purses. I see a shoulder disappear as one woman shifts herself behind her neighbor; she is trying to hide behind the others.

The dog is lead past the women. He walks sedately along, impressive in his poise. He growls deep in his throat when he nears the woman who is hunched down now, using the other women for cover. He dives into the ranks and grabs her purse with his pointed teeth; he's not pulling but he's not letting go either. The other women back away, leaving the victim alone. Losing herself to the drama of it all, she screams and begins to pull on her purse, ready to fight the dog over it. Stupid, stupid woman.

The cops have been here less than five minutes.

I study the woman and right away I want to kick myself. The cop was right. She's been dealing out of my bureau and I should have realized it days ago. She's been around, moving forward in the line but never meeting with a caseworker, conveniently needing to use the toilet when it was almost her turn. She's been sitting in the waiting area, never putting herself forward.

I saw these things but never thought about them.

Two of the cops move in and push her against the wall, put the cuffs on her, read her the rights. One of the cops, the woman brought along for just this job, feels the offender's body up and down. The purse is confiscated.

I'm still on hold. I hang up the phone and go over. I'm angry at the cops, angry at the woman for using my branch and most of all I'm angry at myself for not seeing what I should have seen.

And I'm scared to death of that dog who's been lead away now and my fear makes me mad, too.

"Let me see your warrant," I say.

The one I talked to earlier pulls out the warrant. It's a blanket warrant which means he can search wherever he feels there's a need. Already he's opened the woman's purse. Like an eight year-old showing off, he lets me see the baggie full of crack phials.

I'm furious with myself. I go to my office and slam the door for all to hear. The presence of the dog has upset me. That slut brazenly dealing her drugs right under my nose has embarrassed me. Embarrassment. That's something I don't handle well.

I hide there, behind the door, a mass of humiliation, self-disgust, and frustrated rage. I stay for a while and give myself a good talking to.

Are my children afraid of dogs? Are my children afraid of anything?

They have me thinking that they have no fears but surely this is not so.

Sandra, moving into this marriage - does she fear marriage differently than any other woman because her marriage will be different? Or are her fears ordinary fears, fears not taking into account the huge reality of her color?

And Mark. He dances around light-hearted like nobody's ever called him 'nigger'. He glides and waltzes through his life like he's never heard the word, like he's never looked it in the eye.

Maybe this is so. Times have changed.

This evening Sandra will want me to help her pick out her china pattern.

China pattern! Can you believe it?

Q. W. F. Magazine
(Quality Women's Fiction)

Single Issue £3.75 (UK), £4 (Europe), £5 (outside Europe)
3 Issue Annual Subscription £10 (£15 Europe/£20 rest of world)

1995 Short Story Competition
1st Prize £150
New Contributors Welcome!

Enquiries/correspondence should be sent to:
Jo Good (Editor), Q.W.F. Magazine, 80 Main Street, Linton, Nr Swadlincote, Derbyshire DE12 6QA

John Gower

Home

He had intended to stay no more than a week, long enough simply to see his mother through the first few days and to attend to what remained of his father's financial affairs. But a month after the funeral he had still not departed. He was depressed by the neglected state of the place: the outdoor paintwork cracked and flaking like a pale-green lichen, the garden gone to weed. A dead wisteria clung to the purplish brick front, its thick wrist tensed, its fingers reaching still for the large eaves above. It had always been an ugly house, a monument to some obscure, melancholy past, but it had never presented a more closed and gloomy face to the street than now. The tall Victorian chimneys imbued the place with the air of a small sanatorium. The fence sagged out over the pavement, the dead whorls of knots staring spectrally down.

The longer he stayed the more difficult to leave it became; and when, that October, in the space of a few weeks, his mother seemed suddenly to lose her grip, shrinking to a senile old woman whom he hardly recognised, and who was hardly any longer his mother at all, he realised at last that there had never been any question of his leaving.

Even at night, sitting at the desk in the back bedroom, looking out over the woods behind the house where the church steeple stood like a dim obelisk above the dark mass of trees - even then, he was not allowed to imagine he was alone in the house, or had any life other than that of a dutiful son...

"They have *chosen* us, Michael."

She was teetering in the doorway, clasping a bundle of white to her old breast, her face lit with happiness like a child's.

He pushed back his chair, wearily got up from the desk and went across.

"Go to bed now," he murmured, taking the bundle from her arms.

"The angels have *chosen* us," she said, and smiled up at him, touching his cheek with trembling fingers as if he were her little boy again. He took her out, and then along the passage to her room, leaving the washing at the top of the stairs.

No sooner had he resumed his work than there came a creak on the landing. He sat staring at his lamplit reflection in the dark pane before him, thinking of the night he would finally lose his temper,

Home

grab her frail old shoulders and shake the senility out of her once and for all. He heard her reach the bottom of the stairs and go down the hall to the kitchen. There was a clunk and a judder from the tank in the loft; the pipes began to rustle. He put down his pen...

Sleeves rolled, she was standing at the sink, the first of the whites slumped wet like a steaming strudel on the draining-board beside her. She was mumbling to herself, suds sliding like amoebas down her bony arms as she dunked and squeezed. She seemed quite unaware of him watching from the doorway. He decided it would be simpler not to disturb her; he turned, went back along the darkened hall and up the stairs.

He sat in his room, writing, half listening.

Eventually he heard the back door open, her footsteps on the path, the bump of a tub. There followed a brief silence as she hung the washing out, then the sound of her returning, clicking the door shut, locking it.

The stairs creaked. He had switched off the light and was lying on his bed; but the door was still ajar.

"Michael?"

He could sense her out there on the landing, her eyes glistening with happiness in the dark.

"Michael?"

He lay quite still. He found himself thinking of his father, already seven months dead.

*

Glancing through the window as he dressed, he saw not sheets on the line below, but, swaying in the cold windy sunlight like a bodiless choir, a row of white albs. He swore under his breath, buttoned his shirt and went downstairs.

"Does Father Durcan know you have those, Mother?" he said, sitting down at the kitchen table.

She poured his tea, watching intently as the clear brown twist vanished into the milk at the bottom of the cup.

"Where's he *got* to," she said suddenly, getting to her feet. She trotted out into the hall. He heard her calling his father's name up the stairs.

The place at the table was laid as it had been each morning for the last three weeks: plate, spoon, knife, the napkin in its brown plastic ring. Each morning was the same.

"His tea will be cold," she complained, returning.

John Gower

She sat down and gazed out through the window at the albs, stirring her cup. Slowly she licked the spoon. Her eyes grew wide - and then filled with tears.

"Daddy's gone away," she whispered. "The angels have taken him far away... Don't be frightened. You mustn't cry."

Outside, the albs flapped like empty popes, miming benedictions.

He ate in silence.

Even when he picked up his coat, and kissed her soft cold cheek goodbye, she did not stir.

He left her sitting at the table with the bare-ribbed chairs, the place for his father as ever undisturbed.

*

From then on, every few nights, he would hear her downstairs, washing, softly singing. Next morning the line would be once more inhabited by the neat row of albs. If it was raining she'd bring them indoors, hang them like some celestial quorum, dripping in the hall. In the evening she would iron them, wrap them in a plastic bag, and place them carefully on the step outside the back door. She'd grasp his arm with her bony fingers, whispering, feasting her large old eyes on his face.

He was going to have to speak to the priest. Someone else must be found to look after the vestry; his mother was no longer capable. God alone knew what next might invent itself in her head; it was absurd that she should continue to be entrusted with the key.

He had still not approached the old priest however, when, the first gloomy week in November, his mother fell ill. On the Sunday she was so unwell that he insisted she stayed in bed. To his surprise she acquiesced without a murmur. She stroked the quilt and smiled up at him when he brought her a cup of tea, and by the evening it seemed there was even some prospect of a day or two's unexpected peace; she had hardly bothered him all afternoon...

But late that night he was disturbed once again by the judder of the tank in the loft. The sounds of a familiar commotion carried from the kitchen below. Pulling on his dressing-gown he went down the stairs.

"Nearly finished," she said, wringing a last steaming alb over the sink and dropping it into the tub. She was flushed, her eyes staring and lustreless.

"You should be in bed," he said quietly, and went across.

"Shan't be a ticket," she said. She opened the back door. The

Home

night swilled silently in. Holding the laden tub against her hip she stepped down the three stone steps and into the alley.

"Leave them till the morning," he said.

"... they just need to fetch the air a bit..." Her voice came floating from out of the darkness, her slippers flopping down the path.

He followed her out and began to help peg the albs up. (If nothing else it would at least get her indoors.)

They hung like ghosts, stilled in the eerie light from the kitchen window. She made her way back to the house, mumbling to herself, the empty tub in her arms.

He remained where he was.

He raised his hand, ran a finger slowly down one of the albs, tracing a cold, wet slit. He turned to another. Each, from shoulder to waist, had the same two vertical slits in its back...

Her bedroom was dark. He stood in the doorway. She was not asleep; she was listening.

"Goodnight Michael," she said at last, her voice sounding close, as if it were the darkness itself that had spoken.

"Goodnight," he said.

"Daddy's coming home," she whispered.

He went to his room, sat down at his desk by the window. Opening a report from the office he began mechanically reading it through. The words lay meaningless on the page, seeming not remotely to concern him. His attention wandered as he heard his mother coughing in her room. He thought of her carefully cutting those slits one empty afternoon, alone in the sitting-room, her large dress-making scissors in her hand... He put down his pen and began to stuff the papers back into the folder with a frustrated sigh. At that moment something stepped into his mind. Even before he looked up, his scalp crawled.

He didn't move. Beyond the dark pane - as though his own ghostly reflection had been somehow subsumed or transfigured - gleamed an ugly, long-boned face. It was framed in lank hair. Its lips glistened softly in the light from the lamp on his desk. Above, upraised in the stillness of the night, hung two white and ethereal wings.

The chair creaked as he leaned involuntarily forward. His hand slid across the desk and put its fingers to the latch. At once, like some grotesque doll drawn up on a string, the pale winged figment

John Gower

receded swiftly into the darkness. He rammed the window open, craning out for a glimpse, a shadow in the dim night sky. There was only the faint *whew whew* of two far wingbeats, and then silence. Nothing.

The night shrank back to a streetlamp, the dark rooftops. He looked down at the albs hanging motionless in the garden below, pulled the window shut.

For a long while he stood, listening, again and again imagining he could hear that faint beat of wings...

He woke slumped at his desk. It was dawn. Sparrows were chirruping in the eaves outside. Cold and stiff he stumbled to his bed, lay staring at the ceiling until his mother came pecking with her fingernail like a bird at his door, calling his name.

She was beside herself, trembling, sobbing. Her frail old hands kept reaching up, trying to pull his face down to hers. He found himself taking her into his arms. It was several minutes, holding him tightly, clutching and plucking at his shirt, before she quietened.

All day that corporeal face at the window haunted him, clung to his thoughts like a slug in a jar. It had not been a dream. He knew it had not been a dream.

That evening, arriving home late, he found his mother at the ironing-board, her gaze lowered and bright like a girl's. The iron sloughed its whispers as back and forth she ran it, deftly turning the white alb beneath. So absorbed was she that she jumped when he spoke. She looked up, smiled. He was tired, he said; he was going straight to bed.

It was after midnight before she came up. He heard her talking to herself in the bathroom, then going through to her room. The house fell quiet.

He lay awake, unable to sleep. He got up and stood at the window...

Down in the kitchen, he opened the back door, looked up at the clear night sky. There was only the moon, high and white and alone. The alley lay bathed in an icy glare. He looked down at the albs lying wrapped on the step, hesitated, and went out.

Opposite the back steps stood the old shed. The small wooden door was open. He peered in at the starved posse of brooms and rakes that cluttered the dark interior. A bucket glinted dully. As he reached to close the door there came a slight sound from the garden behind him. He moved from the moonlight into the little doorway,

Home

and stood there in the darkness, looking out, feeling like a man standing in his own lucid dream, unable to move, unable to step away.

Then it came - between the laurels, walking round the corner of the house. It passed so close that he could hear the rustle of its wings held folded behind it. They shone like snow, drooping sharp and white in the moonlight. It went directly to the back step, stooped, and picked up the albs. It turned. He drew back a fraction, seeing again the bony sunken cheeks and lank grey hair, those eyes that seemed no more than the shadows of their sockets. It departed the way it had come. There was a beating of wings. He stumbled from the shed and through into the back garden and saw the apparition rising into the night and away over the woods, the black limbs of the trees upraised as though frozen in alarm.

He returned to the house. Inside, the darkness swarmed at his back as he bent, shivering, fumbling to lock the door.

*

There was something down in the dark well of the years that he did not want woken, did not want to remember, something he could feel inside him, climbing to greet this figment come like a dybbuk in the night. Each evening after work he tried to bury it in the lonely babble of the pub, but it would not be dispelled, would not be deprived. He grew obsessed with the horror that his mother was going to bring it floating out of his head, its icy wings spread there between them in the gloomy hall. He began to avoid her, shutting himself in his room, even though she seemed utterly oblivious of him, trotting round the house in her dressing-gown and slippers, her grey hair awry, her old eyes agog with a tearful, almost evangelical happiness, as if some long-cherished prophecy was at last to be fulfilled. Late into the night she would bustle about, dusting and tidying in preparation. He'd hear her talking in the kitchen as though his father was already sitting there, those fat pallid hands clenched on the table.

Within a few days a familiar smell of sweat and stale tobacco hung on the landing. He felt poisoned suddenly by an old dread, anger, a confusion. The ghosts of bitter supplications rustled in the corner of his room. No more able to work than sleep he would sit at his desk, staring into the night; if he ventured out it was only to trudge the glistening streets, where even a newspaper stirring in the gutter became his father's pale arm reaching from the grave.

*

John Gower

He'd slept all afternoon. When he woke, the room was dark and quiet. It was raining, the house sinking silently below him. He got up and looked out through the black silvered pane. Something had woken him; not the rain, not the wind in the trees...

His mother was in her room, getting ready for church. He told her he was going out.

Outside, he turned and went quietly down the side-alley to the shed. He unbolted the small wooden door and stepped inside. The wind squalled.

Presently he heard the front door close as his mother left for church. Her footsteps dwindled, leaving the street as silent and empty as the hills.

The rain stopped; the wind died away. Beyond the woods the church clock struck a lonely quarter...

... and then another, the cold chimes warping in the dank drift of air. A few pinched stars gazed indifferently down.

Still he stood.

The apparition had not come. He heard his mother return. The kitchen light flickered on, and the back door opened, spilling light down the steps and into the alley. She appeared on the threshold in her coat, and for a moment it was as if she were about to call him in for supper as she had when he was a child.

But it was not him she was waiting for...

It must have been watching, attent in the dark. It was carrying the albs. It went up to her in the doorway, and placed them white and folded in her arms. From her face in the shadows came the faint gleam of tears, and a breath of wind drifted down the alleyway and stirred the apparition's wings, here and there lifting a milken feather translucent against the light. Then it turned abruptly and departed, swallowed by the darkness.

She retreated into the stark-lit kitchen, shutting the door.

For an hour he walked the empty streets, nothing in his head but a vertiginous horror and the pounding of his feet. When he got back he found her in the kitchen still.

"Did you have a nice evening, Michael?" She smiled. She was happy. She twisted the white cloth in the suds, squeezing it in her fingers. A gaunt-boned face floated up into his mind. Her thin hands looked almost as pale and luminous as the alb she lifted dripping from the sink and held up to the light. He was standing beside her. He saw himself reach out.

Home

"Why..." she whispered, her gaze following his finger as he traced a wet slit. "Why, for their wings, Michael. For their lovely wings..."

The kitchen gleamed. He stood motionless, feeling part of himself running out and up the darkened stairs, blundering into a musty half-forgotten room where his father was still leaning over him that night thirty years gone, those large tobacco-sour fingers pressed over his little mouth...

She was not looking at him now, her grey head lowered, her eyes thick with tears. "Musn't... *Musn't...*" she was mumbling. Baring her teeth in a grimace she held the alb under, as though to drown a deranged old mind.

*

The house had woken. A melancholy bitterness brooded once more above the old slate roof. It was as though the walls themselves had coldly incubated that one dark memory held enclosed all those years.

He came home early. It was still light. Sharp limbs of cloud were poised above the street. Climbing the front steps he felt a sudden compulsion to look up. At the spare-room window his father's grey waxen face was gazing down at him, a face lying buried in the cemetery beyond the woods, starved to old flesh and cloth in a box. It did not stir. Stolen from eternity it stared down with a look of steadfast loneliness, hunger, then slowly faded, or was withdrawn, until only the dark and empty window-pane remained.

He walked round behind the house. A long white feather lay on the path. So morbid and incipient a stillness clothed the trees that he went indoors at once.

She was sitting in the kitchen, softly moaning, rocking back and forth. The albs lay crumpled all around her on the floor; he took from her the large scissors she was clutching in her lap, and she shrank into herself and started to weep.

Upstairs the rooms stood vacant and quiet. There was a suffocating silence that would not be dispelled. He returned to the kitchen and sat with his mother the hour or so till evening. He made her a cup of tea, which she left untouched. When, later, he got up and went to the back door, she did not even raise her head...

It was a cold, fog-bound night; the alley seemed divorced from the street, the street in turn isolated from the town beyond. The eaves dripped; the night hung thick and silent above the little shed.

Almost at once the creature appeared from out of the blank soup

John Gower

of darkness. It went to the back step. He moved from the shed, walked soundlessly across. He was standing behind it. Nothing seemed real. Raising his hand, he touched its wing. It was cold and soft, the white feathers jewelled with the fog's wet breath. The creature paused, and as though distracted not by his touch but by a presence merely, or some faint unfamiliar smell, it half turned. He saw the sunken profile of its cheek, its thick repulsive lips. It swung fully round. Cold feathers brushed across his face and he caught the glint of an eye, an oil-black gleam shrinking into its socket. The creature made to move away. He grabbed at its wing near the shoulder. Warm muscle convulsed beneath the feathers under his hand. Was it fear or malice that crouched in the face it turned upon him then? There were teeth, bared and glittering, two globed eyes, dark like glass. It opened its wings and began to beat them, hissing in anger or distress, its icy hands clawing at his arms that he had clamped impulsively around its torso. He was gulping hoarse sobs. It smelt of the night, of all the dark and lonely miles... So strongly was it beating its wings that had it not managed to twist free he would have been carried bodily aloft. It rose vertically from the alley. Looking up he saw its huge shadow projected through the fog by the lamp in the street, the fog itself swirling turbidly like a sluggish smoke, long spokes of lamplight flickering and shuttering from the creature's wings. It cleared the gloomy eaves, and suddenly he was aware that the night beyond was thronged with a multitude of other beating shapes and shadows, and that the dank cold alley was filled with cries, hisses, whispered screams falling from a furious host clamouring malevolently about the roof of his father's house.

Not A Pushover Quiz

Answer to Panurge 21 Quiz. It was **Blaise Cendrars** who wrote Dan Yack (*and* they have it in Carlisle Public Library) but no one got it. Hence and while we are on French poet-novelists:

Panurge 22 Quiz. Which French 'poet of existentialism' wrote a curious novel entirely devoted to praising *soap*? First correct answer wins a £20 Book Token. Answer to Not A Pushover Quiz, Panurge, Crooked Holme Farm Cottage, Brampton, Cumbria CA8 2AT. Deadline 16.5.95.

Peter Slater

Fires

It is always possible to move on, to go to different places, if you really want to. You don't just have to accept what you're given. So one Saturday morning, I asked Mrs Phipps if Philippa and I might be allowed to go to Brighton on our own.

"Of course you may, dears," she said. She was standing on a chair in the hall trying to reach a cobweb with a feather duster. She was a kind woman, and although she knew about my little problems in the past, she was prepared to let bygones be bygones because I had made a real effort to be responsible and helpful over the past two years. I was changed. Wherever I've lived, I've never been like the others, but because of my little problems, they've never known quite what to do with me. At Hope Lodge, though, I had made a real effort to put the past behind me. I wanted to stay. I only ever did the bad things when I wanted to move on. Those episodes were all behind me, now.

"Be sure not to talk to any strange men, won't you? and avoid empty compartments on the train."

In my strong carrier-bag with its picture of Snoopy, we packed cheese and tomato sandwiches, a flask of coffee, two *Mars* bars and two apples. We wrapped up well in anoraks, scarves and woolly hats and I selected a couple of magazines from the pile behind the TV to read on the train.

Mrs Phipps drove us to the station, bought our return tickets and found out the time of the trains home. After making sure that I had the tickets and times securely in my zipped coat pocket, she wished us a Happy Day and waved us Goodbye.

In the train, Philippa gazed out of the window. It seemed that the houses and fields and trees were moving, and that the train was perfectly still, but mostly I looked at the pictures in *Homes and Gardens* and kept an eye on Philippa, because she was my special responsibility.

Brighton was gloomy, damp and cold: a hard, grey town beside a grey blur of mist and sea. We walked shivering along the sea-front. We were disappointed, to be frank. We'd expected sunshine, warmth and children playing on the sand - after all, that was what you saw in pictures of the seaside. It was never like this. The promenade was deserted except for some fishermen huddled in waterproofs. The waves battered against the sea-wall, and the larger

Peter Slater

ones sent spray spattering onto the road in crashes of exploding water.

I had no idea what to do. I kept looking at my watch, to see if it might be nearly time to go home. What did you do in other places? We sat in a shelter, looked at the sea, and ate our *Mars* bars. It was something to do but it wasn't exactly enjoyable.

"It's cold!" said Philippa accusingly, several times, and I felt terribly guilty and miserable. I checked my watch again.

We went to a cafe. It was deliciously warm inside, and smelt of spicy teacakes and coffee. I led Philippa to an empty table beside the steamed-up window.

Presently, two men who had been sitting nearby, came up to us.

"All right, girls?"

"Two teas, please," I said.

They laughed and sat down opposite.

I blushed, and wanted to go home. I wished that we had never come here. It was all a disaster. I would have walked out, at that moment, had I been sure of Philippa's response; but I was worried Philippa might get into one of her states, so stayed put.

"You'll never get served in this place unless you ..." One man held up his hand, snapped his fingers and called, "Hello!"

The waitress came immediately, and the man pointed at me, "You better say summin', girl!"

But I could only shake my head, and stare at the table. I couldn't remember why we were here. My green coat was thick and heavy.

The two men looked at each other, then the first one ordered, "Four coffees."

I was about to say that we hated coffee, when Philippa said, in her slow, stupid voice, "We're on holiday."

"So're we."

"At the seaside."

"That's it. My name's Graham, and this is my brother, Stuart."

They were skinheads, with the crumpled faces of unhappy bulldogs. They wore frayed denim, and their hands, forearms and neck were crawling with tattoos.

"So what's your names?" asked Stuart.

"We're at the seaside," said Philippa and I shook my head.

"That's it!" said Graham. "How long ya stayin' for?"

"In Brighton."

"Come up from the zoo, have ya?" asked Graham, before his

brother kicked him. "How's Chi-chi?"

"Mrs Phipps said we could go."

Whilst Philippa kept up the conversation, I said nothing. I could hear the blood pounding in my head. I knew I wasn't looking after Philippa as well as I should. It was all going wrong. Something terrible was going to happen. These were the strange men that we had been warned about. When strange men approached, you just walked away. You were very proud and very firm and you did not say anything, you just turned on your heels and walked away. But how could we turn on our heels when we were sitting down? Mrs Phipps hadn't said anything about sitting down.

"Where's yer Mum'n Dad?" asked Stuart.

"They've taken the heavenly path," said Philippa.

"Where's that, then?"

"In Heaven, with God and Uncle Bill and Grandma and Grandad."

The waitress gave us our coffees.

"Did they remember to give you names, before they went?"

"She's only my friend, she's not my sister!" So my first words were a betrayal of my friend. "Her name's Philippa and my name's Deborah. We've come to Brighton for the day, and we can look after ourselves. I look after Philippa. Mrs Phipps trusts me, she knows I can do it."

"She's a very trusting woman!" said Stuart.

So they knew her, too! I almost smiled, but then thought better of it: of course they would know Mrs Phipps - everyone knew Mrs Phipps.

Philippa pushed away her coffee, "Don't like it!"

"So what ya think of Brighton?"

"Mummy and Daddy have taken the heavenly path."

"Have you seen the arcade on the pier?"

"We'll all go there, one day."

"We can go now, if ya like."

"And see Uncle Bill and Grandma and Grandad."

"Are you sure Mrs Phipps made the right decision?" asked Stuart.

"Have you got boyfriends?" asked Graham.

"Yes," I said.

"What are their names?"

"Mark."

Peter Slater

"What? Both of them?"
"Yes. I mean ... I think so."
I was getting terribly confused. On my good days, I knew that I could be really clear-headed and sensible: I could do anything as good as anyone; but this was turning out to be a bad day.
"You haven't run away, have ya?" Graham asked. "They really did let you out?"
I felt a sudden, urgent need to check our tickets. I was certain that they were missing. What were we going to do? How would we ever get back? We would have to walk. But in which direction? I stood up abruptly. "We have to go," I said.
"Oh, stay for a bit," said Stuart. "Keep us company. We don't know anyone here, and we get lonely. It comes on ya, a feeling like mist - you ever get that?"
"It's heartache, really," said Graham.
"Yeah. We've been bruised by life."
They talked on and on, but I didn't listen. I couldn't follow it, they talked so fast and what they said seemed to make no sense, anyway. In the end, I seized another chance to say that we had to be getting along.
"So do we!" said Graham. "I'll count to three - right? Ready. One, two, three, *GO!*"
The men sprang up, knocking over their chairs, and ran from the cafe.
"Oi!" called the waitress. She came over. "That's three pounds sixty."
I counted out the money carefully and slowly, checking the amount several times before I passed it over. The waitress took the money, but didn't go away. Then I remembered. "Oh, and thankyou very much. Say thankyou, Philippa."
"Thankyou."
The waitress took away our still full cups, only turning to ask, "You finished with these?" when she was halfway across the room. She was odd.
The men were waiting for us outside.
"Thanks, girls!"
"We have to go home, now," I said. "We've got a train to catch."
"What time's the train?"
"I don't know."

Fires

"Then how d'you know you've got to go to catch it, now?"

This was what always happened in the outside world. People laid little traps, and made you into a liar, when you didn't mean to be. You never knew where you were. It wasn't fair.

"You're a dizzy pair, aren't you? Never mind, you've met us, now. We'll look after you. We'll spend the day together. Where shall we go?"

"We've got to go home."

"No, you haven't. Mrs Phipps told us we might meet you and we had to look after you."

Philippa smiled. She was happy. She said, "We can go to the pier. Play on the machines."

"Come on, then!" Graham linked his arm through Philippa's, and off they went. I resisted Stuart's attempt to hold on to me, but I had no choice but to follow along behind. Perhaps these two men were quite nice, really, and everything was working out for the best. I would say to Mrs Phipps, 'Everything worked out for the best.' No harm in hoping. Deep down, though, I felt that things were going terribly wrong. How could I be certain that these two men really did know Mrs Phipps? I allowed the others to walk on several steps ahead, and then slipped into the doorway of a boarded-up shop. From my handbag, I took out my small wallet. Inside was my photograph: mum, dad and four children smiling in a garden. I stared at this picture for a long time, before putting it away, and hurrying to catch up.

We walked out onto the pier. The lights of buoys offshore were like red smudges in the mist rising from the sea. The pier was deserted, and the atmosphere desolate. I trailed behind the men, who were now walking on either side of Philippa, like policemen escorting a prisoner. Some people's lives become part of history, and are read about in books and newspapers. If you were murdered you became a story and you were interesting and people either said you were silly or that you deserved it. Another thing that happened was that you lost all control of your life at certain times. Sometimes, this was because you did not know what you were doing, and at other times it was simply because other people took you over. They needed to make you go to some particular place and do some particular thing in order to satisfy themselves. I knew that governments did this: ordered people about, took money, gave money, took homes, gave homes, wrote messages, talked about you as though you were an

Peter Slater

object or a pet animal. Once, standing outside Mrs Phipps's door, I had overheard someone from the government talking about me. The words burned into my brain and, even though they were strange, and not like ordinary-talking, I could never forget them. *'Deborah has had an unhappy life. Rejected by her parents at an early age, she has lived in a succession of children's homes and has also been resident in two care institutions. It is hard to define her.'*

'It is hard to define me.'

'She could not be classified as mentally-ill, nor yet "educationally subnormal." Although she may be given positions of limited responsibility in a secure environment, it is doubtful whether she could ever cope by herself in the outside world for any extended length of time.'

And here was the outside world, and I was not coping. I had lost control. Another force had taken over. The voices of another power. I wanted to run away, but I couldn't abandon Philippa.

When we got to the arcade at the end of the pier, they said that they had no money for the machines, because they didn't get paid until Wednesday, so they asked if they could borrow some. They said that they would pay us back and that we could keep all the winnings. I said that we didn't have any money, but they said that Mrs Phipps had given us some and so of course I knew that they knew the truth, and gave them the five pound note.

They seemed to forget about us, then, and played the machines, rode in the speedway cars and fired the guns in Terminator. I kept trying to leave quietly, when they weren't looking, but Philippa was involved in the games and whenever I pulled her by the arm, she pushed me away. I was scared she might scream, so I couldn't try too hard. So we wandered through the arcade, following Stuart and Graham. The music was loud and the machines bleeped and roared and made the sound of firing. You couldn't think straight. You couldn't think. I began to hate Philippa so much because she was so stupid. She didn't know what she was doing. She didn't know that she might be leading us into danger. 'Be sure not to talk to any strange men,' Mrs Phipps had said. I liked to think of her voice, it was soft and comforting in my head and helped me forget all the noise. Don't talk to any strange men... but that was exactly what we were doing. And not only talking. We were being friendly.

When they had spent all our money, they asked me for more. I said I didn't have any.

"Show us yer purse, then," said Graham.

Fires

I supposed it was all right to show him. It didn't seem to me like quite the right thing to do, but they obviously knew about the world, and I didn't. He took my purse and looked through all the pockets. There was only thirty pence. Then he opened the zip section.

"Don't do that."

"Why not?"

"There's nothing in there." I tried to snatch it back.

"This is where you keep your real money, ain't it?"

"No, there's nothing in there." I grabbed and grabbed, but he held it high above his head and then threw it to Stuart, who ran out of the arcade. We all chased after him.

It was cold outside, and beginning to get dark already. When I caught up with Stuart, he was standing by the pier railings. He had opened the zip, and had pulled out my picture. I could only stand. Sometimes you get so heavy with sadness you can't move at all.

"What's this, then?" he said, unfolding it. He read, "Mum, Dad, Charles, Andrew, Edward, Me ... Eh?"

I couldn't say anything. I wanted to say *I know it's not real, I'm just pretending,* but I couldn't say anything. I was stuck, and heavy, and I didn't know anything.

"Cop a loada this, Gray!" He passed the picture to his friend.

I could only breathe.

They looked at me. Graham said, "You think you're Princess Anne, do ya?"

No, I didn't. Of course I didn't. I knew who I was. I know I'm stupid, but I'm not stupid. But I knew that if the Queen was told about me, she would love me just as if I was really her daughter, and I knew she wouldn't mind me carrying her picture about with me. Everyone needs a Mum and Dad and a family. You need people who are special and who love you even when you are not very bright. *Again and again I ran into that room, and again and again Mummy snatched my teddy and threw him out of the window: 'You soddin' little brainless bitch!' How was I to know? How could I have known? Another child would have known, though.*

"You're a coupla loonies on the run, aren't ya?" said Stuart. "What's to stop us screwing this picture up and throwing it in the sea?"

A seagull called and its cry was snatched by the wind.

"You're nuts."

"Your friend got any money, has she?"

Peter Slater

I couldn't think of anything to say.
"Forgotten how to speak, have ya?"
"D'ya wanna come back to our hotel with us?"
I could only look at my picture in his hand. People can hurt you so easily. It isn't good.
"You could come back with us."
"It's not far."
"Only ten minutes."
"Nice room."
"Well-appointed."
"A sea-view."
"Armchairs, a telly, a kettle ..."
"Bathroom, double-bed ..."
"Well-sprung ..."
"Warm in Winter."
"We could spend the rest of the day ..."
"And night, if you wanted."
"Ten minutes."
"Ten minutes."
"Truth is, we've fallen in love."
"Now that we know you're Royalty, eh?"
"Eh?"
"It'd be a very great privilege if you came back with us."
"Your Majesty."
"Royal Highness."
"Let's make a Prince together."
"Or two."
"Please."
"Please."
"Me."
"Me."
"Us."
The words scattered through my head: they didn't have any meaning. I only heard them as lumps of sound.
"You coming, then?"
"Please come with us."
"Princess."
I turned around. Philippa was standing a little way off, examining her hands.
"She can come, too."

Fires

"We couldn't separate you."

"And then you can have the picture of your Mum and Dad back."

"Lovely picture. You don't often all get together as a family, do ya?"

Stuart took hold of my arm. I didn't want to create a scene in case I worried Philippa. We walked on. I looked back, and Philippa was following, holding Graham's hand. Perhaps they were kind men, after all, and everything was still going to work out for the best. I wasn't scared, I just wished that I was home.

When we entered their hotel, I looked at my shoes all the time. I knew that the owner would not make us welcome.

We went up a narrow staircase and along corridors that smelt of toast. I only looked up when I heard the key scratching in the door.

It was only a small room, with a bed, a table and a chair. On the table, facing the bed, was a television. The curtains were grey, but through the window you could see the sea, and that made me hopeful. Graham brought out a pack of beer cans from under the bed and gave one each to me and Philippa. "We can all sit on the bed," he offered. Stuart was already there, with his back against the headrest, and Graham joined him.

"We prefer to stand," I said.

I took a sip of beer, and swallowed, even though it tasted like old metal. Philippa, though, was not so polite and spat her mouthful onto the carpet.

"What the hell you doin'?" shouted Graham.

"She doesn't like it," I said. "You shouldn't have given it to her."

"Hasn't she ever learned manners?"

"Everybody has their own little ways," I said.

Stuart pointed the remote-control at the TV, and a football match came on.

"Excellent!" said Graham. "Come on, girls, watch the match! Excellent!"

"I think we'll go now," I said.

They didn't say anything, so I went to the door. It was locked. I turned. Stuart looked at me and smiled.

"Come and watch the football."

"Come and sit with us. You don't want to go nowhere. Cold day like this. Sit by us."

When I am in a place where I don't want to be, I know what to do. I went into the bathroom and sat on the seat. For a time, I

Peter Slater

simply twirled the toilet paper on its holder, and then I trailed it down to the floor and along and round and round. It wasn't a very large bathroom, but I could make a couple of spirals. When I was finished, I struck a match and lit one end of the paper. I always hoped that a small bright snail of flame would creep slowly along, gently eating the paper and shivering with delight until it reached the roll where it would burn in cheerful circles like a catherine-wheel. But it never happened that way. This time, a little bit burnt in a quick *whump*! and then went out. I tried again and the fire shot along the trail, up onto the roll and straight to the curtains in less than a moment. Suddenly, it seemed that the whole room was ablaze. I was scared by the heat and unpredictable movements of this great, curled animal that I had made alive. But I also loved it. Fire was so wonderful because at its best it was huge and unstoppable and it always released you from where you didn't want to be. I went back into the room, closing the door behind me.

"Your hotel's burning to the ground," I said.

They didn't properly believe me, at first. They didn't want to look because they were involved in the football. Then, I saw it quite plainly, Stuart's nose twitched as he caught the first scent of smoke, and the whole shape of his face changed.

They went crazy, shouting and swearing. They dashed into the bathroom and tried to hit the flames with their hands and stamp them out with their feet. Then they pulled the blankets off the bed and threw them at the blaze. But nothing did any good. I was proud of Philippa, who just stood near me and did not get upset. Things like that rarely do upset her, though. It's emotional stress that makes her get into one of her states - people arguing, and that kind of thing.

We all hurried outside, in the end; and in the confusion, with everybody gathered on the pavement, Philippa and I walked quietly away. I didn't want to hurry, because that would have upset Philippa - she takes her emotions from me, so I have a great responsibility.

On the train home, I gazed at Philippa. I really loved her, and she loved me.

"We won't say anything to Mrs Phipps about the fire, will we?"

"No," she said, and I knew she would keep her promise, because she never told Mrs Phipps about my little fires.

It is always possible to move on, to go to different places, if you really want to. You don't just have to accept what you're given. You have to be yourself.

Dorothy Schwarz
Matriarch

"Always tell lies, Lottie," Grandma used to say. "A woman's job is to keep the peace."
In spite of that, I always hoped that her version of her own story was true.
Born eldest child and only daughter of Romanian Jews, fleeing one pogrom or another, which one was never told us, she was born and grew up in Whitechapel where her parents kept a dairy. At twelve, she learned to play the piano; at eighteen she fell in love with a violinist. Her parents forbade the marriage - no money in fiddling. They encouraged (she'd never admit forced) her into accepting the courtship of Abraham Levine, a small-sized, small-time businessman. The telling always ended with a triumphant: "Never married, never, my violinist. Died fifty years later - a bachelor."
That was another of the lessons she taught; true love is never consummated and never dies.
And love, for my grandmother, had nothing to do with sex. Thirteen children were born in twenty-three years, "And he never once saw me naked."
"So how'd you *do* it, Grandma?"
"In the dark, of course. He lifted my nightie."
Out of those thirteen babies, only eight survived. Scary tales were told of flu epidemics, of diphtheria, of charwomen substituting bleach for barley water in the baby's bottle. Not a single one was ever breastfed.
"Never had enough milk." With a pleased delicacy, she patted her black crepe bodice and added confusingly, "Blood is thicker than water."
And she taught other lessons, bewilderingly contradictory in their message. Girl babies were inferior to boy babies, daughters came second to sons but women were *always*, in every respect, superior to men, "the dirty beasts."
Shortly after baby Percy's curls were cut, Abie Levine succumbed to a heart attack. Had he indulged in too much nightie-lifting? She was in her early forties. Grandma never accused him of being, 'one of the dirty beasts'; you were expected to draw your own conclusions. For the rest of her life, she wore black, enlivened with crocheted lace collars, except on special occasions like weddings or barmitsvahs, when her grey silk made an appearance.

Dorothy Schwarz

Once during her long widowhood, an eligible bachelor of seventy-two invited her to the cinema.

"How was it, Grandma?"

"The dirty beast." His hand had brushed against her arm during the performance.

Thereafter, she would only visit the pictures with grandchildren. We quivered with embarrassment as she'd call out to the heroine, "Watch out. he's coming up behind you."

In her seventies, she developed a fascination with sex. I became a prime source of information. *That sort of thing* had never been discussed when her two daughters were growing up, except that both received a thorough grounding in its horrors. As a result, I suppose, the elder Ginni, emigrated to America and no one would ever tell me what she did for a living; the younger, my mother, would never discuss anything that occurred below the waist.

But now Grandma asked questions of a startling intimacy. Did I or my mates make love *before* marriage? How did we stop babies coming? Old age had unbuckled the blinkers of that Victorian upbringing. She was travelling on a journey of discovery but whether she ever regretted having set out fifty years too late, I never found out. The violinist was often mentioned during these sessions.

The ghetto in which she lived had walls stronger than brick and cement. Never admitting to fear or dislike of *goyim*, she said that they smelt peculiar. And since you could never marry one, why bother with social intercourse when sexual intercourse put you beyond the pale?

A blessed and fortunate old age she had, compared to listless semi-circles of grannies watching the flickering screen in old age homes. She *owned* her semi-detached in a tree-lined street off Golders Green High Street, where she lived with a married son, an unmarried son and Aunt Ginni, who, from time to time, visited on a vacation from her nameless occupations. Other sons and my mother lived locally except for Moishe, who had forgotten his duties and run off. He went *mesuggah*, said Grandma.

The household at number twenty-seven bickered non-stop, with Grandma the still centre of their turbulence; the eye of the hurricane when a real storm blew up.

She owned a slave. Whatever the United Nations definition of slavery, any human being dependent upon the whims of another working wageless a seven-day week, must come pretty close.

Matriarch

Hannah, a pear-shaped woman with a sweet, childish voice was married to my Uncle Nahum. After one still-born son, Hannah remained barren. "A curse," said Grandma. Auntie Hannele's life consisted of shopping, cooking, cleaning, washing, ironing, sewing and running errands for Mama and the household. Auntie Ginni gave her cast-off costume jewellery, my Mum, cast-off clothes. Aunt Hannah was smaller than my mother. The skirts dipped and sagged above her ankles. The shoulders made her look like Charlie Chaplin as she waddled about her duties. Both her husband, Nahum, and her unmarried brother-in-law, Percy, bullied her.

"*Nebbich*, my poor Percy," Grandma would lament, "never finds one good enough."

And I believed every word. Whenever Percy brought home a Miriam or a Rachel, (nice girls every one, although 'girls' became increasingly euphemistic as Percy's paunch increased and hair decreased) Grandma always spotted some flaw; some subtle reason why she *wouldn't* do. In any case, none could stand comparison with Mama. Early photos showed a black-haired, dark-eyed beauty. In old age she stooped, only her size nine shoes remained as evidence of her once imposing height. Grandma's tone never varied; she never complained and never argued. An appropriate cliché emerged for every situation. When Evie, one of the granddaughters, ran off with a commercial salesman and left inoffensive Harold literally holding the baby, Grandma'd say: "Never mind, Harold, as good fish in the sea as ever came out." When my own father suffered a minor heart attack, she told my mother: "No use crying over spilt milk. Arnie's got a good man, hasn't he?" When Hannah made one of her rare revolts, like tending a headache instead of frying fish, Grandma would say: "She's a difficult girl but least said soonest mended and I'll do anything for a quiet life." Hannah, smothered by the feather bolster of Grandma's tolerance, could only sigh herself back to the stove. And for the rest; the subterranean currents of family tensions ran through the sewers of our unconscious and no one dared lift the manhole covers.

In Grandma's house, you felt secure; bad things weren't allowed. In a war which nearly wiped out European Jewry, all that happened to our family was that my Dad got piles in the ARP and a distant cousin developed Multiple Sclerosis, which he would have done anyway. Grandma sent Cousin Laurie chicken soup. Aunt Hannah had a two hour bus journey to deliver it but we all thought Grandma

Dorothy Schwarz

very kind.

After the war, on Sunday mornings, my cousins and I used to play in her narrow, unkempt garden, at the bottom of which two trees guarded a shed crammed with discarded objects that, "might come in handy someday." We'd spend hours crawling through tunnels of furniture, cardboard boxes, trunks and parcels of old newspapers. One summer's day, I found a silver web hanging between lilac branches, a spider waited at one corner with a soft, grey-bodied insect trapped at the other, its mouth opening and shutting in a scream too high for our ears. I almost worked up my courage to tear down the web and let the insect fly to safety. But Grandma had taught us to be afraid of creepy-crawlies. And this was such a large, ugly one. When we finished playing explorers in the dark shed and came blinking into the sunshine, the insect's body was eaten. But the spider had stopped at the head, leaving the beaky mouth opening and shutting in that soundless scream. The web was still there, weeks later, binding the minute, intricate skeleton. In that cosy private world Grandma spun around her family - each of us so special - that incident remained the only bad memory I've kept from number twenty-seven.

Even so, once I'd grown up, I'd spent a year going out with him before I felt brave enough to take Clive to Golders Green. Was I ashamed of Grandma's Jewishness in front of Clive, or the reverse?

The front room smelt as usual of fried onions, Grandma's cologne and dust. A gas fire, burning full-blast, used up any spare oxygen. The brown velvet curtains were already drawn and a one-bar electric fire waited ready in Percy's corner.

"He can't stand draughts," said Aunt Hannah.

Every surface was spread with a lace doily crocheted by Grandma herself, each covered with family photographs, three and four deep. Tacked to the flocked wallpaper, pictures of Crawfie and Lilibet, torn from *Woman's Own*, faced framed postcards of Ben Gurion and Chaim Weizmann.

"Don't do anything special for us, please, Grandma."

"Who me? As if I would."

Clive was told to sit in a leather armchair in front of the gas fire and fenced in with two occasional tables.

"What's the matter, Clive? Tea not right?" asked Grandma.

"No, no. A trifle warm, isn't it?"

"Keep your coat on a while. It's cold out."

Matriarch

"But Grandma, it's stifling in here."
"As you please, Lottie. I hope the young man won't catch a chill. She's obstinate. Have you noticed yet, Clive?"
Without offending one of us, Clive couldn't reply, so went on eating bread and jam.
Meanwhile, Hannah had been preparing the supper. The 'boys' were aged at that time fifty and thirty-five respectively. On top of the upright piano, Percy's plaster bust of Shakespeare jostled a Spanish doll brought back by Nahum from a week in Majorca. Uncle Nahum arrived first, wearing overcoat, hat and muffler, which he kept on and sat facing the wall; he ate three and a half pieces of fried fish, bread and butter, tinned peaches and custard. Hannah laid last week's *News of the World* in front of his plate. She confided to Clive: "So exhausted he is from his work his brain needs a rest." Throughout the meal, she waited behind his chair, rocking on her bunions, waddling out to the kitchen for more pickle or fresh tea.
Nahum remarked to Clive: "Can't drink the muck they've given you, young man. Need a special brew. Delicate stomach, y'know." With a grunt, a belch and a fart, he pushed back his chair, picked up his paper and left the room.
Then Percy arrived, sitting down at the same card table but facing us. Both returned from work at six o'clock but each preferring Grandma and Hannah's undivided attention, they took turns to eat first.
"Kept a nice bit of boiled for you," said Grandma, adding to Clive, "He can't take fried. Delicate digestion - just like mine."
Hannah whined that boiled should have been kept for Nahum's delicate digestion and retreated into the back room. Her husband's answering roar shook the partition wall. "Silly cow! You know boiled lies on my guts."
Aunt Ginni was staying that month, on one of her visits from New York. She lolled at the dining table, wearing purple and yellow flowered crepe de chine, showing glimpses of lace-edged slip, pink bra and blue-shadowed armpits. Aunt Ginni, waited on by Hannah, ate two plates of fried egg and *würst* and complained that the tea wasn't freshly made.
"Hannah," she added, "what are you thinking of? This young couple've had no supper."
"That's true," agreed Percy, picking his teeth with a split matchstick and reading *The Jewish Chronicle*.

Dorothy Schwarz

"We can't possibly be hungry, Grandma, now can we?"
This remark was ignored and a three course meal appeared. Chicken soup ("you won't get soup like this out of a tin") *latkes*, meatballs and strudel.

Clive ate with dogged politeness.

"Nice to see a young man with a proper appetite," said Grandma, heaping Clive's plate. "My boys won't eat a thing."

Walking up the Golders Green Road towards the tube, Clive asked: "Is it always like that?"

"No, not exactly. Everyone was on their best behaviour."

"But no one said a word."

"Exactly. If you'd not been there, they'd have been rowing non-stop."

"Gosh," said Clive, "Cold Comfort Farm - kosher."

But Clive, like everyone who came into the aura surrounding Grandma, fell under her spell - that bewitching knack of making each visitor feel that he or she was the one person she had been longing for. "*Nu*, how's it with you?" she'd pat your arm. My Mum visited every week and sometimes twice. All the daughters-in-law, all the grandchildren, visited often, except of course Moishe, the unmentioned. Eventually, Grandma told me that he had run away from Aunt Ethel, married a blonde barmaid, changed his name to Max and bought a Betting Shop.

"Do you miss him, Grandma?"

Grandma went deaf.

On Festivals and High Holy Days, sons with their wives, daughters, grandchildren, nephews and nieces, arrived for many-coursed meals, cooked by Hannah and served by Grandma, who knew by heart each person's favourite portion of chicken. Everyone came except for Moishe/Max, whom she never mentioned anymore than her dead husband. Surrounded by descendants, she presided beaming over the long, white-clothed table. I imagined I was her favourite grandchild; we all did.

My Dad, ("Blessings on his head," said Grandma) paid most of her household expenses. She persuaded him to part with middling to large amounts to underwrite Percy's and Nahum's crack-brained schemes; opening fur-shops, selling Army surplus by mail-order, writing a book on hypnosis. "Such wonderful ideas, they have, my boys," said Grandma. "Just a little *mazel* is all they need." And she would pat my father's knee. The fur-shop went bust; the Army

Matriarch

surplus cluttered the shed; the book gave rise to two law-suits and the 'boys' never returned the loans.

Her own generosity became a legend. Whatever you gave her, she'd say, "Put it away for later on, *Bubele*." The gift joined the chocolates, scarves, perfumes, piled into a mahogany cupboard in the hall. When she grew old, over ninety, she would forget who had given what, and give back your own bottle of cologne or box of stale chocolates. Old Jews with wispy beards, wearing fur hats and caftans, came begging to the door and left clutching ribboned boxes and murmuring blessings in Yiddish. Your pockets would be filled with boiled sweets, "for the journey," although you weren't going anywhere.

After she became too frail to bake and too purblind to sew, her days passed sitting on a high oak stool beside the open front door, reading *Talmud* through a magnifying glass, her lips mouthing the Hebrew words. My father's brother, the only person I ever knew who didn't admire her, claimed she did it to show off. If true, she spent many hours just to impress us, her hands icy cold to touch, her eyes milky-blue.

"Why don't you like Grandma, Uncle Louis?"

"Ask her kids," was his laconic reply.

*

Slowly, slowly, the reins of her household slipped her grasp; her zest diminished. We knew that a niece did the shopping, a lady was sent in from the Jewish Welfare Board to give her a bath. When granddaughters visited, she would call them by their mothers' names.

Death entered that unlocked front door in the guise of one of the wispy-bearded *yeshiva-bokkers*. She stretched up to pull down a box of biscuits from the present-stuffed upper shelf of the cupboard and suffered a heart attack - fifty-five years after Abie. Her children, grandchildren and great grandchildren shook their heads: "Things will never be the same." And they were right - the family fell apart without its holding centre.

I didn't attend the funeral. I'd like to think that I've forgotten why; I remember clearly that I had busied myself with some plans for my children. My mother pursed her lips; Moishe and I were the only ones missing. They'd sent a telegram but Moishe missed his own mother's funeral! Everyone remarked on it.

The household at number twenty-seven staggered on for more than a decade. No one summoned the family together again; no more

Dorothy Schwarz

celebrations were held. Aunt Hannah gave away the monster serving dishes and the 20-pint saucepans. What had seemed so well-knitted unravelled so fast! Could the aunts and uncles have *hated* one another?

Twenty years on and all her sons have joined her, except Moishe. My Mother said that she believed he lived in America. "Curses on him." Ginni never came back.

When number twenty-seven was finally sold, the grandchildren rushed to grab souvenirs. There was very little collectable in the dusty cupboards. I bore off a photo. When I got it home, Clive said the ornate frame didn't match our cream leather settee, so I put it in the spare bedroom, where I don't see it all that often. She's about fifty in the picture - that smiling, gentle, olive-skinned old lady, who remained a beauty all her life.

I've never forgotten her. None of her children held a candle to her. Now the aunts and uncles are gone - I never give them a thought.

When I remember Grandma, I see her holding my first baby, Berenice, her eleventh great-grandchild. Babies adored being on her lap. My Dad stands behind, looking happy without his crutches. But another image shadows the first; I see the web that the spider had woven between the lilac branches and the insects trapped within the sticky folds of its thread.

Pushover Quiz

Answer to Panurge 21 Quiz. It was **Christine de Rivoyre** who wrote the best-seller 'Boy'. No one got it, to our surprise. So here is a real push over...

Panurge 22 Quiz. **All the following novels about women were written by men who had the same Christian name. Identify the authors of all four books:** First correct answers win a £20 Book Token. Deadline 16.5.95

Answers to Pushover Quiz, Panurge, Crooked Holme Farm Cottage, Brampton, Cumbria CA8 2AT.

1 A Clergyman's Daughter 2. Esther Waters 3. The Odd Women 4. Diana of the Crossways. Hint; two of these novels are published by Virago.

Frederick Lightfoot

Funny Things

There are some very funny things said about drinking. We may come to some of those. Perhaps all. You know the sort of thing: Dean Martin: *You're not drunk if you can lie on the floor without holding on.* Everyone who drinks in this pig-sty, this hacienda of ethanol, this twenty-four hour watering hole for self-deceivers, the most unpublic of public houses, has at least one. I for one have said, which caused Nora to grin malevolently, but justifiably, or so her witch's intuition (Thespian) would say: I started to drink at 8 p.m. on a Friday night and stopped at 10 p.m. on a Sunday. In the interim there has been some thirty odd years. Absurd, my fellow imbibers with comparative, equally unenviable, L.F.T.'s, (liver function tests) declare. And it is true. I haven't stopped at all but I do take a rest, pace depression, in peril of my life, at 10 p.m. on a Sunday night. A rest, it must be said, which is not religious in any shape, form or consistency. (Surprisingly, perhaps, I even despise communion. Transubstantiation my arse! Eat black-pudding and offer the devilish response: Blood of the pig! Blood of the pig! Why? Because the world is so shitty. Therefore, of course, it is aptly symbolic.) But! I hear the complaint sound out. And, it must be admitted, drinkers always are great complainers. And, of course, that is it, the whole point. (Story complete? Well, not quite,)

A funny thing No 2: Me: *The only consistent factor in human relationship is power.* I would also say that alcohol is a weakness. (You see, there is no way out! Well, naturally, the doors are locked! Of course, it is only Sunday morning and Nora, the patroness, insists upon the appearance of law.) But, what I was going to say, to get back to the complaint, was: Pigs are perfectly clean animals when allowed to be by their human masters. I know this for a fact because my father was a pig farmer. He has spent many a night with his nose in the trough, not overcome by ordure, over which he was scrupulous in the collection and disposal of, but by Powers, (which is, of course, whiskey with an e,) just about holding on. He led a pig man's life just about holding on. To what? Did someone ask? To the thirteenth teat of a fecund sow. And I his runt was bottle fed. Excuse me, as there are a number of hours until ten I will just refill my glass...

People are mooching about. Anna's T.V. is on; Darryl's music is winding up; Nora is washing, much in the manner of Lady Macbeth.

Frederick Lightfoot

(I played a somnambulist Duncan all night.) She kept screaming: You never say you love me. I should have said: You have the wrong man. I am only the king. *(Knock, knock, knock. Who's there...* We need a drink, open the door!) I said: The more you want the less I find I can give. I suppose that that is sad. It certainly appeared to make Nora sad who had to console herself with more than ample liquid remedy. But, she complains periodically, intoning her voice dramatically with a quite prolific venom, I never drank until I met you. I answer with: You must have been very thirsty. (Funny thing No 3: *You see when I'm drunk but you don't see when I'm thirsty.)* But that, an 8 o'clock start, shall we say, was a long time ago. (Can she even imagine how much piss in the pot has transpired since that?) Am I to carry the blame all the way? All the way to no longer holding on. Anyway, to carry on; Mr Candido is asleep. I should give him a nudge as he hasn't much time left. He also began at 8 p.m. on a Friday and will stop at 10 p.m. tonight. Interim: 2 weeks. It is recurrent, of course; an annual event. I knew his time had come when he stepped in front of me, his sanguine features burning up, a controlled man about to rupture, his laryngeal voice catalysing in his throat prior to the emission of the single word: Rum! A word which was followed up by the auxiliary command: The bottle. He is, of course, an ex-seaman, devoid, momentarily, of crew, of which more later.

I would, then, like to offer a toast: Absent friends everywhere! Those who are and those who we wish were. In particular, for purposes of elegy, Angel, known as Arch. In full, Archibald Angelus, Nora's retarded (my word) brother, known variously as Archie, Arch, Ark, Angel and, which I agree is trite, though cosmopolitan, Archangel, a name given, I presume, because he was, from birth, fat, sloppy, baby faced and slow (probably thyroidal): a cherub, a grotesquely overgrown, and over-bearing, infant who now in adult life has also been accused of rape. Nora, though not denying the possibility, defends the half-wit with the premise, Well, you raped me! as if the assertion of a collective guilt somehow mitigated the particular. I! I! My exclamation was quite real. When? I demanded. Four weeks after we met, she declared. Is it even remotely probable that a woman would carry that for thirty years? Her justification: What else was there for me to do?

Of course, it is almost impossible to imagine someone obese in the act of coitus, reciprocal never mind forensic. Forensic coitus

Funny Things

perpetrated by an over-weight baboon! It is almost more than my already damaged sensitivity can countenance. And to bracket me in the same disgusting image! Really! Me! Well, perhaps she saw it in a fragmentary moment of alcoholic horrors to which I am sure Nora must be prone. The horror of living and other such commonplaces.

Mr Candido claimed: The only bird in the animal kingdom capable of rape is the duck and quite often the female duck drowns. I suppose it came as no shock to anyone; the duck, not the drowning. Perhaps that too. I would rather it was the mallard which sank its eyes and drowned after the crime which to the dimwit might have seemed a precedence that he could not refuse. Anyway, no one took issue with MrCandido until he began to sing a navy song; well, recite: By the street of the half-strung tit, By the sign of the hanging arse... at which Nora took strong objection, which she expressed by rattling her fist on the counter, to which behaviour MrCandido responded by stepping back and shouting: Never gate-crash someone else's game. He then snatched up his bottle and glumly imbibed.

On the question of rape, I once accused the pig man of fingering one of his sows because I'd seen one of my friends do it. Not to his face, of course, but in my mind, which was like a catechism, a saving remark, indeed, a moment of real illumination. From bestiality to bestiality life quickens apace. And Anna watches T.V.

Darryl said: You need a T.V. to be human these days. He was, of course, being sarcastic because he can never prise Anna from her entertainment. He is a fool, naturally. Some one should point out to him that should he succeed in extracting Anna from passive pleasure she would cease to ignore his infidelities. (True ignorance or achieved ignorance? Who knows?) All I know is that she cleans perfectly, cuts vegetables, retires to her room, the chef's afters, (That is, Darryl! Actually, chef is far too flamboyant a word to describe him. Say rather, a preparer of sundry adequacies.) and once was heard to state: (She said it to the screen, I heard her, in response to Darryl's disparagement.) The television is my very best friend. Darryl retorted: Entertainment must not exist in Finland. Anna haughtily, (a relative word) replied: We have excellent T.V.

As an aside, Darryl's previous girlfriend, bearing in mind that the preparer of meals is also renowned for his own brand of homespun bigotry, was also Finnish. In fact, she was a lean, contemporary, charming beauty, meaning no disrespect to Anna who is simply not

Frederick Lightfoot

in the same league, and had us all reaching for the drawing board in order to calculate her pleasure. Suffice to say, avoiding unnecessary personal remarks, Darryl is an entirely ugly specimen, not obviously burdened like Archangel but simply badly put together; non-specifically unwholesome. The end found the Finn in fits of tears and Darryl seemingly unrepentant apart from the fact that a tape of *The Swan of Tuonela* issued from his room at maximum volume for six hours. Grief, unlooked for or created, assumes a multitude of forms: I suppose Darryl is a different man after a bottle of vodka but then I believe everyone is a different man after a bottle of vodka. Even Nora.

Mr Candido has slipped. He is on his side in some obvious distress. He must be very happy by now.

I took Darryl at his word and acquired a T.V. A great brown giant of an affair that cost me £10. I spent two hours attempting to render the vast, old-fashioned box discreet, positioning it in every corner of our rather cluttered room, and then finally sat down to a strange delight, and yes, a human delight, despite being ghosted and snowy, of advertisements, news and finally a late night showing of *Arsenic and Old Lace*, during which I drank a bottle of gin, fell asleep and vomited. I could guess by Nora's urgently vicious expression that she only wished I had inhaled the offensive matter and expired on the spot. She padded naked around the room while I did the proper thing and cleaned up. That night I learned that she was not a pretty sight but was more or less contiguous with the Archangel cherub. Sad what flesh is ere to. Incredible how much we conceal in the dark.

Mr Candido shouts out, obviously stimulated by his recent fall: "I don't feel pleasure any more but I don't feel pain."

"The ambition of any marriage is to achieve neither pleasure nor pain but simple neutrality," Nora agrees tartly, responding with practised casualness to Mr Candido's resurfacing. "Mind you, rum has much the same civilizing effect," she adds and reaches gleefully for a further tipple of one of her particular favourites, Bacardi with crushed ice impregnated with lime, a refinement she considers sophisticated and in keeping with the necessary character of a proprietress. As she earlier today said, when offered black-pudding for breakfast when she was obviously dreaming of baguettes, (are both those images sexual?), wrapping each word with prickly conviction which is an expression of her belief in gesture as the sense of a thing, a person, a character: A gourmet wouldn't eat eels. But, I should have said, a glutton would eat their own excrement. Instead I declared with an unnecessary surfeit of temper: You are a very poor snob. She immediately retorted with, Damn that noise! and stormed away to rectify the affront to her.

Question: Noise? (Noise is the scourge of civilized man: we are rendered neurotic, shot to hell, by progress.) Which assailed Nora? Anna's T.V.? Darryl's reminiscences? (Dodecaphonic laments suggestive of tangled relationships.) Or was it something less mechanical but as equally unnatural. Archangel's blubbering? (Why was he so emotional? Hungry, perhaps.) Mr Candido's alimentary snoring? My unforgivable flatus? (She believes that I succeed in the rendition at will. Sadly it is more pathological than that. I have a future of gastritis, pancreatitis, hepatic impairment, water on the brain and premature ageing. But at my age, thirty years minimum just minding the pump, (being also a late starter), it is all irrelevant. It is bad enough challenging life without taking on death. One would end up like Archangel feeding fear with the result: obese neurosis. Because, of course, he is neurotic: he has bouts of anxiety states. His fatty, androgynous, voice sails inconsolably: I can't cope; I am being annihilated. Help me! He is immediately ignored. I think he is a fraud. But Nora loves him. If love is a gesture, if rape was love, then we are all in love.)

"No," Mr Candido continues, staring neutrally at Nora, "it is not rum that neutralizes the brain but children. They steal your life away."

"Your daughter loves you."

"On the contrary," I interject, "his daughter wants to be loved by him. That is all anyone wants."

Nora looks winsome. Her mind sees babies. At her age it is positively disgusting. Her mouth opens and she emits a short, reassuring, babbled syllable: "Ah!"

Mr Candido, who is not a general practitioner but an ex-seaman turned boiler room attendant, scowls in reply: "Beast."

Nora puts down her glass, smiles rather viciously, and, looking him straight in the eye, pronounces: "You!" Mr Candido, oblivious to the fact that his body is incapable of erect posture, (the sexual overtones being not unintentional) attempts the military posture but only succeeds in projecting the rather impotent appearance of someone attempting to put on a jacket with only one functional arm.

Frederick Lightfoot

In other words he cannot physically pull himself together. "You," Nora repeats, sotto voce, but with damning emphasis.

Mr Candido looks like a man at boiling point. "Oh, give me a drink," he says remorsefully.

Nora produces the Navy Rum with a cheerful, told you so, swank, leans on the counter and confides: "I have been abused from the very beginning."

Mr Candido counters with: "I was a gentleman."

"He says it wasn't rape but what would you call ripped buttons, a hand over your mouth and the other hand where it was uninvited?"

"I never forced myself on her."

"He thinks it's the done thing."

"I waited. Post-natal complications, they said. Psychological. The shock. Surely post natal abstinence doesn't last thirty years."

"They think women enjoy it. Animals." Nora pauses and scrutinizes Mr Candido and then sympathetically asks: "What did you do?"

"Over time."

"Over time?"

"To send her on holiday."

"Holiday?"

"Every year. They are back in the morning."

"What will you do then?"

"Over time. They like to go further and further afield. My daughter is a geography teacher."

"You must be very proud."

"Of course I'm proud. Who wouldn't be."

"Have you never strayed."

With great deliberation Mr Candido looks wistfully to the bottom of his empty glass, refills it, sips three times and says: "No one is perfect but I at least am innocent."

"And you a seaman," Nora says.

"The navy is a great friend for a man. A friend for life."

"How is your dog?"

"In need of water, food and exercise. But... All in the morning."

"The poor pet. Two weeks without a drink."

"I have been home."

"But you were carried there and back."

"They wouldn't have ignored him. Not a Yorkshire Terrier."

Funny Things

Mr Candido stops speaking and looks afraid.
Nora smiles and quietly enquires: "Have you got the date wrong?"
"No, but I'm sober. How has that happened?"
"Alex," Nora demands, "did you give Mr Candido's little pet a drink?"
That, by the way, is me, if I had not already mentioned it. Alex dogsbody, live-in skivvy, reprobate, acting partner, and whatever else we deign to admit. I respond: "You were right in every detail regarding your over-ripe sibling. It was just how she described it. Rape."
"You!" Nora screams. "You!"
"His only defence is defective equipment i.e. no sighting for years."
Nora screams again: "Bastard! It was you! I was talking about you!"
(Funny thing No 4: W.C. Fields: *Anybody who hates dogs and loves whiskey can't be all bad.*)
As Nora is screaming we may as well consider noise. Nora's investigation and remedy.
To go back a step, then; Nora's implied investigation and remedy of a noise nuisance. Resumé of sources. Anna's T.V. Content; Sunday soaps being a replay of weekday soap. Rationale for viewing; possible revaluation of narrative procedures in the light of new knowledge, because, of course, Anna saw the original. Darryl's music. Geographic origin; European (style), attic (location, eliciting much criticism for lack of skylight which in turn serves as justification for virtual cohabitation with Anna and T.V.). Mode; popular. Instrumentation; simulation. Archangel's blubbering. Causation; criminal activity. Content; self pity and regression as opposed self-reproach and maturation. Mr Candido's anal somniloquy. Olfactory consideration; absence of food in the gut plus excess of rum resulting in diminution, possible destruction, of natural alimentary flora; also, absence of bulk resulting in possibility of accident. Olfactory implications; not for the sensitive! Outcome of Nora's activities? Nil. No change. One can only assume that the noise in question was something different entirely to those mentioned, a product of particularly acute hearing, specific sensitivity or hallucination.
I would not be shocked by the latter. She has played Lady

Macbeth, plus all other minor female roles, once too often (amateur dramatic huff is the other alternative possibility governing Nora's behaviour). Almost from day one we began to play. It was a commitment to the libertarianism of the establishment. (Her dream then was of turning one of the rooms into a small theatre. As to her dreams now, the baguette aside, I cannot say.) Even then, first rehearsal, scene one of our retarded affair, it was Macbeth (amateur attraction: witches, madness and over-ambition). I caused an immediate souring of Nora's enthusiasm, shattering her willing suspension of disbelief, by responding to her proposal that I could be Duncan with the assertion: I am too ugly to be a king. Her composure and complacency snapped together. You will be a king, she insisted. One could almost believe that she actually was Lady Macbeth except for the fact that she was commanding the wrong man. Anyway, I stuck around for the requisite acts and we went through the old theatricals: at first I didn't love enough, then too much, then not at all, then who knows, then indivisible. If Macbeth didn't die in Act 5 (indivisible) then there would never be another Act 1. It is a terrifying thought. (Act 1: Drinking is such fun.) Did I learn anything from my theatrical days? A way of saying that I was a pig farmer's son in a manner that implied I was entirely classless. What other conclusion could be drawn from the juxtaposition of property and excrement.

But, of course, the pig, that most human, cloven, of creatures, is a greatly misunderstood creature as all pig farmers will agree. The pig is the most clean and sophisticated of animals when it is allowed to be. Allowance is the first principle of successful husbandry. Allowance, obsession and fear plus brush and spade work. A well-groomed sty is a sty in which a pig will produce a little piggy toilet which in the end reduces one's labour dramatically. My father was never tardy with such advice.

Indeed, one could quite successfully manage a pig in an establishment like this. But I know before I even allow myself to become mildly intoxicated by this idea that it would be fruitless: when it finally came to it Nora would refuse to eat the bacon (on grounds of sensitivity, not, religion, Nora being Greek Orthodox). In fact, Nora claims that the religious disparity between us, lapsed G.O. and lapsed Anglican, accounts for my, to quote, absolute incomprehension of family life, by which she means, absence of loyalty, absence of compromise, absence of faith, propensity to

Funny Things

amorality, with an overwhelming sense of alienation. I, naturally, would argue the point. I would admit that from my father I acquired (genetics, learned behaviour, who knows) a surfeit of fear. He was, as all pig farmers must be, I suppose, impregnated with fear. The fear of not holding on, nurtured with the nurturing of runts, pipette and bottle feeding, leading inexorably to rapid senility and the grave. I am sure he died of accidentally letting go. In fact, I am sure most people die of similar absent-mindedness. Happily I also acquired his cure which, incidentally, is empty. Time: mid afternoon. Full. Ah!

(Funny thing No 5: W.C. Fields: *I always keep a supply of stimulant handy in case I see a snake - which I also keep handy.*)

I must say that I was greatly disappointed that Nora did not eradicate, and I do not use the word lightly, Darryl's noise. I would have preferred something rather more liturgical in keeping with the gravity of the day. After all, it is the day in which both Mr Candido and myself will have ceased drinking. And that horror awaits us all. In fact, being forced to be so continually cognisant with her failure, I was quite resolved to eradicate it myself and having the benefit of an entirely liquid lunch (therefore, no gratitude owing the chef) went to the attic to further my ambition.

"Consuming laughter and applause," Darryl said vindictively and as if he supposed that the tenor of his comment was entirely universal in comprehension, an effect slightly lost by the fact that I only heard him on the third attempt at articulation. (Consuming laughter and applause. Consuming laughter and applause. Consuming laughter and applause. Fortissimo.)

"Are you sick?" I inquired, which was purely interrogative and not sympathetic. For me he was sick.

Darryl reached out his arm, located his half-consumed half bottle of Smirnoff vodka, brought it meticulously to his lips, swallowed deliberately and then, remembering previous efforts, shouted: "Probably."

I must be more precise in my description: Darryl was lying on his bed, which was tucked into the roof space so that the distance between his face and the covering ceiling was only a matter of inches which rendered his vodka drinking awkward; indeed, he had to wipe his sleeve across his cheeks after each mouthful. Impression: slovenliness, arrogance and depression. I should also point out that Sunday is not particularly a day of rest for Darryl which has rather been procured over a period of time by the making of beef and

Frederick Lightfoot

horseradish sandwiches, cellophane-wrapped, on Saturday which are then retailed as fresh on the Sunday. It is, of course, of no matter. The only people here on the seventh day were certainly here on the sixth and not unusually were here from the very beginning of the seventh. (Mr Candido for example.) And as can only be expected from such a set of circumstances the exercise of taste buds is not sophisticated. (The serving of horseradish is particularly generous.) As a coda to the sandwich situation I must add that I insist upon the inclusion of pork although, as already suggested, I do avoid consumption myself. In fact, I find that I eat very little. I have been warned that, due to the pathology of alcohol, eventually my pancreas will ingest itself which strikes me as such an intriguing condition, symbolic in the extreme, that I look forward to it with relish, if you will excuse the pun. Anyway, to return to the aesthetically displeasing cook.

Whilst Darryl was consuming his vodka, in what I could only describe as a snivelling manner, I took the opportunity of surreptitiously seeking out the word I was looking for: Stop. And once I had located the said command wasted no time in executing it. Momentary ferocious, fragile, peace! Darryl's response to the cessation of his music, was the morose remark: "There it is, the Sunday matinee, the thing I tried to drown."

"You should take her out."
"She couldn't cope."
"You could support her."
"I couldn't cope."
"The responsibility."
"Being seen."
"You're no athlete."

Darryl grunted and, moving in a circular motion so as to avoid collision with the ceiling, sat up abandoning his vodka bottle to the floor, (empty, of course). "This must be sanity!" he said impressively. I vaguely nodded assent. "Do you want a drink?" I nodded assent even less forcibly than before but all the same he comprehended my answer. "Vodka?" Repetition of previous two actions even more dilute. "People were not meant, were not designed, to live in single rooms," Darryl said as he handed me what I must admit was a particularly generous glass of vodka from a newly opened (whole) bottle.

I responded with yet another curtailed repetition of the previous

Funny Things

assents until, having taken a large measure of the said vodka into my mouth and oesophagus and from thence into my failing stomach and pancreas, I said, liturgically: "I don't want to die here."

Darryl smiled, offered an uninterpretable toast, followed by the matter of fact comment: "You will die here," and then, as if it was a comforting remark, "You will die here, Nora will die here, and Anna will probably die here, and you will all want to be somewhere else. And I wish you were. For my sake, not yours. There are too many people in this city who don't belong here."

"If I have to die, in the classic phrase, I just don't want to be there at the time."

Darryl smiled, replenished my not entirely spent glass, and said: "You won't be, don't worry about that. Where are you from anyway?"

"A pig farm."

"Sorry I asked," Darryl said and resumed his former docile position on the mattress. "Is that the truth?"

"I lied."

"Everyone lies."

"Everyone?" In response Darryl indulged in one of my dilute assents. I followed it up. "Anna wouldn't know how to lie," I suggested.

"Anna has lived in furnished rooms too long. She doesn't really know fact from fiction but as we all know she has a propensity for the latter." He took another drink (still direct from the bottle), considered a moment and then said: "It would be very pleasant to marry a virgin."

"Anna?"

"Anna is a virgin after intercourse. No, a proper virgin not a perverse one. The trouble with all of you is that you expect to be humiliated. You think it's normal. You have no self respect because you have no property. I'm not going to die here."

I smiled, drained my glass, and said, victoriously: "You won't leave here. Not in any real sense. You are destined for poky rooms."

Darryl shook his head, lay back, stretched out both arms, his right holding the bottle neck, and said: "I'm going to have a house." I put down my glass and made to leave. "Don't tell Anna," he said in a manner that I would happily interpret as threatening.

I unplugged his cassette player at both the wall and the machine

Frederick Lightfoot

and kept hold of the lead. "Everyone lies," I said.

Darryl yawned, closed his eyes, and said: "I could never love a woman the way I could love dogs and children."

I made no reply but exited with the cassette lead. As I walked down the stairs I put my head around Anna's door and told her: "Darryl wants to go for a walk." Anna turned from the screen, smiled pleasantly enough, and shook her head. I put my index finger to my lips and backed out on tiptoes. Anna must have been viewing a comedy because I could hear her laughter before I descended another step.

"I dread her coming back," Mr Candido explains to Nora, "but I dread her being away more. Is that crazy."

"Of course it is," Nora says. "Drink your drink."

Six o'clock. Little pleasure in drinking, but the obligation is overwhelming. Port, for variety and effect. Nora looks down her nose, her nostrils actually flare, suspicious but also, quite obviously, impressed. Port is so, what we would say, sophistical.

"What about me?" she says.

Why not, I think, after all, I never expected to marry a virgin. What could be more tedious. I pour her an Irish Cream which she contemplates at first disagreeably, then with some surprise, then with trepidation, and finally with gratitude. "Thank you," she says, as if she has evinced a symbol in my action.

I would like to say that I am sick of symbolism. In future I will take everything literally. But already I've drunk too much and, after all, there is my pancreas.

"For old times' sake," I say despondently, pregnant with symbols.

"Which old times?" Nora counters defensively, reacting to the glass in her hand as if it was stage poison.

"La Ronde, our first screenplay together."

"Shut up," she says. Already my literalness has failed me. Nora does not mean shut up, at all. She means: All my life is symbolic: Thank God. "Fill me up," she adds and proffers her cup.

"Of course," I say. It is a shame, a human weakness, and perhaps fallacy, that we have to live with what we say. No one, who drinks, should be so encumbered. Is that not the point. Funny thing No 6: *I want a drink. I want a drink. I want a drink. Fortissimo.*

"What was so great about La Ronde?" Nora asks, manipulating her voice so that it issues forth in the form of contentious drawl. It is a worthwhile trick as it leaves me with no means of verifying her true state of sobriety. She can now do and say anything.

I answer: "Because all I ever wanted from you was an equal amount of fidelity and infidelity."

"I didn't want abuse," she counters.

I don't hesitate in consuming another two drinks.

This is perhaps the moment to list the unknown properties of alcohol:

The ability to patronise (the lie comes out!).

Hypersensitive recall (without the adjunct of analysis).

Latent power (the absence of doubt).

The ability to mash swill (and refuse to accept what the animals made of you).

Therefore, given preternatural activity, and actuality, given the power to annul a world of wisdom (and boredom), plus boar and sow - my father always made a point of watching pre-planned swine copulation: in order to see whether the boar had become too heavy for the willing female (or unwilling: patronising on some part). He claimed, with unusual vigour, to have seen a sow crushed to death by a too liberally fed boar. There was something too tragic to countenance watching one's livelihood vanish in the shape of crushed bones, embarrassed breathing, expiration, in the pursuit of such, analogously, enjoyable activity. But he always drank to watch, though he strongly refuted all accusations that he found the performance an entertainment. He steadfastly maintained throughout his long, second-rate, slops-portion life, sucking the thirteenth teat, that: Performance is not an entertainment. I suppose, with the evidence of amateur dramatics on my side, I would support his claim. His every action had one motive: Fear. He was scared of wives (women), children (mixed gender), and swine (obese and under-ripe) and fear made him patronising, begrudging, dogmatic and obsessional (of unknown properties). All in all: gargantuan efforts to simply hold on.

But, I hear you say, yes, I really do, what of the pigs man pig woman? Oh, lyrically and elegiacally, to allow at least some note of reconciliation into this building, I refuse to call it a house and certainly not a home, she was the complete opposite. She was driven by fear. Fear of the terrible human power she wielded. There is a rule that all addicts are aware of: Human life loves and needs its own weakness. And why? Because weakness can only result in tragedy

Frederick Lightfoot

and tragedy is the only optimism known to man (collective i.e. woman too). But, I go on... weakly, diminuendo. A drinker rapidly learns his own weakness: bladder insufficiency, sentimentality, surrealism, violence. Though, I must say, I am not particularly prone to any. I simply suffer the psychic condition of being alienated from my own poison which renders it both symbolic and real - but, to come back - given, etc, etc (and an absent propensity to violence) I can state categorically that Nora is lying. I never raped her; never have, never will. (God help me!)
   Question: Motive of accusation?
   Glibness.
   Destructiveness.
   Boredom.
   Fear.
   From such dangerously simple beginnings as a memory involuted by surrealism, diluted by delusion, abstracted by need, re-vamped by necessity, has terrible wrong occurred. But, I am afraid, she is not going to have her own way. This performance is not an entertainment. We are too mutually destructive to destroy each other. And the moment is rapidly approaching when I will stop drinking. So, what would I say to defend myself? Very little, in fact. The nature of defence is that it must be located in the fantasies of the accuser. So...
   Nora, proprietress of this house, known to a select multitude of serious no-hopers, daughter of a manic depressive Cypriot woman of very unmoderated performance disciplines, and a father... (But why bring such things up? All right - probably not a pig farmer, or lost at sea, or anything at all like that, but, quite possibly, very nice, quite possibly a victim of his own compassion i.e. Mrs Angelus, who, whatever, is absent from this account.) is, Nora that is, the sibling to an endocrine (or exocrine?) victim whose imbecility, eunuchoidism and neurosis masks an undisclosed viciousness.
   All right, the central object of this account...
   The Archangel.
   The Archangel came into being in the year anno Domini 1945, five years adrift from his closest relative Nora. (Never tell a lady's age, she admonishes me.) And now we are in the year, the thirtieth of my addiction... No, forget time... Well, the Archangel grew big, fat and ugly and what is worse was possessed of a totally obnoxious nature. He was, though, loved by the elder sister, (trite, trite) who struggled

and sacrificed, without the aid of a male progenitor and with the handicap of a manic-depressive mother, whose only respite and adult pleasure was amateur dramatics, particularly Lady Macbeth and at one stage, I promise you, (briefly, perhaps) La Ronde, in which she took five parts, (I took six) which by any standards is open to misconception... Enough of this...

The Archangel, Archibald, committed the crime of rape. Reasons: weakness and fear. Characteristics of victim: weakness and fear.

If any one has not yet realised: this is an account of addiction. The object: pigs.

It is the eighth stroke of ten. My glass is empty. Pancreas and stomach relax. (Liver? Maybe.) I have stopped. Mr Candido has left without so much as an adieu. He has fifty weeks in which to dream of his wife's (and daughter's, who seems remarkably disinterested in men) vacation. It has been, of course, a very long protracted excursion, these journeys, for all of us. Why have I paused at this moment? Moment signified by parenthesis ().

To begin. If there was no ending there would be no beginning. Tomorrow at eight p.m. I am going to make (perform) the most destructive decision of my miserable life: I am going to start drinking. It is a game; a personal game. What will come first, the first stroke of eight, delirium tremens, or fear? I am convinced that all three occur simultaneously and are therefore of no true significance. The end has begun.

The tenth stroke. End.

Coda: The most important character of this narrative has not had any say at all; in fact, is missing.

Panurge 23 (October 1995)

The three winners of the Lancaster University 1995 Fiction Competition, judge **Janice Galloway**. Note the deadline for entry is **15th April 1995**.

Richard Beard

The Three-Rope Trick

If you've been to Paris, you might know me. You may have seen cigarettes vanish in my bare hands. Seen me performing miracles on the square in front of the Pompidou Centre, all tubes and truth behind me. You know, the Algerian-looking magician dressed in black who hypnotises two boys, and then two girls, that's me. You make a ring around me, two or three deep, and you always laugh when the boys and girls can't move their arms or their legs. I line them up side by side so you can see their nervous faces.

Money please. I scamper round with my leather bag the size of a small rucksack. It zincs encouragingly with ten franc coins.

The broad-shouldered boys laugh and twist around their frozen limbs, at least until I say Alakazamee and make their penises disappear from their neat pleated trousers. They stop laughing. Wide-eyed, they touch the flies of their trousers tenderly, like fruit. I free them and they run to a corner and tear open their belts and gape into their shorts. This part of the show is more entertaining in winter. Then the boys run back and start shouting at me. They don't know what to believe.

The crowd loves it, you love it, you stand on tiptoe at the back. You clap. You laugh. The two boys always think I've given their penises to the two girls (who are still hypnotised to the spot), and maybe I have, so they all start arguing amongst themselves.

I collect more money before giving everyone back what was once theirs. The boys search out their friends and walk quickly away, towards the Forum, glancing back at me every few yards. The girls sometimes stay and talk to me.

If you haven't seen me, and you're ever in Paris, you should come and watch; it's a good act.

"But it can't be true," you say. "How do you do it?"

"Are the volunteers paid accomplices?"

"Is it simple hypnosis?"

If it can't be true, I say, I can't do it. If you haven't seen me, you really should. Every Wednesday and Friday afternoon, outside the Pompidou Centre, Paris.

CHATELET

I always go home on the Metro. As soon as the ticket barriers slide

The Three-Rope Trick

shut behind me I feel as if I'm disappearing underground, and vanishing from the real world. Escalators fold me into miles of moled underground, and if you look at the right angle, in the right light, with an illusionist's eye, the Metro is very similar to the Pompidou Centre, where all the surfaced pipes and ducts, unhidden, unclad, make the building somehow true, as though everything ugly must always be true.

Elsewhere, the truth is always beneath, behind, under, below, anywhere but the surface. The naked truth lies beneath the clothes, beneath the skin, under the shirt-cuff, below the false bottom of the false top-hat, and the Metro knows this - it is underneath, and holds the secret of how things work, and the truth of them.

It's like magic. On the one hand it scares you nearly to death. On the other (below the shirt-cuff) it holds out the hope of instant remedies and elves at the bottom of the garden. It is mysterious, a place where everything can change, and be changed. It's another world.

I met Sumi in the Metro, which is another reason I like it.

"You're the guy who does the dumb tricks," she said.

It wasn't a question. By now she'll already be home in Abesses, which is where we live, the end of my line.

Underground at Chatelet you can walk endlessly through tunnels and feel you're never getting anywhere. They have these moving pavements, which means you pass people going in the other direction much quicker than normal. You feel superhuman, walking a hundred miles an hour. You feel like an olympic passer-by, passing the world by at olympic speeds.

You reach the platform and you wait for a train. A train arrives and you slink into a seat and wish the woman next to you weren't so fat so you could stretch out a little. You're jostled away and disappearing, you catch a poster advertising instant love, and the name of the dating agency is CUM, which doesn't even make you laugh anymore.

LOUVRE   LOUVRE   LOUVRE   LOUVRE   LOUVRE

First stop. The fat woman leaves. I spread myself out.

I think of Mrs Grip, and decide that one of her problems was that she never travelled by Metro. She was an art collector, which was another thing in life hard to believe, considering. I'd just finished a show, and was checking the concrete for any stray coins. She touched my face and I jumped away.

"Are you for real?" she said.

She was soft, ripe, pungent with money. Her clothes were too expensive and too small, but she wasn't unattractive. She was older than she wanted to be.

"Do you do private stuff?" she asked.

I said maybe.

"Oh, so you speak English?"

She never tried any other language, so it was just as well.

"I can pay," she said.

Painted on the walls of the Metro, in the tunnels themselves not the stations, just above the train-tracks, are advertising slogans which read ECCO, ECCO, ECCO, in green letters on a white rectangular background. It's something you have to see to believe.

I asked her what she had in mind.

"Something private," she said.

I asked her name, in case she was famous. She giggled and said her name was Grip, Mrs Grip, Kirby Grip, which was like throwing the hat over a rabbit and not even pretending to make it disappear. Besides, she had the initials MM woven in miniature pearls on the lapel of her canary-yellow jacket, which angled sharply over her breasts, back into her waist, out over her hips.

Sumi's body, before our little accident, was a shade lighter than those painted by Gauguin. (Gauguin was a painter who became a hero by leaving miserable Europe for a Pacific island where the sun always shone and women wore no clothes). Japanese skin, behind the myth, under the clothes, is like European with a slight tan, is the truth of it. I told Sumi she was beautiful. She sneered and told me to take off my make-up. I wear eyeliner and a little blusher (for my cheek-bones). It makes me more dramatic for the audience.

Mrs Grip said that her art collection included several Gauguins, some Renoirs, Monets, and one Van Gogh. She explained that her father had made a fortune importing bidets into America, and then spent the profits on European art.

"If you do what I ask I'll give you any painting you like," she said, "except the Van Gogh."

I thought Sumi might like a Gauguin, so I followed Mrs Grip to the taxi rank (she never travelled by Metro).

Sumi never promised me anything.

Royalty and Empire Exhibition, Windsor

Philip Wolmuth

Richard Beard

"What you see is what you get," she said, sitting cross-legged and naked, pulling her black hair out of her eyes, then blowing her nose into her hand.

PALAIS ROYAL   PALAIS ROYAL   PALAIS ROYAL

Mrs Grip was surprised when an Algerian-looking entertainer in France spoke to her in English, but I was born in Port Talbot, a large industrial town in the South of Wales. Apparently when people from Port Talbot speak French they sound exactly like people from Algeria who speak French. I know this because a friend of mine from Port Talbot once came to stay and he was told he sounded like an Algerian. People only mentioned it because he doesn't have the same dark skin as I do. They could therefore tell him the truth because they didn't think it could possibly be the truth.

Sumi was born in Japan, originally, but she tells me she's been reborn all over (she scratches her apple-smooth bum and rolls herself in the sheet). She once lived with a native tribe in the jungles of Papua New Guinea. One night, moonlight splintering the dark branches of the trees, she was cut from the navel to the hip with the broken neck of a Coca-Cola bottle. The moon-god then entered her womb in a reversed Caesarian. It was a local ritual.

The long scar is a strange colour, white and almost silver. I like to kiss it because it has the texture of a lip and I imagine sucking moonlight from her body.

"You remind me of the tribe in Papua New Guinea," she once told me.

I asked her why.

"Because you're full of shit," she said.

She was once reborn in Los Angeles, U.S.A.

Mrs Grip came from Kansas, U.S.A. In her own words, "I came to Paris because I got the culture thing."

She planned to stay in Paris until she'd finished writing a poem called Papillon Longing, and had taken a six month lease on a luxury apartment near the Luxembourg Palace. I told her it must be a long poem.

"There," she said, "I knew there was something special about you."

The taxi crossed the river, on the way to her apartment.

The Three-Rope Trick

TUILERIES TUILERIES TUILERIES TUILERIES TUILERIES

I knew Mrs Grip was going to ask me to do something I couldn't do. It happens all the time. If I told you magic was a skill only, I'd no longer be a magician, but a trickster. But say, just for a moment, that magic was only a skill (even if people genuinely disappear and penises too), then it's a skill like any other. If a banker makes your money double, you don't think he has superior powers. But all the same, you don't know how the markets work, or how to time a sale, or why to trust one stock and not another, or why he has the skill and you don't. It's the same with magic.

The difference is the banker probably can't be magical, but people suspect a magician could also be a banker, by magic.

This is the best kind of skill to have, one which makes other people suspect all skills are offered you. It's like being a king, who also has the resources to have all skills. He can order the gardener to hoe his garden and the tiler to tile his roof and so has access to the skills of a gardener and a tiler. To have access to all skills is the difference between power and expertise, and most people think that magic is more than a skill, and an access to power. This means they end up with very high expectations.

Mrs Grip's apartment was large and leafy, with plants and flowers scattered everywhere between the soft furnishings; rubber plants, irises, umbrellas, spiders, elephant's ears, traveller's joy. It could have been a version of Papua New Guinea.

I asked her where were the paintings.

"Back in Kansas."

I asked where was Mr Grip.

"Disappeared for a few months," she said, and giggled.

I asked her what she wanted me to do.

She giggled again, and put her hand over her mouth, and smudged her lipstick.

"Oh not much," she said, pretending to be calm. "I want to be transformed, be a ruler, a lover, an engineer of world peace, an enchanted traveller, a terror to all enemies, and a woman of passion."

I asked her if that was all.

"It was a line from my poem," she said.

I once asked Sumi what she wanted from me. At the time I was still trying to impress her, so I squeezed a billiard ball from my forehead as though I could give her anything she asked. She was sitting cross-legged and naked on the floor, as she does, eating a bowl of yoghurt. She looked up at me through her hair, and her narrow Japanese eyes made her look as though she never believed a thing, and anyway, had seen it done somewhere before, and better.

"I just want someone so dull they won't run away," she said, pivoting on her bum and turning her back. Sumi has the most beautiful back. Her shoulder blades are angular, and the skin smoother than her breasts. She wears backless dresses.

I have to change at Concorde. I stand up and lean against a pole. A small boy is watching me. I pull a cigarette from my nostril.

CONCORDE   CONCORDE   CONCORDE   CONCORDE

The sleeping drunk-woman with skirt rucked above her hips is the old age of the girl-punk burning sweet hashish is the daughter of the head-scarved woman clinging domestic shawl-space around her shoulders is the mother of the boy in polo shirt and ironed jeans looking tough because to scared eyes everyone looks tough.

So many people out of agreement with themselves, and all collected underground.

Each square tile on the curved wall at Concorde is enamelled with a white letter on a blue background. Snatches of what might be the Declaration of the Rights of Man appear and disappear in the Babel of letters like answers in a find-the-world puzzle. FREEDOM. CHOICE. TRUTH. CHANGE. You can also find your own words, as if answering an entirely different puzzle, and choose and change them like ingredients which make any number of meals. If you look hard, there is a diagonal which says bacon and eggs. Tuna is all over the place (in French).

There is a girl, also waiting for the train, and standing a dangerous diver's distance from the edge of the track. She seems good-looking, but I stroll closer, in case there's something I'm missing (behind the make-up, hidden by the clothes etc.) She has long cool legs and a neat little black dress. Her arms are crossed over her breasts and the material stretches just beyond her elbows onto her freckled forearms. She looks one way then the other. I smile at her. She is all cheekbones and big round hazel eyes, and she shakes her fine blonde hair which looks very clean, almost commercial.

There is a breath of air and a rumble of train. Clumsily,

The Three-Rope Trick

beautifully, her long-boned hand pulls open the hissing door.

I step into the same carriage, because I like to have something nice to look at on the Metro.

MADELEINE   MADELEINE   MADELEINE   MADELEINE

Might be the name of the blonde-haired girl sitting opposite. She looks as though she could be a model, which is one way of mixing with talented people if you have no talent. Beauty, after all, is not a skill, unless you're ugly, and models are never ugly. I think I resent them. They always seem able to conjure poster-beautiful boys to wear on their arms, then they walk around like photographs, as though they were unreal, and not part of our world.

Earlier in the year the outside of the Madeleine church, which is a square of pillars with a space in the middle, was being cleaned. Instead of covering the facade with scaffolding, which is what a building always seems to need when people look at it too much, they covered it with a huge tarpaulin, on which was painted a picture of the facade of the Madeleine. It was a rosy pink colour, sunset all day long, and it looked much better than the Madeleine church itself. Above and below, in front and behind, on top and underneath.

Mrs Grip said that in order to finish her poem, Papillon Longing, she needed something she'd never had. I told her I was better at making things disappear than appear.

"I thought magicians also brought rabbits out of hats?"

I said we could bring tower-blocks out of hats, if the hat was big enough.

"It's quite a big thing," she said.

Like the Madeleine building, Sumi is no longer what she once was. She is bigger, her breasts are rounder, she is about to pull a rabbit from a hat. What she is about to pull from her body is a bigger and better magic than any of mine. We call her box of tricks our little accident, because neither of us has any idea what is happening, nor any control over it. She is a paler colour where her skin has stretched; the scar from navel to hip has flattened and dulled to the colour of mercury. She would love a Gauguin, I think.

It was about time Mrs Grip became all tubes and truth. She explained that her poem would teach people how to stop crawling and become butterflies, metaphorically. She believed the soul could rise above the body and fly over cornfields and flutter over the world, but she was missing the one thing she believed proved this.

I asked her how she could believe it then.

"I just know it, but evidence helps."

To transcend her body, and become a butterfly, she wanted an orgasm. This didn't strike her as strange.

The girl Madeleine keeps glancing at the map of station-stops. I wonder if I mixed with her I could mix with the talented people. I will her towards me, just a little.

ST LAZARE ST LAZARE ST LAZARE ST LAZARE ST LAZARE

"Messieurs, mesdames."

He leans against the door in the middle of the carriage, and stares at nothing. He is a broad man, older than middle-aged, down on his luck. He wears a silver-grey jacket which is creased with dirt, and a wool tie over a shirt that was never made for ties. The dark Airtex collar curls limply under his chin. He has a fine clear voice, as though he is used to talking to children. He's a beggar.

"I'm a joiner by trade, and I've worked all over the world. I used to craft the world's finest reproduction furniture, Louis Quinze, Louis Seize, every Louis there ever was. Alas, I work no more because of a great tragedy that has befallen me."

He pauses. He holds up his right hand, which is missing the two middle fingers. The stumps shine like polished red-wood. The other fingers are flat and square-nailed and dark with dirt: hard, work-scarred hands.

"I lost these fingers to a shard of glass from a smashed wing-mirror in the Gambia. It was a punishment. My crime? I fell in love, this was my crime."

With his fully-fingered hand he wipes away a tear that has lodged in a worry-line stretching from the bridge of his nose to the corner of his mouth.

"She was a warrior's daughter. Her hair was as black as the eyes of a snake. Her eyes were as brown as the skin of a bear. Her skin was gold. Her tribe was famed for its ferocity, but I became friends with them all, one by one, and for each one I made a chair from the local banyan wood, until they all had chairs and as payment they invited me to choose a wife.

"The warrior's daughter was my whole purpose for living. She was so beautiful. So beautiful and sly. So, so beautiful. I chose her to be my wife. They said I could have her, if I was to make something special from the banyan tree, better than anything I'd ever made before.

"I couldn't wait. I had no patience. I wanted her. I worked all that night and the next day, sweating in the sun and the jungle black of night, carving and chipping and smoothing and varnishing, until on the second day, as the sun began to set, it was finished. A Louis Quatorze Bureau, the best I had ever made, and fit for any queen.

"I went to claim my bride. Tomorrow, they said, tomorrow. Give her your gift, if she is pleased with it you will marry tomorrow. She seemed pleased. She climbed into the desk like a child, and her father gently pulled down the perfectly slatted roll-top. If she has pleasant dreams, he said, she is yours.

"I didn't sleep that hot night. As soon as dawn broke I rushed back to the bureau and the whole tribe was waiting, gathered in a circle around it. Now we shall see, the warrior said. He went to pull back the top of the bureau and the tribe closed in to see more clearly. Then he threw back the lid, and the girl was gone. She wasn't there.

"There was a high-pitched scream from the river, and she came running, her golden skin burnt red by the undried varnish.

"They rounded on me, chanting a death chant, their teeth flashing in the morning sun. They said my magic box had cursed her and accused me of the blackest of black magic. There was no reasoning with them. They held me down and cut off my fingers with the broken eye of the devil's steed, which was the smashed wing-mirror of an old Renault 4. They chased me from the village with the burning brands of my own furniture, they chased me back to France.

"Messieurs, mesdames, for a poor joiner, who suffered for love, and the impatience it breeds, I beg you, a few francs."

TRINITE   TRINITE   TRINITE   TRINITE   TRINITE   TRINITE

Sumi wants me to be a banker, so that the three of us have a solid future.

"Think of your family," she says, "and how unexciting an exciting life is, from the inside."

She stays home often, now she has the baby inside her.

My father was an Algerian who married a Welshwoman and went to work in Wales as a car-welder, a job he learnt at a Renault plant in Lyon. He taught me my French and my magic and how to make penises disappear. In fact he used to do the same trick in Covent Garden in the late sixties, after my mother left us.

My mother went to Algeria to meet my father's family and never came back. Me and my father were left like a triangle with only two angles, with two lines waving like antennae but never managing to cross. The base was my mother because she was the only thing we had in common, apart from the magic.

It was my father who gave me the most useless piece of advice I've ever had. Take opportunities he used to say.

He gave the same advice to my mother. It was as if you could take an opportunity like a loose orange from a market stall, even though an opportunity is just the same as a choice - it sounds like one thing but comes as a pair. Each one you take leaves another behind.

I wonder what it would be like to walk hand in hand with Madeleine in Algiers. She's looking nearly everywhere in the empty carriage except at me, which is just another way of looking at me.

All sorts of triangles, irregularly shaped. Mrs Grip put her hand on my thigh and I wondered how much less firm was the thigh of Mr Grip. I coughed. I asked why me?

"Because you can do anything," she said.

She kissed my neck and her lipstick was sticky and cold. Gauguin left his wife and family to go to a Pacific Island where he was fed passion-fruit and slept with naked native girls for the sake of his art.

"Papillon Longing," she whispered in my ear, and unclipped an ear-ring.

ST GEORGES   ST GEORGES   ST GEORGES   ST GEORGES

She has beautiful hazel eyes, and I refuse to look away. She tosses her hair and looks out of the window where all she can see is her own reflection and, painted on the tunnel walls, ECCO, ECCO, ECCO. She crosses her legs. She's telling me I can't have her, she's dismissing me.

If I was the perfect man, her dismissal tells me, I wouldn't have wanted her, and so I would never have had her. Because I want her, I cannot possibly be good enough to have her.

There was Sumi, as Mrs Grip undid the buttons on my black shirt. I was excited by the candy smell of her breath and the artificial talcum of her skin. Sumi said I was dependable. I slid beneath Mrs Grip, who had taken off no clothes except her underpants and her

The Three-Rope Trick

ear-rings.

Again I asked why me?

"Because you're not scared of letting other people believe in things you don't believe yourself."

She started moaning, like a sexual cassette.

Sumi says our child will be the first thing I've ever created which is true and without trickery.

"You won't be able to run away from it," she said, "as if it doesn't exist."

She has such a low opinion of me that I believe she's always right. What is ugly must be true. The Pompidou centre, conspiracy, science (he has a spring beneath the table), the hidden, the sinister, the tortured and the tubular are all true. The truth is underground and underneath, it's the drunks on the Metro and rats in the cellar and bowel movements and the urge to muss the underclothes of twelve-year-old girls. This is the real world.

Saint George, the patron saint of England, is well-known for killing a dragon. Some people think that fantasy is the dragon to their St George, and they kill it in order to live in the real world. Other people think the dragon is reality, which they kill in order to live in the unreal world. Either way, it's because reality is bad more often than good. Me, I believe everything.

And anyway, Sumi tells me the planet will be dead in fifty years, like a northern forest. And if this is true, everything real now becomes slightly unreal. The baby is only true as a flattened scar and rounded breasts but we have no idea what is to come after, not even the skin-colour of the hybrid we have made.

The Gauguin is in the post. The boys' penises have disappeared. Madeleine is a model. The girl is called Madeleine. The sleight of mind needed to live makes us all magicians.

Madeleine stands up and stretches her long legs by arching her back and punching out her non-existent belly. With long fingers she smoothes her skirt at the hips. She's leaving. She sits down again. She's staying.

PIGALLE PIGALLE PIGALLE PIGALLE PIGALLE PIGALLE

At night, at exactly eight o'clock, whores appear in the streets of Pigalle as if by magic. They wear shiny red handbags with gold clasps, and fishnet stockings cover their angular legs like the mesh on a

Richard Beard

microphone. Often, they are very beautiful, and their eyes seem kind, but the truth has to be an ugly basement with plaster peeling from the walls, and a dying mother, and an undernourished baby girl, and eventually, underneath and behind even this, sexual disease and death.

Gauguin ran away to a desert island, leaving his unprepared wife and his under-developed children and his butcher's bills to go in search of innocence. The truth is ugly and far from innocent.

No deception is truth.

Therefore all deception is innocent.

The three-rope trick, which even an Algerian schoolboy in Port Talbot can do.

But this is a trick which belongs to a trickster, not a magician. Ugly things only seem true because it's easy to distrust what you don't understand and ugliness is simple to understand.

Mrs Grip didn't get the orgasm she wanted, but she tried hard. Afterwards, she said,

"Well, if I can imagine it, it must be true, mustn't it?"

I said no.

Madeleine yawns theatrically, and glances at her black-strapped wristwatch.

Sumi is waiting in Abbesses, brooding on her body and some cutting remark to welcome me. I can think of a hundred cruel things she might say, and all of them would be true.

ABBESSES.

Paul Lenehan

Old Flames

Mr. Johnson allowed himself to be led to his place. He allowed the nurse to manhandle him into a chair.
- This is Mr. Johnson, she said, eyeing his name tag.
She introduced the table companions nearest to him.
- Mrs Wright and Mr. Newman...
They smiled at him and he gave the minimum of recognition, allowing his head to rotate a distance which only a micrometer could measure.
- ...and Mrs. Fitzroy.
She gave no greeting, and he replied in kind.
- Mr. Johnson, said the nurse, this is a special day. Please try to be a little more sociable.
- No. Why should I?
The nurse left to find more hapless ancients. Mr. Johnson tried to shut out the bleating of the crowd, tried to ignore their counterfeit excitement. He saw a window at the end of the hall. Outside, sunshine lit the calm trees. That was where his attention would lie, he decided. He longed to feel on his face the sun which warmed the panes. The chatter continued round him like sour birdsong. His glance came back from the window to inspect the woman opposite him. No one was more surprised than Mr. Johnson that he should take an interest in another person.

Mrs. Fitzroy paid him no attention. She was as old as he was, surely. But should she be younger? How could he tell? At their age, time has ceased its work of transformation. Time has left them, and gone in search of malleable flesh. Beneath the lace scarf she wore on her head, only tufts of waxy hair still clung to her skull. The eyes in her head were hazy, like shattered glass. Skin in loose wads clung desperately to the bone structure of her face. Aware of his examination of her, she turned her head away. Such displeasure, such a pursing of her parched lips. Familiar, almost. In his memory he heard a voice calling, calling...

They had been brought to Cypress Grange by the Administration to pay homage to their benefactor, Mr. Argyle. He was tycoon, landowner, millionaire, philanthropist. His money endowed the Homes which bore his name. They had come, the ancients, from all the Argyle Homes in the region, and beyond, subjected to drowsy

Paul Lenehan

journeys in sweltering buses. And here they all were, hundreds of decrepit specimens, ready to goo and grin and wave flags as Mr. Argyle and his entourage passed by. Mr. Johnson wanted no part of it. Why couldn't they be left alone? If God had mocked them with the curse of aging, of decaying, surely that was humiliation enough?

A nurse ran down the long room.

- Here he comes! she cried. Here comes Mr. Argyle! Trumpet player, play your tune!

Mr. Johnson watched some old fart spit and splutter into a trumpet in a failed attempt to play something jazzy and welcoming.

- Pennant holders, wave those flags!

The pennant holders performed as instructed.

- Singers of song, sing your song!

Some kind of off-kilter droning began, like the sound of a seagull being dismembered. Mrs. Fitzroy continued to ignore him. In his mind the voice still called, and he saw the outline of a face. But, as yet, he could give that face no name.

Mr. Argyle entered then, a smiling public man, followed by his wife, his son and daughter, and by the directors of the Argyle Homes. He shook hands; he cracked jokes; he laughed aloud. His family were models of politeness and decorum. He stopped by Mr. Johnson and addressed him.

- What about you, old-timer? How are you keeping?
- Leave me alone, mercenary.

Those nurses who knew him nodded to each other and contained their laughter. They knew Mr. Johnson wouldn't let them down. Mr. Argyle grinned, after a moment.

- You've still got spunk, he said. I like that.

Mr. Johnson tried to spit, but his mouth was dry. No phlegm came.

After the President - Mr. Argyle's official title - had made the rounds of the stick-men and stick-women, speeches were made, and prizes presented to deserving ancients. These fragile souls crawled to a podium to receive tankards for achievement in draughts, crochet, skittles. Then the Head Nurse took the stand and bellowed into a microphone.

- Lunch will now be served!

Hundreds of tin mugs were drummed against tables, and there was cheering from the assembly, all of which had been rehearsed before the President's arrival. Plates were placed before each old man and

Old Flames

woman, plates on which were laid slivers of beetroot, egg fragments, lettuce leaves shredding at the edges. Each mug was filled with tea, or lukewarm milk. Those who could not feed themselves were fed by the orderlies, and they gurgled between servings.

Mrs. Fitzroy kept her hands by her side and left the food untouched. He watched her, and this time she returned his gaze. It was that stare - such contempt - that convinced him. It was her! though Fitzroy had not been her surname then. Yes, he was certain, almost certain, that fifty years ago - no, more - he had fumbled with her clothes while she kissed him on the cheek. He remembered her skirt distinctly, a pleated skirt, dropping to the floor beside his uniform. It must be her; they loved each other in the spare room with a chair jammed against the door, while downstairs her parents listened to a tenor sing songs of loss on a crackling wireless. So why did she ignore him now? If it was her?

Simon, who had driven Mr. Johnson and his group to Cypress Grange, roamed the tables tending to his charges.

- You're all right, Mr. Johnson? You can manage?

Mr. Johnson nodded.

- Food's not bad, is it? You're enjoying yourself?

What could he say? That he was loathing it, the food? Loathing every minute of this circus show? Loathing every second of his life, and waiting for death to release his brittle body from its miming of deeds and involuntary motions? And if there were others present - only the few, perhaps - amongst these gurgling shadows who were of the same mind, how would he know them? What could they say?

After the food, after more speeches and prizes, they were released, the ancients, into the grounds. Cypress Grange was surrounded by three hundred acres of parkland, with streams and woods and gardens. They were wheeled, led, chaperoned, from the banquet hall into the welcome warmth of mid-May. They struck fragile poses on the lawns and hummed, like the inmates of an open-air asylum. They raised their arms and faces to the sky, and some would feel the sun a final time with that one glance. Before night came, some would be released. Mr. Johnson pursued Mrs. Fitzroy as he had pursued her so many dozens of years ago, though with less apparent fervour. She had the advantage of years, he the disadvantage of the frame he pushed before him with no dexterity. And so she maintained an unbridgeable divide between the two, even accelerating from time to time to increase it.

Paul Lenehan

He followed her diminishing figure past clogged fountains, cracked sundials, chipped cherubs, a wrecked gazebo, past wheelchairs whose occupants had disappeared and occupants whose wheelchairs had been mislaid. He saw her glide - no, hobble, crawl - into the flower garden, so prodded the pathway furiously with the walking frame to increase his pace. But it was necessary for him to loiter by a willow to recover breath and calm his heart. He knew - he could not say how he knew - that she was evading him deliberately, exhausting him maliciously. But he had not lived four score years and more on this earth only to learn the world is round and the seasons four in number. He decided to apply cunning to the chase.

Instead of entering through the gate she had chosen, he shambled round the hedge which marked the perimeter of the garden. He chose an alternative gate and entered there. He did not find her by the yellow tulips, nor by the bluebell grove. The purple hyacinths did not conceal her, nor the blue violets afford her shelter. He found her by the creeping ivy, with her back to him, expecting his entrance where she had entered.

- A fine day, he told her.

By the time she had manoeuvred - should he help? what good could he do? - to face him, whatever surprise there may have been had left her countenance.

- You know who I am, don't you? he asked.

She looked bemusedly at him, as if he were the village idiot.

- You do know who I am? he repeated.

- I wish you would stop...stop following me. Anyway, you don't look well. You should call for help.

- We should sit down. Please. There's a bench not far from here. I...I would be obliged.

She did not refuse his frail offer. So they slouched together towards this oasis, her skinny wrists helping to haul the frame forward. From the corners of his mouth spittle trickled now, when he did not need it.

They reached the bench and sat down, he first, sinking onto the wooden slats, she next, shaking. They took their time.

- What a chance, he said. Finding you here.
- You never replied to all my letters.

For a time they heard only the sound of breathing and of bees.

- All? You only sent...one. Much you must have thought of me.
- You were worth no more...I forgot you easily...

- Did you marry?
- Twice. You?
- Just once. Yours are...?
- Dead. Both of them.
- Me too.

Then she was crying, and he did not know why. Tears appeared at the corners of her squinting eyes. Tears trickled down her cracked cheeks. He did not know why.

Because she said nothing, the thought crossed his mind that he had broken her heart all those years ago, that a pain long lost was found again. He felt quite proud of this achievement.

- My God, she said, the look on your stupid face.

She dabbed at her eyes with a cloth.

- If you had not met me today, if...you would remember a girl with dark hair and dark eyes...

He said nothing, and neither did she, for a time; but when she ordered him to look at her, he did.

- Would you want me now that I am old and... Do you think I enjoy being reminded of what I was?

- I understand.

- And look at you. The stye in your right eye is...repulsive, you must know. Your teeth fit you...not at all. And, and, despite this, you wear that ridiculous hat, like some dandy sixty years younger than you are...You old fool...

He took the boater from his head and laid it on his knees. On his grey cropped head, one surviving lock of hair fluttered in the breeze. He bit his lip to stop from sobbing, and she knew.

- There is nothing rare in my life anymore, he said. These days dry me and give me...no rest.

She was silent now, so he hoped her anger was spent.

After a while, he set his hat back onto his head, leant back and closed his eyes. The sun shone on his face, its warmth on his skin like a promise which could never be kept. Tired, he had never felt as tired. The white light on his shut eyes lit up his skull with sparks and flashes. Sleepy, he watched this lightning rage on the thin screen of his eyelids. Then her lean hand rested like a stone on his lean hand. He felt the coldness of her touch, at first, then a curious warming. Her hand moved to the flesh and bone of his forearm, wrapped in corduroy, and rested there, gentle, soothing. His slow breathing was soft as a flower. Then the hand moved to his cracked face, stroked it with a touch which was not old and hard, but warm and strange. But - strangest of all - he felt lips pressed against his own, but not cold lips, not old lips, fresh lips, lips plump with love. The warm hand traced the lines of his life, then left his old face. Tired, he never felt as tired, sleepy, sleepy...

When he awoke, the sun still trembled in the sky with heat. No hand, no lips...but surely they had only snoozed in the sun - the old woman, the old fool - separate, apart. She sat beside him with her head bowed. He heard a bell ringing, ding-a-linging, ding-a-linging. Easing his head forward, he saw her eyes were closed, so he shook her shoulder, gently.

- O...Are they calling us? she asked.
- Yes. Time to go.
- I'm sorry, she said.
- No, no. You told the truth.

She smiled then, but careful not to widen her mouth. He was glad to see it again, her smile.

- Pointless to write, she said. We might be dead before the ink is dry.
- Do you think that's best?

She did, so he agreed, though it shook at his vanity. They saw no-one else in the flower garden. Perhaps, he thought, no-one else had come this far. They helped each other up, and made their slow way back, stopping once to ease the pain.

All the road home the sun lay at his shoulder, orange, fading, trailing lesser light in its wake, aiming towards the west. He watched it from time to time, noticed its changes in position, noted the sky darken in the wake of its decline.

- Good King Wenceslas first looked out-

Some spirited ancient croaked out song to enliven their journey. Some listened to his wailing and nodded; others dozed. Why? Mr Johnson thought; why carols in May? Then he thought: when she said sorry, was it for what she had said, or for what she had done? But what had she done? Nothing happened in the garden. It was the sun, his brain made lazy by the heat. Still, though, he let a smile whisper at his lips.

Simon, alert driver, saw this smile in his mirror. He called out, and all the bus could hear.

- I don't believe it, he shouted. A smile from Mr. Johnson. What has you smiling? What has you so happy?

Old Flames

- No, no, said Mr. Johnson.

The sleeping folk awoke, the singing stopped, the drone of the engine became a roar as the bus took on a hill. Simon laughed, as did all the other faces, laughing at Mr. Johnson because he had smiled, because he was happy.

- It's not true..I'm not...It's not true...

His voice could not compete against the engine and the laughter. So he turned in his seat, closed his eyes, slept. A window was all there was between his face and the sun.

LETTERS

Sarum Twins

Panurge stories are both far reaching and yet accessible and I don't get the feeling as I do with Granta that I'm on the outside looking in. The Sarum Twins(Panurge 20) I thought a masterpiece.

Dorothy Schwarz
Abberton,
Colchester

I agree about Christine Hauch's story though it got very few fan letters, compared with say Clare Portman and her fine story in the same issue. A clue may be that our female typesetter and mother of two came back looking green after keying it in (it was about the fathering of a child upon one half of a nineteenth century Siamese twin). I thought it was beautiful and gruesome at the same time and told with immense style and control. On the one hand, had it been written by a man I wouldn't have printed it. On the other hand it could never have been written by a man in the first place. Ed.

Endless Quest

I would like to thank you incidentally for the helpful comments you've made when rejecting previous stories. They give the bottomless pit the beginnings of a bottom; if you see what I mean.

Andrew Hook
Norwich

It's hard placing a story anywhere in the UK in the 90s and I always tell writers to keep on trying. Andrew Hook has recently had work in Iron which also makes a principle of saying something to all writers who submit. Ed.

Editorial Taste

What sort of story are you looking for?

Phone Enquiry, 1994.

Anything that stands up to at least four attentive readings. Otherwise I have no particular bias about theme or style or length. Publishable work stands up to repeated readings whereas I find that half good ones start to show the cracks on the second and third readings. That is my empirical test. The worst possible thing an editor can do is accept a story after one enthusiastic reading. Ed.

Alfred Nadin

God, Leonard And The Thin Man

1.

Thin evening sunlight shows up the streaks of the window, and casts savage shadows of a coriander across the draining-board. Even the bread-crumbs stand out in relief as I place the tin squarely on the working-surface, then hover above it with the opener. 'Bread-crumb sins' Bobby once sang; and now 'Desolation Row' plays unobtrusively on the CD player in the lounge, though I no longer listen. Dylan is mood-music nowadays. Not quite supermarket stuff, but definitely degree-syllabus, and anyway I know all his sixties work off by heart.

Upstairs a baby cries. I still hover with the tin-opener. It is a memory half-coming back, half-invented. Fog clouds the brain. We remember things the way we want to remember them, our past lives carefully adjudicated by what we've become; but we are our own worst censors. The tin, coming back now. A tin of ham. But it is a manufactured déjà-vû. A déjà-vû of poseurs.

I remember like I always remember. My friend B stole a tin of ham from a village shop in Gairloch in 1973. When we got back to the croft-house we were renting for £8 a week he tried to open the tin on the kitchen table. The tin slipped and he cut his index-finger. A bad cut, with blood streaming all over the floor. When I came into the room he was rinsing it under the tap, effing and blinding. "Is that the tin of ham you stole?" I said, or something like that. Maybe it was the way I said it, or maybe I said something about 'karma', (which would have been a strange concept for an avowed Christian, as I then was), or perhaps I was just smirking. At any rate I must have implied that the cut was his pay-off for the theft. It was all he needed. "If you think like that, then you must be mentally ill!" he screamed, as he pulled on an elastoplast.

I probably did think like that in those days. I'm sure part of me still does. Some unconscious, reptile part of me, unmoved by a thousand disasters of fire, famine, earthquake and volcano; the slaughter of innocents. B has no such qualms. But there again, he almost never did. He was always something of a nihilist. "Why should a human being be worth anything?" he once said. "What makes you think that we are anything special?" The toilet in the croft house was in a small room at the top of the stairs and whenever B was taking a shit he always left the door open. Maybe this was to

God, Leonard And The Thin Man

prove how free he was; or maybe, as he later joked in the presence of others, it was to get me interested in his arse. But when he repeated it later, in private, it sounded like only half a joke. And in 1973, in Gairloch, it was no joke at all.

The baby is still crying. 'Desolation Row' is working its way to a climax. There goes Bob's famous line about half-jokes too, about the 'time the door-knob broke'. This puts me in mind of another friend and an even earlier memory; a colleague called Leonard Jones and the day a door-knob really did break in the offices of Ferguson, Pringle & Co, a firm of accountants I used to work for in the late sixties and early seventies. It was a simple screw-in job, or so said 'Delilah', our 6ft 4ins, 15 stone, office-manager, as he delegated the responsibility to poor Leonard. But half an hour later Leonard was still struggling. "What on earth are you playing at, Leonard?" I said, pausing to help him as the sweat poured from his brow, only to be interrupted again by Delilah who accused us both of skiving as he finished off the job himself in thirty seconds.

Poor Leonard. It is only rarely that a colleague makes a transition into a friend, a universal phenomenon, I feel, caused by our resentment at having been drawn together for purely commercial reasons. But Leonard managed to transcend this barrier. First of all I asked him to play for a football team I was running at the time, an emergency measure forced on me whenever we were a man short. I don't know why I bothered, because we'd have done just as well with ten men. Leonard was bloody useless. He once missed an open goal from two yards, a real work of art, considering all he had to do was stick a foot out. But I forgave him, even though there were some dark mutterings afterwards from the rest of my teammates about revising the selection process. (in this respect, of course, Delilah would have been my first choice, but he was very rarely available.)

But most of my friends usually have some quirk about them. A reflection on myself, I know; but then I always find the conventional so dull and boring. Leonard was a Dylan fanatic, too, so we had something in common right from the start. In Leonard's case, though, the strangeness didn't derive so much from himself, as the company he kept.

In the neighbourhood where I was raised I grew up alongside a mysterious boy called Liam Kennedy. Although we passed each other in the street on scores of occasions, and may even have nodded

Alfred Nadin

from time to time, we never actually spoke. I call him mysterious primarily because of his appearance: he was thin and always seemed to be dressed in dark clothing, augmenting it, as he grew older with a pencil-line moustache and a quiff of jet-black hair. He was only of average height, I suppose, but there was a kind of sinister aura about him which made me extremely wary. As we grew into our late teens my uneasiness began to be justified: Kennedy had acquired a record for violence, including one particularly nasty incident which concluded with a police constable lying face down in the mud at the foot of a low, brick wall.

It couldn't have been long after this incident that Leonard started at Ferguson, Pringle & Co. Over the first few weeks, as I gradually made his acquaintance, it was our mutual admiration for Dylan's work which drew us together. But then I made the mistake of giving out my address. ('A man can't give out his address to bad company' - from 'Absolutely Sweet Marie', *Blonde on Blonde*.) It transpired that not only had Leonard been a friend of Kennedy since their schooldays, but that Kennedy was the leader of a gang, and, by implication, he was part of it. Revelations of Kennedy's activities were soon to follow. Kennedy had made a detailed study of the works of Hitler and Machiavelli; indeed, he liked to be known as 'the fuhrer'. He was capable of great violence, but more often he preferred to use the threat of it, or instead get one of his gang - whom he sometimes referred to as 'the idiots' - to do the deed for him. Leonard's style, whilst he was revealing all this, was to wait for a quiet moment (preferably when Delilah was out), draw a cup of coffee from the office-vending machine and - a bit like a detective trying to crack the nerve of a suspect - sit half-smiling on the corner of my desk. He spoke in a slow drawl, picking his words carefully. For example, he might describe how the fuhrer had 'administered' a 'beating'; or relate how he had 'chastised' a gang-member (an 'idiot') for some 'transgression'.

As the months passed all this talk of Kennedy gradually increased until it became a virtual obsession. The fuhrer had even replaced Dylan as our main topic of conversation, and I was getting fairly cheesed off because I suspected Leonard was taking a secret delight in these stories. It all culminated in one never-to-be-forgotten trip to the Isle of Wight on the occasion of Dylan's celebrated 'comeback' concert in 1969. From the moment we boarded the train at Manchester Piccadilly, right down to Southampton and across on the

God, Leonard And The Thin Man

ferry, Leonard talked about Kennedy virtually non-stop. When Dylan failed to appear on stage for about four hours my patience had finally come to an end. "You have done nothing else but talk about Kennedy," I snapped at him. "You are obsessed with the man. He will destroy you!" Ashen-faced, Leonard meekly protested: "No, no... I will destroy him!"

But worse was to follow. I had warned Leonard not to mention my name to Kennedy, yet sooner or later I knew it was inevitable. Leonard claimed that the fuhrer had been enquiring quite innocently about his colleagues at Ferguson, Pringle, and that naturally he had been obliged to supply the information. There was a barely concealed grin across his face as he said it. A few days later he casually sauntered into the office with the news I had been dreading.

"The fuhrer saw you last night," he said.

"Oh? Where?"

"In your kitchen. You were wearing an orange-coloured shirt, and eating a pork pie."

I was stunned. Kennedy lived on a different road, but from my kitchen window the rear garden of the house in which he lived was visible, albeit at a fairly oblique angle. It was just possible that I had been observed, though it would have required exceptional eyesight. It was the bit about the pork pie that was the real clincher.

"And how did he come about this information?" I demanded.

"The fuhrer has some military binoculars. He had them trained on you."

It was all getting pretty creepy, and, if truth be told, beginning to unnerve me a little. However, I managed to keep cool. I responded with a joke: "Well it's just as well he thought it was a pork pie," I said, "seeing as he's not too keen on the Jews!"

2.

I have mentioned these separate characters and events because they all figure strongly in another memory which dates from soon after I arrived in Gairloch with B. Shortly after the incident with the tin-opener, and with our money rapidly running out, we succumbed to the inevitable and fixed ourselves up with temporary seasonal employment. In 1973, with another busy Scottish tourist season about to start, this was relatively easy. We managed to get jobs in the local 5-star hotel, myself as kitchen-porter, B as night-porter.

Alfred Nadin

The memory which I now describe is a dream which I experienced after I had been working at the hotel for about a fortnight. If, in itself it sounds fairly mundane, then I simply stress that it was not so; even to dismiss it blandly as a nightmare is to do it an injustice. Since this experience I have read Jung's theory about certain dreams being distinguished by a special numinosity; some of these may contain 'archetypes', or they may occur at, or presage, junctions in an individual's life. I can only go along with Jung's theory. This isn't to say that I agree with everything in Jung, it's just that in this particular area I find his ideas are quite helpful.

This, then, is the dream I had in the Royal Gairloch Hotel on Tuesday 22nd May 1973: Along with nine other people I am starting work on some kind of building site. It is adjacent to, or near, the sidings of a large, covered railway station. We arrive for work, as a gang, on the back of some trucks, and straightaway disembark to the site which seems to consist of nothing more than a massive pile of rubble. (It is hard to describe the atmosphere of menace and foreboding which permeates the scene, but the best I can do is to say that it takes place in a kind of twilight, a murky half-light so dense that it is impossible to see the ceiling or roof of the building. The impression I have, though, is that it is supported by a mesh of iron-girders, both horizontal and vertical.) To gain entry to the place with the rubble we have to pass through some sort of barrier and show a ticket; but then we quickly get down to work. We begin to sort through the rubble. Almost immediately one of us triggers off some kind of lever and an overhead girder plunges to the floor, killing one of my colleagues instantly by squashing him into the ground. This is repeated continuously. I dislodge the lever myself a couple of times, killing several others, whose bodies are later found beneath one of the trucks. (I don't know how the trucks managed to get past the barrier, but this was, after all, a dream.) At the end of the day I feel inside my pocket : I still have my ticket; but out of the ten of us who started work in the morning only four of us are still alive. Even within the dream-logic I can remember thinking: 'At these odds, I don't think I'll bother turning up for work in the morning. I'll pack the job in!'

The identity of the four survivors were: myself, B, Leonard Jones, and one other unidentified (male) person. Over the years I have often thought about the dream, and it has always been the identity of this fourth person which has been the biggest mystery to

God, Leonard And The Thin Man

me. I say his identity was unknown, but I strongly suspect that he was one of two people. He was a dark, thin man, of medium height, with black hair. He was either Bob Dylan or Liam Kennedy.

This was the first, and most dramatic part of the dream. There were other bits to it, but they seemed lighter, silly and innocuous. The end of it is noteworthy, though. There was a complete switch of scene. I was with B on some land which was near to the croft we were renting in Gairloch. Suddenly, in a distant field, we see a man on a tractor. There is something about the way he is driving which causes us great concern; he is going up and down the field, zig-zagging erratically, out-of-control. Then he starts to move in our direction. We begin to run, and enter a narrow lane, lined with trees. Before long we look behind, and already we can see that he is at the top of the lane, in hot pursuit. We run faster and faster, and in blind panic, when we get to a fork in the lane, shoot off in different directions. We have put quite a bit of ground between us and the guy on the tractor, but myself and B are moving further and further away from one another.

It was at this point that I woke up, or, rather, was woken by a knock at the door of my room, an early morning call from one of my new colleagues, Donald, the hall-porter. I washed and dressed quickly, feeling totally disorientated as I descended the hotel's long spiral staircase, through the staff-quarters and into the kitchen. I remember that it was a beautiful sunny morning, and it was hard to reconcile the freshness of Gairloch with the malevolence of the dream I had just experienced. It was as if my mind and body were in different places, and it was well into the afternoon before I had regained any sort of equanimity.

Of course, the dream still played heavily on my mind, and in the evening, over a couple of malt whiskeys in the lounge-bar, I told B all the details. This proved to be a big mistake. He gave me an analysis of its meaning, using a string of half-baked Freudian metaphors. I should not have been too surprised. A few years earlier, when we were both still in our teens with little or no ego-position to defend, he had confessed a 'brief homosexual adventure' with a room-mate at college. Maybe he'd regretted telling me; and now this was his opportunity to get even. He told me that he felt the trucks were somehow indicative of my sexual motor or sex-drive, and that having to leave them outside the barrier indicated my 'incapacity' or 'impotence' to function properly. The falling girders,

Alfred Nadin

on the other hand, were, of course, penises; and the fact that the bodies were found beneath the trucks indicated my fear of normal sexual expression. By the time the bell sounded for last orders I was more or less a latent, passive homosexual with 'morbid' or 'suicidal' tendencies. It wasn't quite what I'd been looking for.

*

In one respect, though, the meaning of the dream was obvious. It occurred during a period of rapid transition in my life and merely reflected the accompanying anxieties and uncertainties. There was no reason to look any further. To use more modern jargon, I needed a period of rapid personal growth; perhaps the manner in which I effected it had been a bit too dramatic, and, that consequently I had experienced a little fall-out.

The year previously I had handed in my resignation at Ferguson, Pringle. After five years in the job I felt I was being treated like part of the office furniture; and I'd had enough of it. I figured that if I was going to work for shit wages I might as well get a bit of entertainment out of what I was doing. The business about Leonard Jones and the fuhrer had merely been the final straw, and though it had caused me some momentary discomfort I tried not to let it influence my decision.

When he heard that I was about to quit Leonard was very upset and tried to get me to change my mind, but I was adamant. Perhaps he was afraid that I was going to spoil his sport, for out of the confines of the office he naturally found it harder to raise the subject of the fuhrer. On the few occasions when I saw him afterwards he seemed quiet and subdued.

After Ferguson Pringle I moved rapidly through a succession of stop-gap jobs - like you could in 1972 - including labourer, amusement-arcade attendant and brewery-clerk. Then myself and B hit upon the idea of our Scottish adventure. B would give up his teaching post and we would rent a croft in the highlands. Over the years, fuelled by flower-power and the spirituality of the late-sixties, we had developed a romantic, Thoreau-like vision of the rural idyll, and now seemed like as good a time as any to put it into action.

It was something I had to do. My life was going nowhere and I was getting stale. There was one underlying reason, though, which was greater than all the others. Despite a few brief liaisons with girls I still hadn't established a relationship. Worse than that, I was still a virgin.

God, Leonard And The Thin Man

Over pints in our local I confided my problem to B. My virginity was hanging over me like a giant eagle, I said, or at least a brooding wood-pigeon. B listened intently, then pronounced his verdict, nonchalantly sucking a long, thin cigarillo: "You're just going up there to get a woman," he said, then paused for a moment to exhale the smoke from his lungs... "Well I don't think you're going to be very successful."

*

B was wrong. When I started work in the Royal Gairloch Hotel for the first time in my life I had moved into a sexual milieu. Most of the staff were young, female, and available, and, like ourselves (myself at least), had embarked on working holidays with one thing in mind. Like Jimmy Grogan, the barman from Birkenhead, said: "If you can't score here, you can't score anywhere."

There was such a surfeit of opportunities that we couldn't really miss. It was only a matter of time. Friday nights were best. There was always a dance in the village hall, and everybody who didn't have to work would usually attend. Beforehand we would gather in the lounge-bar to ensure we were sufficiently intoxicated; and on one occasion we were joined at our table by a group of waitresses and kitchen maids.

I had already been giving one of them the eye, and now I found, to my utmost joy, that it was being reciprocated. When the bar closed and everybody started to move across the street to the dance, myself and B retired to the hotel kitchen to discuss tactics. I was dismayed, however, to find B reluctant to commit himself. Exasperated, I said: "If you do not go to this dance even I will be convinced you are a homosexual!"

B thought for a moment, intent on his revenge, then said, smiling: "You're after that woman, aren't you?"

I nodded.

"Well for God's sake, whatever you do, don't do it from the back!"

*

But everything went according to plan. By the time the dance finished, spurred on by Jimmy Grogan and what seemed like the best part of a bottle of White Horse, I found myself arm-in-arm with my waitress on the streets of Gairloch. Her name was Liz. I was soon where I wanted to be. The staff quarters where I made my first fumbled attempts at intimacy were situated in an annexe, away from

Alfred Nadin

the hotel itself; and it was there, to the accompaniment of Gary Glitter and Osmond Brothers records from a nearby all-night party, that I finally strangled the wood-pigeon.

It was a nervous affair, all arms and legs akimbo. Most of the time I was half-limp with tension. I didn't really enjoy it.

The relationship ended as quickly as it had started; but at least I had gained the experience. Now, more confident, I began to chance my luck. I started to date some of the other waitresses and kitchen staff, some of the local girls I met at the dance. Quickly I moved through a succession of relationships, each one lasting a few weeks. By the end of July the eagle had long since taken flight, and I had shot and stuffed the wood-pigeon time and time again. It was then that B, who had been taking things much more sedately (having lost his own virginity three years previously at a teacher-training college in Weymouth), decided that he had had enough. He claimed that he had only really gone up there in the first place for the climbing and trekking, and that now he would have to think about his future. Another friend from home had been on the phone, telling us of his plans to tour round Europe for a month and asking if we wanted to join the party. B promptly accepted and handed in his notice at the hotel. He would try to get back into teaching in the new term, he said. I would stay on at the hotel until the end of the tourist season. I was having much too good a time to chuck it all away, and anyway I had no other plans.

Once B had gone, it was as if I had severed the final link with my old life. I was in a new place, making new friends; for the first time in my life I felt truly independent. Sooner or later I knew that I would return to my roots, but for the time being there was no hurry. Then towards the end of August a new girl called Joanne started work at the hotel. Soon we began to date. This time it was different. I knew I had gone in at the deep end. At the moment she is upstairs, changing our baby. It is our third child, and we have just celebrated our fifteenth wedding anniversary.

After I got involved with Joanne I naturally stayed on at the hotel for as long as I could. Periodically, at this time, I would talk over the phone to B, who seemed fairly bemused by what I was doing. I would also speak with my parents to keep in touch with events at home. It was during one of these routine calls, about eighteen months later, when I was beginning to settle into my new life, that I received news which stunned me to the core.

God, Leonard And The Thin Man

After her customary preamble my mother suddenly said: "Did you know someone called Leonard Jones?" The way she said it made her next line superfluous, but I took a deep breath and prepared myself. "... Well he's dead."

"How?" I said, my voice still shaking.

"There was an accident. He drove off the edge of a cliff. There were four of them altogether. It's in all the local papers."

"What?"

"It's in the local paper. I can send you a copy if you want."

"No. That bit about four of them. You said there were four of them altogether ... Are they all dead?"

"Yes. I can tell you their names, if you wait a minute till I get the paper."

In a lonely telephone box, at the foot of a cold highland moor, with Joanne next to me, who could understand none of its significance, I held the line whilst my mother read out the other names: "Patterson... Briggs... Fitzpatrick." They were the names of the 'idiots'. I had heard Leonard speak of them occasionally. But the name I was half-expecting to be on the list was missing.

She did give me one other piece of information, though. They were driving in a large estate-van. I suppose some people would call it a truck.

3.

'Desolation Row' has finished now, and Joanne has brought our baby son downstairs. Soon it will be time for him to take his food. I have already put his highchair in the usual place by the corner of the lounge.

Our two older children have just come in. They are called Roald and Seonaid. All our children have Gaelic or Scandinavian names, a concession I gladly made. On the mantelpiece there is a photograph of Roald and Seonaid with my father-in-law. He has a croft just outside Gairloch. In the photograph the children are riding on his tractor.

It all seems so long ago now, looking back to the time I met Joanne and I was working in the hotel. So much has happened. In the late seventies we moved to Aberdeen, where I attended university. Then we moved back down here. I have a job in local government.

Alfred Nadin

As for B, six years ago he went out to Japan and earned himself a packet, teaching English. When he came back he was accompanied by a Japanese bride. He was 36 at the time, she was 18. A lot of people were surprised but I was half-expecting him to pull a stunt like that. His ego demanded it. I still see him occasionally. He clings to his Freudian metaphors.

Whenever I think back to those times now, it is always with serenity. The past is a friendly country, and even the darkest mysteries take on an air of well-being. The dream was a puzzle, its quality seemed to suggest something extraordinary; but was it really a foreboding of Leonard's fate? If so, it was garbled and esoteric; like peering through a muslin bag, darkly. What purpose did it serve? Couldn't it all have been just a strange coincidence? For a long time I was preoccupied with trying to unravel its symbolism, if any. I read Jung repeatedly. The symbolism of numbers. Four was a significant number as far as Jung was concerned. It represented wholeness, completeness; the fourfold consciousness. It was all very intriguing, but didn't seem to be leading in any particular direction.

Then, when I moved back down here, I hunted out the back copies of the newspapers covering the reports of Leonard's death. I wanted the official verdict. The accident occurred at a notorious bend in the Peak District. No other vehicle was involved, and there were no witnesses. The few details I managed to gather merely added to the mystery. Evidently Patterson had been driving. His body was still in the seat, but the others had been thrown out. The report stated that they were found around and BENEATH the vehicle.

It all seemed like a conundrum that had gone wrong, a damaged interface, a jigsaw with a piece missing. Perhaps the missing piece was Kennedy. For a while I became obsessed with Kennedy. I wanted to know what had become of him. Where had he been, for example, at the time of the accident? Why had four of his gang - 'the idiots' - been together in the estate-van? It was almost as if Kennedy had dispatched them on some secret mission. I tried to make subtle enquiries about him in my old home neighbourhood. I unearthed a few sketchy details. I found out that he had left his parental home, but was still living somewhere within the district. In 1979 he had stood as a National Front candidate at the local seat in the General Election, but had, of course, lost his deposit. Whether that had been the end of his political ambitions I could not tell, anymore than I

God, Leonard And The Thin Man

knew what had become of him during the last decade.

But then, just as the puzzle was beginning to fade, I was presented with a postscript.

*

A few months ago I visited an exhibition at my local gallery. The subject was Dylan; and it was part of a display which had been put together originally to celebrate his fiftieth birthday. It was really little more than a collection of artwork by Dylan fanatics intermingled with an occasional photo or personal insignia, a few poems and drawings, which dated from the earliest, most celebrated phase of his career in the sixties right up until the present day.

I attended on a Saturday lunchtime, and it was fairly crowded. The usual types you associate with Dylan concerts were well in evidence: the home-brew, open-toed sandal brigade; now, I'm afraid, mostly bald and pot-bellied. I did the rounds fairly quickly. The only thing of interest to me was a painting which someone had done to illustrate Dylan's song 'Ballad of A Thin Man' from the LP 'Highway 61 Revisited'. It was a misty, abstract thing; a pair of sunglasses (Dylan's, naturally) floating on top of a cloud surrounded by a series of objects which are annotated in the song: a hand holding a pencil, a naked man, a circus freak, a lumberjack, a cow, a tax-deduction form, and some F. Scott Fitzgerald paperbacks. I don't know why it interested me so much. Perhaps it was because Leonard once told me how he had played 'Highway 61' to the fuhrer, and that the only track he liked had been 'Ballad of A Thin Man' with its famous, ever-so-appropriate chorus... 'Something is happening but you don't know what it is, do you Mister Jones?'

What happened next was like something I had conjured up from my wildest fantasies. Perhaps it is true that if we become obsessed with something so strongly we can give substance to our thoughts. A transubstantiation of our imagination; an alchemy of our senses.

A small public house is adjacent to the gallery: I went in and ordered a pint. All the seats had been taken so I just remained standing at the bar. I had almost finished my drink when I noticed, at the far side of the room, to my right, a figure who seemed vaguely familiar. His hair was less plentiful than it used to be, a bit greyer round the sides, and the famous pencil-line moustache had turned into a thick bristle; but he was still thin, even if a little podgy with the start of middle-age spread. It was unmistakeably Liam Kennedy, the fuhrer.

Alfred Nadin

He must have been watching me for a while, even before I spotted him, and now, unbelievably, he began to approach. My first instinct was to finish off my pint quickly and leave the pub, but, deep inside, I knew that I didn't really have that option. I had to stay. I had already left it too late anyway. He was by my side, and smiling.

"Alf, isn't it?" he said.

I affirmed softly. If this was fate there seemed little point in struggling against it any more. Besides, he had put his hand in his pocket: the fuhrer was going to buy the next round.

When the drinks were served I asked him what he was doing with himself nowadays.

He told me that he had 'business interests' in a local nightclub. As he spoke the chimera which had haunted me for so long disappeared, to be replaced by the reality. He had a broad, northern accent. Close to, the hair which I had first judged to be thinning was indeed balding. The notion of a balding fuhrer with a northern accent suddenly struck me as being particularly ludicrous.

Quickly I gave him my own potted history of the last two decades. Then he told me that the nightclub in which he had an interest was staging a special evening of entertainment during the following week. It was a kind of relaunch, he said, and he wanted as many people as possible to attend. He began to reach inside his coat-pockets. One of them was so padded that it was easy to imagine he was 'packing a piece'; but instead he withdrew a handful of tickets and gave them to me. "Complimentary," he said. He hoped I would be able to come along.

I thanked him and said yes, I would think about it. He smiled. Rather than the hoodlum or monster I had imagined, before me stood a man who, like the rest of us, had mellowed with age. Now he was trying to play the suave, sophisticated nightclub owner; but somehow it wasn't quite coming off. Instead he seemed a slightly comic figure.

He said he had to leave. He had business to attend to. I thanked him again, and watched as he started to sink the last third of his pint. But before he left I knew there was one subject I had to raise.

"Do you remember Leonard?" I asked, suddenly. "Leonard Jones?"

His face darkened, but only for an instant. Then he began to smile again, this time a little whimsically. "Ah yes, Mister Jones," he said slowly. "Yes I remember Leonard very well. Tragic affair, wasn't it? ... Yes, Leonard was a good friend, one of the best, even if at times he had a very fertile imagination!"

He said goodbye. When he had gone I looked at the tickets he had given me. On the front of each one there was a list of artistes scheduled to appear. Among them there was a local heavy rock band called 'The Demolition Crew'. He had given me four tickets. The name of the pub I was in was called The Railway Arms.

*

Was this it? After nearly twenty years had I finally broken the dream? It seemed, simultaneously, both bizarre and mundane, trivial and profound. For the events I have described to have occurred by chance seemed to be about one-in-a-million. And yet - give or take a minor detail for the sake of dramatic clarity, and the usual switch of names and places - this is what happened. It held about as much sense and significance for me as that celebrated cliche about monkeys, left to their own devices, eventually playing a Beethoven symphony.

There was, however, one other, logical, explanation; and in those moments when I particularly want to feel in control of my own destiny I cling to it like glue. When I went up to Gairloch I naturally took a selection of Dylan tapes and a cassette player. One of my favourite Dylan LPs is 'Blonde On Blonde'; and one of my favourite tracks on this is 'Stuck Inside Mobile with the Memphis Blues Again'. Monday nights at the hotel were always quiet. I remember that B used to start his shift earlier, and I usually stayed in my room and played the cassettes. It is quite possible - more than likely - that on the evening of the 21st May 1973, immediately before going to bed, this is what I had been listening to:-

> *The senator came down here*
> *showing everyone his gun*
> *and handing out free tickets*
> *to the wedding of his son.*
> *And me, I nearly got busted,*
> *and wouldn't it be my luck*
> *to get caught without a ticket*
> *and be discovered beneath a truck.*

In an earlier verse there is a warning to 'stay away from the railroad line'. Could this have been the origin of my dream, I wonder?

*

Alfred Nadin

However, if fate really had decreed that I should be the recipient of cryptic messages, who was I to argue? Having endured the mystery for so long, it would have been a pity to spoil things just as they seemed to be moving to some sort of climax. Accordingly, I took up the fuhrer's invitation. It would have been churlish not to. I even compounded matters by inviting along B and his young wife, Eiko. After all, if this was fate B had his own stake in it, too.

So that made the four of us. B and Eiko, myself and Joanne. We met outside the club, then gave up part of our tickets to get through the entrance. Once inside, I made a careful examination of the ceiling, which seemed sturdy enough, and on the position of the fire exits. However, I am pleased to report that nothing untoward occurred, either in there or on the journey home, for which I hired a mini-cab which did not remotely resemble a truck. Halfway through the evening the fuhrer came to our table, asked us if we were enjoying ourselves, and presented us with a free bottle of wine. 'The Demolition Crew' were quite good; but I preferred a solo singer lower down the bill who even played one of Dylan's songs. And yes, I do believe the people at the next table were part of somebody's stag night. (The fuhrer mentioned in passing that he knew one of them, though it wasn't - I hasten to add - his son.)

During the course of the evening I kept intending to bring up the subject of the dream again with B; but somehow the opportunity never presented itself. I was going to tell him about all the bizarre events that had occurred, and the meaning I gave to them. But by the time I'd had my fifth glass of wine even I realised that I had perhaps been going a little over the top in some of my conclusions. It's amazing the effect alcohol can have on you. By that stage even if the ceiling had collapsed I don't think I'd have noticed. Anyway, I'm glad I didn't say anything because I know the sort of conversation we'd have had: I'd have talked about 'Jungian synchronicity' and the 'collective unconscious'; he'd have talked about 'coincidence' and a 'load of shite'. In the final analysis we believe what we want to believe. So I just sat back, listened to the music and watched the dancers. Keeping one hand on the ticket-counterfoils just in case, I took consolation in the wine and told myself that the interpretation of dreams has never been my strong point.

FIRST PERSON

Success

Kathy Page

It's clear that success comes in three distinct forms: personal or artistic of which only the writer can judge; public, verbal; and public, financial, which are absolutely relative. The three kinds of success weigh differently with different people at different times. The best thing is to have all three at once, but I don't think it happens often.

Some ten years ago I spent two years writing and rewriting a novel. I wanted it to be published, but protected myself from failure by assuming that it was unmarketable and bursting with structural faults I couldn't as yet detect. Nonetheless, a friend made me to put it in the post. A year passed; I was writing another novel and thought of the first only occasionally and with horror when I received a rather enigmatic letter inviting me to come for a chat with an editor. I expected to be given tips and encouragement. When I walked out of Virago's office having signed my first contract, I felt so insubstantial with joy that knew I would have to wheel my bicycle home if I wanted not to be run over and utterly obliterated.

My route took me up Charing Cross Road, past the book shops, and I thought how my advance might just about cover the amount of print I bought in a year. The lack of profit or the notion of success didn't then bother me at all. I felt that writing was a huge conversation, maybe a song, and all I cared about was to join in. My expectation was that I would go on feeling like this, and that perhaps my voice would grow gradually more confident with time. Still dazed, I wandered on into Covent Garden and bought myself a purple dress in a sale. When I emerged from the shop my bicycle had vanished, clipped from its lock.

I substantially rewrote the novel, and it came out another year later. After this, I began gradually to see myself as a Writer, then, insidiously, to see writing as a Career, which it is not, and sometimes to wonder whether I was successful or not. Like most writers who don't make much money, I made a point of counting my blessings, and still do. Currently they would go something like this:

Overall, I love the activity of writing, though sometimes I struggle at it and sometimes it comes easy. I still like some of the things I have written, though not all. I feel I am getting better at it.

In ten years my work has been published and broadcast reasonably often; I have been awarded various grants and bursaries. I am asked to give talks, readings and workshops and people have even paid wages and air fares for me to do so in other countries. Oh - mustn't forget - I've been translated (into Estonian !).

I can think of quite a few reviews that pleased me because the words I'd written had so obviously done what I wanted them to, and letters from readers which did the same only more so. Sometimes when I read aloud people laugh at the jokes; they have even cried at the sad bits.

On the other hand, after one of my readings, another writer came up to me, dressed top to toe in soft, red silk with a thick gold chain around her neck.

"What a lovely story," she said "Do you make money, then, dear?" I explained, rather nervously because she was hugely successful in all ways and I admired her work, how I scrape a living between writing and part-time lecturing, residencies and so on. I added, almost proudly, how good I was at living on nothing.

"Good heavens !" she said, appalled. "That's not the way! Spend, spend, spend - and then you just have to make some more! That's what I do, anyway. Of course I'm very prolific." I was almost convinced, but remembered the stolen bicycle and realised that it was unlikely to work for me.

On ordinary and good days counting blessings works and the amount of success of all kinds I have had seems OK-for-now or at least better-than-nothing. Slipped between the good and ordinary days, however, are bad and even terrible days - days when achievements both public and personal seem so minimal as to be pathetic and I consider signing myself up for some horrendous vocational course or other in order to become almost anything but a writer. John Murray has an almost psychic ability to detect the worst kind of day; he chooses them to ring and ask for two thousand words on Success, taking in: How Did You Start; Is It Different for Men and Women and Does the Reality Match the Expectation, with a few digs on the MA at UEA thrown in, Please. Your books are all in the library up here, he says, soothingly.

Many publicly successful writers are women, as are many avid

Success

readers, so how much and exactly what gender has to do with any of this takes more explaining than I have the space for. But I do remember (or at least I think I do ; I may not have it exactly right) an October evening which I spent in a bedsit with three other students on the MA in Creative Writing. They all happened to be men and I shall call them Jonathan, Jim and Jason. Another thing they had in common was that they all wrote short stories featuring masturbation. There were minor differences in detail and setting, but the similarity was very striking. Someone had pointed it out in a seminar only to be told that it was not surprising since, all writing was, after all, essentially, masturbatory. Everyone says that on the UEA MA there are good years and bad years, as with wine, and within weeks ours had the reputation of being a bad one.

We sat on assorted brown, second-hand chairs, in front of a gas fire, drinking whisky. The rest of the group had sensibly gone home, having things to do: writing ? changing nappies ? row with husband? (they were all women). Or perhaps they had simply grown weary of our long discussion as to whether it was necessary to Live, or at least *have done so at some point*, in order to Write?

No, said Jonathan, who wore a second hand suit with a bow tie. Jim, in the leather jacket, agreed, as did hollow-eyed Jason who always wore a cream silk shirt. He declared the only living he had ever done was reading the collected works of Oscar Wilde. I wanted to suggest that writing was in fact *a part of life*, but they overlooked me.

"This -" Jim suddenly said, leaning forward, looking us all in the eye one by one, "is make or break for me." Silence fell; we could hear his leather jacket creak, then the sound of his swallowing as he swigged deeply from the bottle, the gasp he made afterwards; the thud of the bottle on the occasional table. Jason then Jonathan agreed: if they failed, they too didn't know how they would go on living (not that they did it anyway). They too drank from the bottle, thumped it down. To Success!

Suppose - I piped up from across the room - to take an old story: you could make a bargain. You could be a wonderful writer, however that's judged, but the price is to be miserable and die unloved in a damp basement flat or even possibly in a lonely lap of luxury. Alternatively, you could have a fundamentally interesting and contented kind of life but not be such a wonderful writer or not even a writer at all. Which would you chose ?

The best answer would have been any one of a number of questions such as why not both ? None of us thought of that: to a man, the other three plumped for misery and artistic success and again I was in a minority of one (though really it was just what I happened to think at the time - asked on a other day and in different circumstances I might well have said the opposite). We sat there - a bunch of what can only be called apprentice wankers - our faces flushed, listening to the hiss of the fire. Some time later Jason said:

"Why, anyway, are you on thish caw ?"

"I want to learn to wry butter," I told him, earnestly. Women have a lower tolerance for alcohol than men: it's a scientific fact.

"Yourready published !" He pointed at me, as if it were some kind of offence. My second novel had just come out. None of them had read it, and none of them would during the year that followed, though all the women did, despite having to change nappies and so on. An aspirant male writer's jealousy of a relatively successful woman - his conviction that her achievements are somehow stolen from him - is not yet scientifically proven, but one learns to cope with the suspicion of it none the less. Of the two commonest strategies the first is self-abasement:

"That doesn't mean so very mush. It was luck, really. Dunno know why they did it. Still feel I've got a lot to learn," I said. The second strategy is flattery but fortunately I will never know whether I would have sunk so far as to use that because Jonathan interrupted me:

"Any man," he said "in your position would be patting himshelf on the back and asking the world to do the same; he would be calling himself a Shuccess."

From the horse's mouth: a difference.

It strikes me now that perhaps Jonathan was wearing the suit and bow tie in anticipation of Booker day.

"Whass wrong with you, then ?" said Jim, jacket creaking again as he leaned into my face and glared.

I'm alive ! I thought, that must be it. I could see it was a problem for them but at the same time it cheered me up, and overall the time in Norwich was a useful one. I was pleased with the collection of stories that I wrote there and reviewers seemed to like them too so I allowed myself for the first time to be optimistic about public success, particularly in its financial form. My publisher didn't share

Success

the feeling and declined to issue a paperback. I found myself thinking of this as a kind of persecution, rather than routine stupidity and lack of imagination, and it was a short step from this to becoming thoroughly bitter and twisted.

In this condition I dismissed genre writers; I railed at the bad taste of the public and at the increasing cravenness of publishers, particularly their growing habit of approaching people with famous names and scant writing ability at parties and suggesting that they write novels. I singled out for my particular hatred successful literary writers, writing badly, boringly and with bugger all to say and yet mysteriously rewarded for it. I observed that almost every almost-successful male writer I knew had a wife supporting him financially or emotionally or secretarially and often all of them, *and* managed not to feel guilty about it... I turned my bitter-twistedness on myself and found it easy enough to think that there must be some dreadful flaw in my personality that made me sabotage my own potential, some kind of public success-repellent which I secreted and unwittingly oozed from every pore, the very opposite of a Midas touch. Finally, it was an absolute doddle to re-read Tillie Olsen's *Silences* and think how nothing changed and how it was almost inevitable that I should become bitter and twisted and so fail to do my best work.

There is truth of various sizes in all of these observations but granting them status of world view did me no good at all. I completely forgot that I actually enjoyed writing, and then, naturally enough, I forgot to do it, then how to, and very soon had nothing of interest to say in any case. This could easily have gone on for ever but fortunately I found myself ridiculous. Also, I realised I missed writing - not public success, not being a writer, but *writing* - the excitement of discovery and expression, the satisfaction of having worked hard, the greater satisfaction that comes when you know you have written something meaningful or entertaining and well made - artistic success, the thing for itself, the attainment of an object according to one's desire (SOED).

Bitter-twistednes was something I would never have foreseen for myself when I emerged Virago's office and decided it would be better to push my bicycle. But just as ex-convicts can tell each other at a glance I can now recognise a writer in the grip of bitter-twistedness across a crowded room: it's something to do with the set of the jaw and the buttoning of the lip and the way their eyes push you away rather than welcome you in, then bore into your back as you walk away. I like to keep well clear in case I am re-infected.

Well: I have a composer friend who has written symphonies, sonatas and quartets with no performance for ten years, and never once seemed bitter about it. I know a woman who has always done pretty well from her novels but says that she would happily write into a void, would do so even if no one on the entire planet could read or had even heard of the activity; in fact, she says she would rather that was the case. She also coyly remarks how pleasant it is to afford a house with three bathrooms. The first used to worry me, the second infuriate; now, I think that we all walk the same tightrope, with various degrees of grace.

Panurge 23 (October 1995)

Margaret Forster on Success. First published stories from Peter Dorward, Michael Eaude, Albert Leventure. Ecuadorian writer Pablo Palacio translated by Stefan Ball.

Edward E. Stonelight
On The Bus

It was a summer afternoon in Sonoma. When the bus finally showed, it was like waking from a long, unmemorable dream. Your mind is full of thought but nothing significant, nothing worth remembering. Just another way of killing time while time kills you.

The Blue and White. Sonoma Transit: Number Twenty. Hiss of hydraulics and the doors unhinged like the jaws of a big snake. I stepped up and in.

The driver had a face like a fist. Bad-boy nose. Scarred lips. Eyes hidden behind 'blue blockers'. Hands as big as hams, one on the wheel, the other on the door lever. His knuckles looked like they'd been through a meat grinder. Two things I always check first: the hands and eyes. Hands for scars, the eyes to see if there's anyone home or if they're filled with a distance you cannot fathom unless you've been down the same road or one like it.

I didn't have to see the eyes in his case because I recognized him right off. My first instinct was to bolt. To turn, jump off the bus and head for the nearest bar. But there wasn't a flicker of recognition on his part. Not one iota. And I guess the fear of six months in County was stronger than a fear that was twenty-five years old. It shouldn't have been, but it was.

You see, I'd missed my ride to work and needed to catch a bus to the Christian Camp where I was a cook. Two weeks on the job and couldn't afford to lose it. It paid five-fifty an hour and I needed it more than I needed a drink. It stood between me and jail. I'd had my third DWI and a DWL. After a stint in detox, they'd put me in a rehab program. Without that job, it was back to the hoosegow.

Riding public transit puts you in with those close to the edge. It's wise to check it out without being obvious. Never hold anyone's eye for more than a second and never let them engage you in conversation. When you're close to the edge yourself the last thing you need is to beat yourself with it.

I couldn't stand the thought of being locked up again. And though I'm a coward, I swear they'd have found me swinging from the bars. Neck stretched and tongue out. I had to keep the job at all costs. Even if it meant riding the bus. So, instead of running, I put a dollar forty into the meter and found an empty seat with some distance between me and him.

I knew what the name tag attached to the visor above him would

Edward E. Stonelight

say before I looked at it: Milo. Milo Sinclare. Sergeant Milo Sinclare. Sergeant Milo Sinclare of the 401. Sergeant Milo Sinclare of the 401, and the I Drang Valley, nineteen hundred and sixty-six, anno diem.

"Hey, Chief," Milo shouted. "Where ya goin'?"

"Camp Meeker," I answered casting him a quick glance. "The Christian Camp."

"Uh," he grunted as if expressing disapproval, then turned, closed the doors and put the bus into gear. It bucked back onto the road, caught its steam like a big train and chugged forward.

I busied myself with the landscape.

West Sonoma County is easy: vineyards, orchards, farms, and redwoods. Hills that drop quickly in and out of sweet, blossomed valleys and rural river townships. The architecture switches from quaint to squalor and back as fast as you can turn the pages of a book. Forestville to the banks of the Russian River. Rio Nido. Stop and go. Go and stop. By the time we got past the Korbel Winery there were only seven passengers left. After Guerneville, two. Me and a slim blonde with a rock-hard face and wren-sized breasts. She pressed the yellow strip just before Monte Rio and the bus pulled over.

"Take cay-ah, now," Milo said.

Bird breasts flipped him the finger.

"I love ya too," he told her. Then he pulled off the sunglasses, rubbed his eyes with the back of his hand, and turned to me.

"Some people," he muttered. "... Ya got that thousan' yard stay-ah... Where was ya?"

"What?" I asked, fear catching in my craw like a shard of old bone.

"Wasn't ya in Vietnam?"

"No," I told him, sorry I hadn't run when I had the chance.

"I coulda swore. Ya got that look."

"No, I wasn't there," I blurted too eagerly to be convincing; heart tattooing as loud as a war drum.

"I coulda swore," he said again, pushed the dark glasses back onto the broken bridge of his nose and put the bus on the road.

"Lotsa vets in this part a California. Oregon an' Washin'tin, too. I was a E7," he continued. "Should-ah made E8, but I los' my stripes. I was inna I Drang in sixty-six. Then did Lurp up by Phu Bai and Kashan. Heard-ah them places?"

On The Bus

"Read about them," I said hoping to drop the subject; praying for more passengers to free me.

"Yeah," he said. "Ya prob'ly saw-rum on the T.V. back then."

"Probably."

"Yeah."

We passed through the run-down little town of Monte Rio in a blink and out onto Moscow Road making towards Duncan Mills from where we'd loop back to Monte Rio on the other side of the river and finally up the Bohemian Highway to Camp Meeker and the restaurant town of Occidental.

Moscow Road twists its way along the south bank as it follows the river towards the Pacific, winding through second growth redwoods that look like giant arrows shot through the earth. The beauty of it takes your breath away.

I sat looking out the window. I wanted to think about Coastal Miwoks and the first Russians up the river. But his words kept bulldozing them under. 'Ya got that look.' 'That look' was the last thing I wanted. It made me vulnerable. Milo was quiet so I began to feel safe. Then he started up again. He wanted to talk. I know now, he was pressing.

"There was this guy," he said. "On my secon' too-ah up North. Squirrely little Irishman, named Flood. Jack Flood. Tunnel rat. Tough little monkey. Born tough. Raised tough. Flood." He waited until it sank in.

"Well, couple a months ago I was drivin' the route from San'a Rosa t' Sonoma when he get's on my bus in Glen Ellen. I recognize 'im right off. 'Flood,' I says. He don' say nothin'. Jus' looks at me with dead-clam eyes. So I says again, 'Flood. Ain't ya Jack Flood?' 'So what?' he says. 'So what?' I says. 'It's me, Sinclare... Milo Sinclare.' 'So what?' he says again. Hey, I think. Maybe the guy's whacked out. This Eye-Ran thing's got guys spooked. George Bush don' know from nothin'. He was one a them glory boys from Doubleyah Doubleyah Two. But 'Nam guys is spooked. Ya know? But I gottah figgah, I gotta figgah, hey, I don' gotta talk t' no prima donnas. I don' gotta. Ya know? So I don' say a word 'till he gets off in Sonoma. 'Flood,' I says. 'Nice talkin' with ya.' Then he stops. Right there on the bottom step. He looks up at me an' says, 'Sinclare, ya always had a way with words.' Then he steps off an' disappears. So I says to myself, 'Hey. I ain' gotta put up with no prima donnas. Am I right, a what?"

Edward E. Stonelight

I couldn't even squeak a reply. Christ knows I tried. But I couldn't.

"Am I right?" he bellowed, unnerving me.

"Yeah," was all I managed as the bus swung onto the bridge at Duncan Mills.

"Prima donnas," Milo said. "Some people."

Resentment clawed at my common sense. I wanted to shout back at him. To swear. To bust him in the mouth. To tell him that he had no right to make judgements. That he was mistaken. But we pulled into Duncan Mills and I did as I always do: I kept my mouth shut.

Duncan Mills. Just another trinket town where American Country Cuteness is carried to the extreme: Granny Goose and cornucopias stencilled on every wall; where the major marketing strategy is fleece the tourists all summer, complain about them all winter.

A young man in a cowboy hat signalled the bus.

"John Wayne!" Milo Sinclare exclaimed. "Hey, Chief. Get a load a this guy. His name's John Wayne. Really! Ain't that somethin'?"

The bus stopped and the kid got on. He was about eighteen. A genetic cross between a brahma bull and Goofy. He wore metal-tipped cowboy boots, jeans, denim jacket, red t-shirt and a wide-brimmed white Stetson with a silver cochina hat-band. He carried a thin, plastic grocery bag that contained videos.

"John Wayne!" Milo shouted again.

The kid flashed a big, dumb grin.

"Hey, M-M-Milo," he said bowing his head slightly as if acknowledging an uncle.

"How's ya ol' man t'day?"

The kid didn't answer or pay a fare but sat in the seat directly behind Milo and placed the videos on the floor between his metal-tipped boots.

"I asked how ya fah-thah is," Milo stated.

"F-F-Fine," the kid stammered.

"F-F-Fine," Milo mocked him. "Fine ya butt. Ya foun' a job yet?"

Worry began to build in the kid's face.

"I'm l-l-lookin'," he said biting his lower lip.

"Hey, Chief," Milo said. "He's lookin'. He's bin lookin' fer a yee-ah since I knowed 'im. A yee-ah!"

The kid looked at me with apprehension then at his feet and the

164

London, 1981

Philip Wolmuth

bag. He knew what was coming next. He'd been through the wringer before.

"Lookin' ain't good enough, John," Milo prodded in a gruff, sing-song voice. "Ya ol' man's still payin' the freight."

John Wayne choked back a short, clipped laugh, looked out the window, then at the floor, at me, and again the floor.

"Yup. I k-k-know, M-M-Milo," he said, rubbing his nose.

"Whadya think?" Milo asked me. "Think this kid needs a job a what? His ol' man los' a leg inna accident an' all he's gotta show fer it's a disability check every two weeks, a wheelchay-ah an' this kid what prob'ly ain't worked a day in his life."

"I h-h-have too," the kid protested.

"Yeah, well," Milo said as he dropped gears and guided the bus around an s-curve. "Ya sure ain't workin' now. An' now ya gotta get a job. Right, Chief?"

"Right. A job," I agreed, reluctant to get into the thing but wanting to be on the safe side.

"See," Milo told him. "Even the Chief here says ya gotta getta job."

"Yeah, I k-k-know," the kid said and swung his head down until his chin touched his chest. He raised his eyes to check my reaction.

"Don' look t' the Chief fer sympathy," Milo told him. "Ya jus' lissin up he-ah. An' lissin up good. I gotcha a intahview at the video store in Guerneville. Guy'll go five bucks an hour an' all de videos ya kin stan' t' watch. Soun' good?"

John Wayne started in on a Saint Vitus Dance. Leg tapping to some silent music in his nervous system.

"Really, M-M-Milo? All the v-v-videos I kin watch? W-W-When?"

"Tamorrah."

"G-G-Great!"

"Yeah. I don' want ya blowin' it so I'll tell ya some more about it aftah. Up in Occidental. I'll buy ya lunch at Negri's when I go on my break."

At last we crossed back into Monte Rio where the road climbs up a lazy canyon toward Camp Meeker and the little town of Occidental. The canyon always reminds me of Colorado: Evergreen. Dry Gulch. Coal Creek Canyon. Except for the trees. On the wall side grows scrub-oak, pepperwood, and the occasional madrone. On the creek side: redwood and douglas fir.

On The Bus

On a bit of straight road Milo looked at me then into the rear-view mirror.

"John," he said. "I wanna tell the Chief and ya a story. Jus' t' cleah up some stuff. Stuff about 'Nam."

My colon wrapped itself into a knot and my head felt like I was coming down off a five-day drunk.

"We was inna I-Drang Valley," Milo began. "Our platoon was pinned down by North Vietnam Regulahs. None a them rag-tag V.C. Hard-core sol-jahs. N.V.A. Uniforms an' all. For three hours we'd bin pinned down by a gun emplacement behind a ant hill. Ya couldn't even lift ya head without gettin' it shot off. I mean we was eatin' dirt fer three hours. We got K's, an' wounded all ovah the place. An' they kept whittlin' away at us. Got maybe only a third of the platoon what ain't bin hit. I couldn't stand it no mo-ah an' I thought I was gonna lose it. I mean I was about bug-nuts... Scared? ... I was so scared I jus' about fouled myself."

"Y-Y-Y-ou was scared, M-M-Milo?" the kid asked.

"Yeah," Milo admitted. "Petrified. I couldn't move. Pretty soon the gun starts findin' my range an gettin' in on me. I was shoo-ah I was gonna die. The Act a Contriti'n. 'Oh my God I'm hotly sorry fer havin' offended thee...' Ovah an' ovah again. All the while I could heah the radioman callin' fer air support, an' the ol' man screamin', 'Git that gun!" Git that gun!' A course nobody ain't movin' 'cause nobody ain't that nuts. And the gun was gettin' in on my positi'n. The roun's wingin' by my ee-ahs so clos' I could heah-rum spiralin.

"All a sudden up jumped this guy screamin' fer bloody murd-ah firin' a M-14 from the hip with one hand an' a grenade cocked like a baseball in the oth-ah an' he ran right for that hill. Those gooks musta bin shocked too, 'cause they started thrownin' so much lead at him the groun' looked like it was a muddy rivah churnin' 'round his feet. I was shoo-ah he was gonna git zapped. Then... all a sudden... Balooweey! Up goes the gun an' the guy charged behin' the ant hill firin' like crazy an' we all took off aftah him.

"He was sent from God that guy! Ya know what I mean? Naw ya can't. It was like God come t'life. God answerin' m' pray-ahs. An' when we got t' where he was there musta bin eight dead gooks an' the guy was layin' face down. I begun t' cry. Like, 'No, God. Please don't let him be dead!' Then we turned him ovah an' he was still breathin' an' his eyes wide open like he can't believe what he

Edward E. Stonelight

done. We finished up there but the fiah, from the big hill we was supposed t' be assaultin', was so heavy that we had a find covah. An' it started all ovah again.

"T' make mattahs worse, the ol' man called in a arc-light strike. Them fly-boys came roarin' down the pike layin' phosphorus bombs almost on top-ah our positi'n. The heat from it was so hot it gave ya sunburn, an' it was so scary that if a guy tells ya he didn't wet his pants ya kin call him a liah. I was huggin' the earth right beside the guy, the hero a I-Drang, I called him. His name was Davis. Remy Davis. Thin, redheaded guy - like Chief heah.

"Now, I didn't know Davis very well, but I loved him then like ya love ya moth-ah. An' he was layin' right next t' me starin' right intah the bombin' like he's watchin' somebody weldin' with heli-arc. Then he stood up an' started walkin' towards the bombin' an' somebody pulled him down. I didn't see him again aftah that.

"T' cut t' a point I'm tryin' t' make heah, four days late-ah, when we got back t' the fiah-base, we heard that the guy disappeared. Scuttlebutt was that he made his way down t' Saigon somehow an' the M.P.'s picked him up drunk as a skunk livin' in some hotel what was where the free-lance news guys lived. He refused t' go back t' the platoon so they charged him with desershin in a combat zone. Aftah a court martial, they gave him five yee-ahs in the stockade at Fort Leonard Wood. In Missouri."

"This guy didn't deserve none of it. They should a give him a medal. But that was Vietnam. Nothin' evah turned out the way it shouldah. An' none of it evah made any sense. An' if ya got through it alive then ya was one a the lucky ones. M' only regret t' this day though, is I nevah got t' thank Remy Davis for gettin' that gun 'cause I wouldn't be heah now if it wasn't fer him."

Milo told the story for my benefit; knew who I was the minute I got on the bus; played with me. At least that's what I thought then. Why wouldn't I have thought that? I was supposed to have been on that expedition into the I-Drang. But I drank half a can of Brasso when I heard where we were going and got myself sent to sick bay. Hell, all the short-timers were trying to get out of it anyway they could. They said the last time they went in with five hundred and came back with a hundred and seventeen. That included the wounded. Sergeant Milo Sinclare, knew exactly what was up and tried to get me out of sick bay. When the doctor refused, Sinclare threatened to kill me when he got back. He said that if he had to

On The Bus

track me to the ends of the earth he would because worse than his hatred for the Communists was his contempt for cowards, especially those who let their friends go into combat without them.

When the platoon returned, I was still in sick bay. The carnage had been as bad as the time before. Many of our own troops had perished in the arc-light strike. Milo found me and tried to make good on his promise. It was my luck that he attempted to kill me when three officers were in the bay. With help, they pulled him off me and had him confined, to quarters, under guard.

I got shipped down to Saigon and spent the remainder of my thirteen months pushing paper in a military warehouse. Milo got busted back to private and transferred out of the unit.

The bus slowed down as we made the corner by the camp, pulled over and came to a slow, clean stop.

"Chief," Milo said, pulling dread from the depths of my stomach with his voice and manhandling me with it. "We... are... he...ah."

I went cold. Every joint in my body felt as if it was held together with screws that had all worked loose. I would have to walk past him. I had no choice. There was no one to save me. I made a mistake getting on the bus. Now I was going to pay for it. I had no choice. I stood. My hands were shaking and I thought I was going to heave.

Milo Sinclare took off his sunglasses, folded them, placed them above the visor, turned and watched me.

I was shaking like I had the D.T.'s. When I got to the front of the bus, my mouth was filled with sand and my face was in fire. But there was something in his eyes. Compassion? Sorrow? I don't know. But at that moment I realized he wasn't going to hurt me. In fact, he did not recognize me. Then I understood: He thought I was Davis! *He actually thought I was Davis!* My walk became steadier. I could take a breath again. I looked right at him. Right at him! Sergeant Milo Sinclare. And I stepped down off the bus.

"Stonelight," he said. My heart fell through my shoes. I tried to face him but I could only turn half-way. I felt stupid and afraid. I knew the word - coward.

"Yeah. I recognized ya," he told me. "Not right off. But I did recognize ya. Ya changed a lot. But ya still got that trapped rabbit look. Man, ya gotta learn t' live with them demons or they gonna eat ya alive. An' I'd say, from lookin' at ya, they bin gnawin' away fer quite a while now."

Edward E. Stonelight

My hands began to tremble and my eyes welled up.

"It was twenny-five yee-ahs ago," he said. "Nothin' made sense back then 'cause it was only rock an' roll an' the tune was all wrong. The secret is ya gotta give up the angah. Ya gotta give up the feah."

I turned and faced him squarely. I tried to speak but an owl sound came from the back of my throat.

"Hey, Chief," he said in a soft, quiet voice. "We all got ghosts. Ya just can't let um live in ya house."

"Yeah," I said.

"Yeah," he said. "See ya around."

He put the bus into gear and as the doors closed I heard him say, "John. About that job."

STOP PRESS

* Congratulations to **Christine Hauch** (see Letters Page also) and **Barry Hunter** whose Panurge stories from 1994 have been selected to go in *Best Short Stories 1995* (Heinemann) aka *Minerva Book of Stories*, published at the end of this year.

* Awful to hear that that wonderful magazine *Passport* has folded for lack of sales and subscriptions. One of the few British all-fiction magazines it published some excellent translations and original writing by new British talents The last all-Portuguese issue was superlative. Congratulations and commiserations to **Mike Gerrard** and **Thomas McCarthy** for their fine work.

* **Ivy Bannister's** Panurge 21 story has been picked up by Radio 4 for transmission on the afternoon story slot some time this year.

Freeda Fitzgerald

No. She *Never* Takes Sugar.

Today is my birthday. I'm a few million years old. I've been reincarnated more times than I care to disclose. This time round, I'm a hermaphrodite, which is unusual for a disease. I really wish though that I was lodging in a sheep. My heart is broken by that twirp there with the MS., that Ms. one slouched in her wheelchair, meditating. She's jigging her leg on the grass at the same time. At first she seemed a nice woman - husband, a couple of kids. Just the sort of family situation a respectable disease like myself really enjoys being with. At the start I thought ten years would do it, fifteen at most. Would you believe, nineteen years later and I am still stuck with her. Oh, I have had my little successes. A standing-frame, an abandoned walking one, abandoned crutches; a wheelchair; a hospital bed with a monkey pole; the ramp she came down on to get to the garden. Most times, winter and summer, she has to wear two pairs of socks and mittens. But she keeps thwarting me. When will she learn? I always win. Always.

I don't mind conventional medicine. Antibiotics, a shot or two of cortisone into the spine. My friend Candida and I love these concoctions, which strengthen us. Because she's been enriched with Candida for years, last month she put drops of fungicide onto her tongue, as prescribed by her G.P. The fungicide didn't harm my Candida friend that time either. Does this Ms. one realise what a fine disease Candida is? If I was not a hermaphrodite, I would probably mate with it. Candida has great potential. Great disease bearing hips.

A few years ago she tried hyperbaric oxygen, which is a conventional treatment for 'the bends'. Luckily for me she didn't know that someone who's acutely affected with MS can improve, while those chronically affected may disimprove. She's a chronic egghead. I loved that hyperbaric oxygen chamber of horrors. Electromagnetism everywhere. It took her a long time to realise that I was winning. Then she called a halt. I'm stuck with her stupid decision. She drives me round 'the bends'.

Now she has me at it too. Those stupid puns. She twists clichés, like 'there is no light at the end of tunnel vision'. I take a dim view of... Oops. See what I mean? She seems to think that life's just a game of Scrabble and she can't even fill in a simple crossword puzzle.

Freeda Fitzgerald

At least I don't laugh at my own jokes. Nor did my last client. He was a retired British Army Colonel. A proper gentleman. He did cryptic crossword puzzles no problem. Smiled merely. Last week that Ms. one said to her poor, suffering spouse, 'Between allergy and Candida, I don't know where to turn. Which came first, the egg or the hen?' She laughed so much, she got a treble chin. That treble chin goes well with her double vision.

I would love someone to take a photo of her treble chin. She's so vain, it might humble her a bit. Last Friday she had her poor sister murdered with dying her hair. On the one paw she preaches about the dangers of chemicals, yet on the other, she didn't even read the formula until she couldn't get up on her hind legs. Her nose didn't detect the ammonia, but her scalp absorbed porefuls. Served her right for being so vain.

After the hyperbaric oxygen treatment failed to harm me, she went back to her alternative stuff. That really gets to me. Honestly, if you knew half the ways she tries to thwart me. For instance, last week she had a bad flu. For a while I thought I might be packing my bags. I hate dwelling too long in a body. I thought that virus and myself would flatten her. Her temperature soared and she could hardly move, even breathe. Then a nurse friend of hers inserted garlic as suppositories. She improved, pulled on her monkey pole and sat up. She had also sprinkled her bed clothes with Olbas oil. She appeared not to notice the stink!

Yesterday a therapist made the mistake of telling her to make her moves, as in a Karate chop. That is, to move swiftly on an out breath. Later, showing this technique to her aunts, while lying on their floor, she kept taking her right leg swiftly from their stool on which her lower legs lay Alexander style. She would then leave that leg on the floor. For her next trick she would take a breath and on the out-breath replace the leg on the stool. Such a show-off!

She is slowly opening her double visioned eyes. Now she is pulling the grab rails on either side of the ramp and her chair is moving up the ramp. Now see her propelling herself into the kitchen. I'm starving. What celebration for my birthday? I can't hope for Monosodium Glutamate. She wouldn't touch that with a paddle from anyone's canoe. But, there's a lovely sponge gateau in the fridge. Maybe... Maybe... The fridge will be her next stop. Will she devour some sponge gateau like she used to? She does not know that it contains, E120. that is Cochineal, which is a red dye which is

No. She *Never* Takes Sugar

prepared from the dried bodies of female cactus insects. Yummy!

At last. Now that she has closed the back door, she is opening the fridge. She's eyeing the gateau longingly. Longingly. She shakes her dumb blond head. Yack! She's dragging her bowl of maize out from the fridge. I should not have built up my hopes. It's not the Cochineal she's avoiding. It's gluten. I should have known she would not satisfy my hunger for a celebration now. She begrudges me the bit of gluten that might be in toothpaste and she would not even lick an envelope for the same reason. I will not be around here for my next birthday. That's for sure.

She was astonished to learn that food dust can be an allergen. Yet, years ago, mixing flour for her gluten-free bread, whenever she had added soya flour, she had farted like a truck.

She had quit eating spinach when she noticed that she slurred the word. Once she used to eat that veg. until it nearly popped out her eye.

She is full of cod. With lettuce and her gluten-free toast, she eats tail-end of it nearly twice a week. Then she eats tuna two days later. The monotony is killing me. She doesn't seem to remember that, 'there are plenty more fish in the sea.'

Thankfully she is wheeling away from the table. What goes in, must come out. Next stop, the loo. This loo's so small, you couldn't swing a fever here.

She does not even wear knickers, because she cannot stand long enough to pull them down before piddling. Whist. She is piddling onto her hand. Now she is dabbing the piddle under her tongue. Ugh! That's really gross!

Her face is like a wall-nut? Crinkly or what? She believes that her bowels cannot act naturally because the loo is too high. I ask you. She would squat at a hole in the ground if she could get up easily from that position. To her, a turkish toilet would be a delight.

Last week, a Spiritual healer advised her to talk to her Mum on a cassette, to listen to the tape, then to record music she liked over this. She did all that. 'I love you, Mammy and please help me to get well,' she cried into a cassette recorder. She was crouched like this on the loo that time too, snivelling and blowing her nose with jack's roll. She whimpered 'Mam, I'm sorry'. Then with music from the radio, she erased her talk with her Mother. She felt as if she had a clean slate. I'm sure she has one missing.

Did you hear her? 'Help me, Mammy'. Her mother is six foot

Freeda Fitzgerald

under. The Ms. one here keeps saying of her Ma, 'May she Rest in Peace'. Then she keeps invoking her. Can she not make up her mind. She is calling her mother now, because she is stuck on the loo again. It's hilarious. Cover your ear-drums though, folks. Yes. I bet you could still hear those 'Up! Up!' bellows out of her. 'Kiai' she calls that yelling, from a method used in Karate - to concentrate the mind, to strengthen the abdominal muscles, to help breathing and to frighten the opponent. It certainly scares the salt out of me.

Now she is buttoning her pad... As usual, she is standing all bent over, like a gorilla. With her right hand, she is grasping the loo frame, while with the other hand... Wow! Like lightning, she has slumped to the floor. Her throat is pushing into the frame. She can't lift her ton weight off of her throat, which is pushing harder into the frame. I've never seen her so frightened. Yes. Maybe... Maybe... Hear her whimpering, 'Help! Help!' It was more faint that second time round, was it not, folks? Maybe... I'm holding my breath. The obituary. I cannot wait to read it. I was never this close before... Sesame seeds! Footsteps. Someone is coming. The dam plumber. I forgot all about him meddling with the washing-machine. Why do plumbers always have to be in the right place at the wrong time?

He is rushing into the loo. "How did she get there?" Great, he is doing a post-mortem.

"Do something!" she says, not moving her head.

"What?" he asks.

"Anything," she tries to bark.

Now he realises what a demanding bitch she is and what I and her poor, suffering spouse have to endure. The plumber is tongue-tied. She is pushing against the sewage outlet pipe. She falls back on her hunkers, just as her poor, suffering spouse turns his key in the hall-door. Seeing the plumber at the door of the loo, sure stops the husband in his tracks.

"Your wife fell," the plumber says.

The poor, suffering spouse rushes into the loo. He is squatting beside her now.

"I nearly choked," hear her sobbing. "I fell against the frame." She repeats my line about the obituary. Her spouse massages her shoulder and kisses her treble chin. There is not even a blemish on her throat. He kisses her on her lips. The stupid wally. If he knew what she just put into her gob, he would not be so quick to swap spits.

No. She *Never* Takes Sugar

I stare at The Ms. one, who has just wheeled herself back to her bedroom. She is supposedly washing her teeth now. Do you know, just because two of her friends at swimming work in Oral B, she leaves their company's toothbrush by her bed. Hear her brushing her teeth with it, without using paste or even a glass of water. She begrudges me the few drops of chlorine in the water. She herself drinks gallons of chlorinated water every time she splashes in the pool. Now that she has skimmed over her teeth, she is spitting into a paper towel. I suppose she thinks her still flashing teeth are an ad. for Oral B.

Now she is taking out her tattered copy of affirmations. Shhh. Listen! 'Everyday, in every way, I'm getting better, better and better!' Did you ever hear the like? She can hardly crawl these days and her getting up from the floor, makes a snail look sprightly.

Why will she not just die and let me do my duty with a more interesting person? There's one lovely young lady I had hoped to dwell in, a business tycoon's daughter. As a bottle-fed baby, had she not been ecstatic about sucking on latex? But at this rate she will have been visited by one of my mates, before this Ms. one snuffs it.

In the wake of Con Colbert dowsing the room and informing her that there was Geopathic Stress under where her bed lay, last night her husband and children, moved her bed for her to the middle of the room. Her husband is a right wimp. He never drank a pink of Guinness in his life. Ballygowan only, thank you very much. He even changes the baby's dirty nappy. My British Army Colonel would never have done that. He would have passed the child to his Mrs., saying 'engine trouble'.

Oh! A sudden change has taken place in her aura. She has just had a lousy epiphany. This Ms. one now believes that her affirmations are going to work. I can't fight that. Birth!... More like my deathday.

Richard C. Zimler

The Pleasant Surface of Things

Dear Joshua,
I'm sorry I missed you when you visited Brazil, but very glad that you got my new address and wrote to me about your experiences. You said that, as an American, you found the contrast in Brazil really startling: the shack-filled slums hidden behind steel and glass skyscrapers; the African spirit worship taking place inside Catholic churches. "In Brazil," you wrote, "nothing is quite what is seems."

True and false, I would reply. Let me tell you a brief story about three people from my past to illustrate what I mean. This story will also answer your question about why I've moved so suddenly to Portugal. (You asked, half-joking, if the security police were after me. No, the threat is more subtle than that.)

Back in 1967, Brazil was being run by the military, as you know. I was a freshman at the University of São Paulo, working on a degree in History. I hated the dictatorship and began writing for a small underground student newspaper, *A Primeira Hora (The First Hour)*. A lot of the journalists and their friends used to go for lunch to a café off-campus called the Vila Indiana.

At the Vila Indiana, there was an elegant old woman, perhaps sixty-five years old, who always sat alone at the back, at one of the square, wooden tables. I remember her well because she was so different from the students and workers who came to the café. She had silky white hair combed up in a wave off her forehead, a pale round face, intelligent hazel eyes and a small, proper mouth which seemed perfect for scolding servants. She had two gold bracelets on her left wrist and three silver ones on her right. The skin on her arms was like that of a turkey's neck. She wore sleeveless white blouses with lace collars and long, floral skirts. And the touch that really made us laugh is that she also wore white gloves. On taking a seat, she would peel them off and lay them neatly over the back of another of the chairs at her table. Then she'd take out a gold pen from her brown leather bag and begin writing in a black notebook which she always had with her. Often, she also had books with her which she would read, but they always had makeshift covers which she made out of brown wrapping paper, so we could never read the titles.

All in all, she looked like the kind of woman who used the royal 'we' when speaking. I came every day to the Vila Indiana at

The Pleasant Surface of Things

lunchtime and she was almost always there by the time I arrived.

The café owner, João, told us that her name was Maria Inès Lancaster. That last name - Lancaster - settled matters for us. We in our little group of student journalists decided that she must have been a member of an aristocratic Brazilian-English family. Most of us were would-be Marxists, and we despised her. It was even theorized that she worked for the police as an informer. We were careful not to discuss politics near her.

The only time I came close to speaking with her was when she dropped her pen once and asked if someone at our table would pick it up for her. "I cannot bend over like I used to," she explained. "I really would be most grateful."

Her tone was gentle. There must have been six or seven of us at our table. We sat there unsure of what to do, suspicious, as if she were initiating a plot schemed up by the dictatorship. I picked up her pen but didn't say a word to her when she thanked me.

The unofficial leader of our little group was Marco Arezzi, the youngest son of Italian immigrants from Naples. He was a philosophy graduate student at the university, several years older than the rest of us, and he considered himself a Marxist theoretician. He was handsome, combed his black hair back with a sweet-smelling pomade of some sort and smoked Gauloise cigarettes. He had a profile like John Barrymore. He claimed to have read *Das Kapital* in German and Jean-Paul Sartre in French. Whatever the case, he most certainly had slept with several of the girls at the newspaper. The boys were impressed by his amorous successes and by his command of revolutionary jargon. We were eighteen, and whatever he told us was accepted as wisdom.

When I picked up the old lady's pen, Marco told me that it was a symbol of how the upper classes will always use the proletariat to do their work for them.

"But she's an old lady," I replied.

"A farmer cedes an inch of land to the Capitalist, and the rest of his land will soon be taken." He put an arm on my shoulder:

"Ricardo, all acts are highly symbolic," he said.

Everyone in the group nodded as if that was a maxim we had to remember.

My girlfriend at the time was Maria Silveira Brouwer. She was petite and dark, very sensuous. When she was wet from the beach, with her long black hair clinging to her back and shoulders, she was irresistible. And I was proud that she was a passionate revolutionary. She wrote editorials for our newspaper applauding the bombings at government buildings carried out by urban guerrillas. In class, I doodled pictures of her with a machine gun slung across her ample chest, just like revolutionary women in Mexican murals. Maria had also recently discovered the rudimentary feminism just then reaching São Paulo from the States and added to Marco's criticism of my behavior. She said, "You men must stop stooping down to help women. Bad back or no bad back, we are perfectly capable of picking up our pens for ourselves."

It seems almost impossible today that such absurd conversations about pens and old ladies were possible. But the Brazilian dictatorship was so perverse and destructive that it produced these kinds of aberrations in young people.

Joshua, imagine plants kept from the sun and constantly rained upon. They will produce some very strange growths, don't you think?

After lunch, walking on campus, I confronted Maria about what she'd said to me. "You didn't need to humiliate me in front of the others," I told her.

"Just like a man to worry about his image," she scoffed.

"Women don't worry about the image they're presenting, I suppose?"

"They do, but only because men force them to. Brazilian men only see women as virgins, whores or a weird kind of transvestite that's unable to switch back."

"I don't see you in any of those ways. And I don't force you to do anything."

She rolled her eyes and said, "All men do."

"All men? You mean, there's no difference between me and Costa e Silva." He was the military's puppet president at the time.

"Politically, yes. But in how you think about women, no."

"And you, I suppose, know my innermost thoughts on the subject."

She reached up and caressed my cheek. "You, my dear, have absolutely no innermost thoughts. That's why I like you."

Her words stung me, of course, and I replied, "You can be a real bitch."

"And being a bitch is precisely what you like about me!" she said, a note of triumph in her voice.

The Pleasant Surface of Things

I'm convinced that for Maria, these hateful conversations were simply like the courtship rituals of certain birds. She wanted me to kiss her passionately like Carlos Gardel in some horrible Argentinean musical. But I've never been good at these sorts of ritualistic games. I think it's why people who don't really know me consider me slow or dimwitted. I simply shrugged and started to walk away. She grabbed my arm and turned me around. Then she leaned backwards and slapped me across the face so hard that tears gushed from my eyes.

Maybe you won't understand what I mean, but it was a very Brazilian thing for her to do. I mean, that she was able to hurt me physically with such ease. Why I stayed with her so long is a question which even today I can't answer. Is it possible that sexual attraction made me insane?

*

In 1969, you may recall that the National Action for Liberation, our main guerilla group at the time, kidnapped Charles Elbrick, the American ambassador to Brazil. He was later released in exchange for fifteen political prisoners. After that, the dictatorship started really cracking down against any and all opposition. I was a junior then at university. Maria Silveira Brouwer had grown bored with humiliating me by then and had started sleeping regularly with another member of our clique, Toninho Rodrigues.

That's about when things started really going wrong in our little world.

Toninho, Maria's new boyfriend, was studying genetics at the university and was a paste-up artist for our underground newspaper. One day, he simply stopped showing up for classes or lunches at the Vila Indiana. We investigated. His car, a rusted old VW bug, was parked outside his garret apartment. The lock on the door to his flat was broken. A package of vanilla ice cream had melted atop his bed and soaked into the sheets. As best we could figure out, he'd taken the ice cream to bed when the police must have burst in and taken him. The neighbors wouldn't confirm any of this, but they were scared out of their wits.

This was not unusual at the time, of course. People were disappearing all over the country, were taken by security police and sequestered in prisons or private houses. Often, weeks or months later, they were sentenced in secret trials to three, five, ten years in jail. Sometimes, they were tortured, killed and dumped in unmarked

Richard C. Zimler

graves.

Until two years ago, I thought Toninho was one of those who never came back.

The next to disappear from our group was a boy from Santos named Paulo. We called him Walrus because he was really fat, and there was that famous line from the Beatles' White Album: "Here's another clue for you all, the Walrus was Paul." He was an economics student, absent-minded but extremely bright. I liked him a lot. He wrote a column on how to 'correct' the Brazilian economy and had already made contact with the National Alliance for Liberation. He was planning on joining their guerrilla war in another year, after graduation.

It may seem strange to you that he was waiting for graduation to start bombing government buildings, but that's how things were back then. Brazil, as you correctly pointed out, is a surreal place.

I grew paranoid with all these disappearances, of course. I started telling my parents where I was going when I went out and when I'd be back - things I'd stopped doing when I was about fourteen or so. For me, giving them these details was like Hansel and Gretel leaving a trail of bread crumbs; I wanted people to know exactly where I'd been if I suddenly disappeared. Not that knowing I'd been eating pizza or playing basketball when the police arrested me would have helped any.

Two more friends were soon arrested. One was Marco Arezzi, our leader. The other was a great soccer player and mathematics wiz named Artur Perez who had grown up in a slum near downtown. He was something of a hoodlum, really only showed up at the Vila Indiana to mooch cigarettes and eat other people's desserts. After Toninho and Walrus disappeared, he and Marco planned a robbery at a neighborhood jewelry store. They were going to sell the goods to a third-rate gangster in Campinas and use the proceeds to print a pamphlet which Marco Arezzi was writing on a 'Ten-Fold Plan for Toppling the Brazilian Dictatorship and Establishing a People's Republic.' Perhaps that title makes you laugh, but as you sit there reading in New York, please remember that we were plants growing without any true sunlight. And if there's one thing Brazilians need to stay sane, it's tropical sunshine.

Just before the robbery, however, Marco Arezzi and Artur were captured. The police burst into Arezzi's home while Artur was there, made his father and mother watch while they beat up their son and

The Pleasant Surface of Things

his friend. Both young men were dragged away, and neither were ever heard from again.

Only recently did I found out that Marco Arezzi didn't die, however, and how he, Maria Inês Lancaster and even my old girlfriend weren't quite what they'd seemed.

One day, about two years ago, I was working on a computer at the library of the University of São Paulo, bringing up documents relating to my doctoral thesis on the massacre of Jews in Lisbon in 1506. I needed a break from the routine and, just for fun, started entering the names of old friends and acquaintances into the computer to see if any had written books. Eventually, I got to Maria Inês Lancaster. A book called *A Context for Democracy* appeared on the screen, published in 1984. All those years ago, she must have been sitting at the back of the Vila Indiana writing this text on the origins of Brazilian reform movements since our independence from Portugal in 1822. I read it, of course, and the point of the book is that we've been duped into believing that democracy can't work in Brazil. Let me explain. A lot of Brazilians - maybe even more than half - believe that our country must be ruled by a dictatorship because such a form of government is *in our blood*. A myth we've somehow accepted says that we are conformist and submissive by nature. All those years that she spent at the back of the Vila Indiana, Maria Inês Lancaster was researching and writing a book that carefully documents dozens of popular uprisings throughout Brazilian history in order to prove that this myth is a lie - that it was, in fact, fostered by our various dictatorships in order to keep us down. In short, we are not submissive, and our people have fought many times to be free. In a way, the little old lady with the white gloves was the only true revolutionary I ever met. I'll send you a copy of her book if it would interest you.

When I typed Maria Silveira Brouwer's name into my computer, I discovered that she'd had a novel published by a small feminist press in 1990. It's called, *Too Late for Tears*, and I read it as soon as I could get my hands on a copy. It's an autobiographical novel about a naive but well-intentioned revolutionary girl who falls madly in love with a young genetics student (after breaking up with a physically attractive but dimwitted history major - me!). To her great surprise and disgust, she discovers that her new lover is cheating on her with a man. She denounces him right away to the police as a homosexual and communist sympathizer. He is arrested and hung up by his feet

Richard C. Zimler

in an old sugar refinery outside Santos and killed.

The surprising thing about the novel is that the protagonist defends her actions from a perversely feminist perspective. In a key paragraph, she writes (my translation and condensation): "All acts are highly symbolic... Two men, sleeping together, sucking each other's cocks, were not just betraying a woman but also an entire gender. And if it took the police, that band of professional women-haters to destroy others of their ilk, then that was the remedy required. It was an ironic solution, but a perfect one."

From the characterization of her boyfriend's male lover in the novel, I realized that he was another old friend of ours named Vasco Costa. He had never worked on the newspaper, preferred music to politics, but sometimes came to lunch at the Vila Indiana. Marco Arezzi hadn't liked him because he swished around in pastel-colored clothing and talked too loudly. "In the new society we are constructing," Marco told me one day, "there will be no faggots like Vasco because they are a by-product of Capitalist Imperialist oppression."

After reading Maria Silveira Brouwer's novel, I contacted Vasco. I was able to do so because he'd become a well-known guitarist in the 1970s and 1980s, had even played on several albums recorded by Caetano Veloso and Ney Matogrosso. It was fairly easy finding his address through Veloso's record label, Philips. Once, when I was in Rio, I looked him up. To my surprise, he told me that Toninho - the target of Maria Silveira Brouwer's revenge - hadn't been killed by the police, after all. He'd survived five years in prison, but had his right leg so badly broken that he needed a steel rod put in. He lived in Rome now, had an Italian wife and two kids. He was working as a radio disc jockey. As for the novel itself, Vasco hadn't read it. He said, "I won't allow anyone to hurt me anymore. Even if it's just someone from the distant past. I take each day as it comes and don't expect too much. I don't want to figure it all out. I just want to be happy."

I couldn't find anyone else's name from our group in the computer. But my success gave me the idea of consulting a database on the secret military trials of the Brazilian dictatorship prepared by a former member of the Archdiocese of São Paulo. It took several days of work, but I found out that both Walrus and our group hoodlum, Artur, had been tortured inside a private house on the coast near Iguape and murdered. No real surprise, of course. But

The Pleasant Surface of Things

sad. Against all odds, you hope that people survive.

I did, however, get one big shock; I found out that at the secret trials for both Walrus and Artur, evidence against them was generously provided by none other than our Marxist fuhrer, Marco Arezzi. He'd been an informer for the military, and had spied on both students and professors. Obviously, he didn't turn in everyone he could have, only those he considered really dangerous. As for why he had been beaten up with Artur and taken away, maybe someone had begun to suspect him of being an informer. Maybe the security police needed to reestablish his cover as a vigorous opponent of the government. Probably, the generals in power had more important work for him elsewhere. Anyway, if he hadn't considered me a harmless puppy, I might not be here writing you this letter.

Of course, by then I began wondering what had happened to dear Marco himself. My only clue was that he'd probably be teaching philosophy at some Brazilian university. So I contacted all the philosophy departments. Nothing. Then I went to São Paulo's central library and looked in vain for his name in all the phone books. I even tried to find his parents, but their old apartment was now owned by a family from Natal. Finally, I just gave up. I took Vasco's words as good advice, decided to forget the past as best I could and try to be happy.

Purely by accident, however, I saw Marco Arezzi about a year and a half later, just three months ago, at the São Paulo Film Festival. It was just before the Brazilian debut of 'Howard's End.' He was in the lobby, dressed in a tuxedo and surrounded by others in formal attire. He still had his hair combed straight back with a thick gel of some sort, looked a little paunchy and jaded, like Juan Peron before he died. He was smoking a Gauloise cigarette; I could tell from that characteristic smell. I stood nearby, hidden behind other people. He was speaking English to a tall, pale, sickly looking gentleman. I gathered from the conversation that this was the British Consul General in São Paulo. Marco obviously had friends in high places.

I decided to confront him. As you know, I'm not a courageous person, and my heart was racing. I thought I might faint. I walked directly in front of him. Our eyes met. He didn't recognize me, resumed his conversation with the Consul General.

"I know who you are," I said loudly.

He looked at me and frowned as if I were a beggar - in part, I suppose, because I was wearing faded jeans and a colorful Ecuadorian sweater.

"I know who you are," I repeated.

"You've made a mistake," he told me. "I don't know you."

I took a step toward him, wanted to slap him across the face just as Maria Silveira Brouwer had slapped me. But I simply couldn't do it. I turned instead to the Consul General. As you know, my English is very good. Calmly, pronouncing each word as if it were a link on a steel chain, I said, "This man was responsible for the torture and death of two of my friends. You can't see it, but his tuxedo is covered with blood."

The Englishman lifted his hand as if he were calling a waiter. Suddenly, two men in tuxedos were rushing toward me from opposite sides - bodyguards, maybe even old members of the security police. I turned and ran through the crowd out of the theater.

*

With a little more research, I was able to discover that Marco Arezzi's language skills and work as an informant had served him well; among other diplomatic postings, he had been Cultural Attaché at the Brazilian Embassy in London from 1983 through 1987. I also discovered that he lives today in Rio de Janeiro and works as a consultant for European businesses operating in Brazil. He is quite wealthy and, as far as I can tell, happy. Through Vasco, who knows a lot of people working in Rio for European firms, I was able to get his unlisted phone number. I called him once. I heard his voice, but hung up without speaking. What was there to say other than that I knew what he had done all those years ago?

This all leads me back to your comment about nothing being what it seems in Brazil. True. But given enough information, we can approach the essence of things. That's why research is dangerous to dictatorships - and why it's a personal risk, too; when I found all this out about my old friends, I felt much worse actually then when they were disappearing around me in 1969. I guess because the excitement of those times was missing. And because the illusions had been destroyed once and for all. I began to feel guilty, too, that I'd done so little to help my friends. In consequence, I pretty much stopped sleeping at night and began to neglect my studies. I started roaming the streets during the day, looking at people's faces, wondering what they'd been doing during the time of the dictatorship. Slowly, I began to realize that if I stayed in Brazil I

The Pleasant Surface of Things

would only have three choices: re-invent the past to make myself look good and honorable, like Maria Silveira Brouwer; sit at the back of the Vila Indiana writing for a decade about the need for a democracy which punishes torturers and informants; or plan to kill Marco Arezzi.

I'm probably making myself sound like some character out of a melodramatic tropical opera, but what can I do?

No, Joshua, as you can see, the police weren't after me - just some people from the past.

Anyway, I simply began to feel exhausted, weighed down by memories. Brazil, if you think about it too hard, makes you tired. So I finished my thesis as quickly as I could, defended it successfully and came to Portugal. I realize fully well I'm fleeing, but with my PhD in History, I've been able to get a good job teaching at a private university in Porto. Besides, the weather is cooler here, the contrasts are less jarring, the Portugese like my accent, and I have no urge to penetrate beyond the pleasant surface of things. For now, that is enough.

Katharine Hill

A Share For The Domovoi

It used to take her an age to study all the labels on the shelves. Sometimes there had been exotics, like pineapple; imported shampoos with pictures of ladies whose magenta lips smiled through waves of yellow or orange or jet black hair, but today there was even less than last time, so she had come to stand beside her uncle at the counter. He was holding a red-and-blue thimble of coffee in his huge hand and his whiskers twitched towards the aroma but his eyes, like those of the shopkeeper, were fixed upon the television set above the bar.

A young man in a fur hat and an unidentifiable uniform raised his gun, let off a few rounds, stooped and dashed down a shattered street. Old women with bundles, their heads tied up in shawls and scarves, covered their mouths and turned weeping from the camera's eye or, standing amid the ruins of their homes, threw up their arms in melodramatic despair.

Was it real or make-believe?

More soldiers appeared; thumbs up and a grin for the camera as they marched along beneath their flag. Whose flag? Both sides favoured tricolour stripes, but all the stripes on the black-and-white screen looked the same.

Here was a town, "Ancient and historic..." the reporter said as the church tower melted like a candle, and what was that going up now, a hospital? The university?

"Tch, can't go on much longer, there's little enough left to knock over," said the shopkeeper. "You'd have thought the United Nations would have stepped in before they let this happen."

"My son," said the priest, setting down his cup, "if we had oil instead of plum brandy and goats' cheese, we'd have had some action by now. Well, I must be off. If this weather goes on, it might be some time before I see you again. God be with you."

"And with you, Father - and you, little one."

The horse was standing patiently in the hard-packed snow. Hardly anyone about in the street, although it was market day; a few women, a child or two. No men. No young men at all.

"Where is everyone?" she asked.

Her uncle was busy loading the sledge and did not answer, so she unfastened the nose bag and put it in the back, then her uncle

A Share For The Domovoi

stretched down his hand and swung her up onto the seat beside him.

The shopkeeper stood outside his bright blue store, waving. The sun twinkled through great staves of ice that hung between eaves and ground like a balustrade of glass. The bells on the harness rang in time with the horse's hooves as they trotted along. Trees on either side of the road, weighed down like folded umbrellas beneath their casing of snow, would suddenly release a branch, sending a cascade of sequins floating about them and she felt her heart lift too with the exhilaration of being alive, here and now. It was all too wonderful for the little grey war in the little grey box to matter very much.

Her father and both her brothers had gone off to that war in their stiff, new uniforms more than a year ago, and no word since.

It was a long way home. When she had first gone to the village school, the other children had crowded round her.

"Isn't it lonely, right out there in the forest?" And when she shook her head. "Aren't there wild boar, and bears - and wolves? Aren't you afraid of the wolves?"

She had shaken her head again, because she found the forest far less intimidating than the noisy playground with the wall all around it.

By the time they got back to the priest's house, dusk was already falling. A woman was standing in the yard, exhausted and half frozen. They took her inside, and while the girl brought tea and replenished the stove, the woman, who had walked six miles from the nearest village, explained that her father was dying and feared to let go of life until the priest was there to ease his passing.

"Yes, of course I will come, as soon as you have something hot inside you. We will eat now, and you, little one, will have to stay here and look after mama. Keep the fire going whatever happens and put a lamp in the window so that I can find my way, but if I am not back tonight, don't worry. God bless; now, let's go."

As he stood cloaked in the doorway, so tall and broad, his beard flowing over his breast and the instruments of the blessed sacrament, carefully boxed, in his hands, he looked like one of the stern, brave saints in the holy pictures that were hidden in the wood. Priests were always more handsome than ordinary men, that was how it should be, for who could fear life or death when he was there to guide them?

When the sledge had gone, she carried a tray of bread and soup to her mother's bedside in the corner, and raised her up, spooning liquid into the slack mouth, dipping gobbets of bread in the broth to soften before the poor woman could manage them, wiping up what she slobbered and spilled, crooning persuasively while she did it.

She was rewarded by a vague, milky smile. Pushing the almost empty bowl quite firmly towards her, her mother said,

"Doi, doi."

"Yes, I will. I always do."

"Doi!" Fretful, emphatic.

"Yes, I'll give it to the domovoi. See, here I go."

She scraped their leavings into a chipped crock, opened the door and put them quickly out.

Some creature always took them; bird or beast, she didn't know, but her mother thought the domovoi came for his share of the meal and if he were slighted or ignored, he might make mischief.

*

The girl awoke to find the lamp had gone out. Only the wick in its jar of oil before the family icon glowed, red as a serpent's eye. All was so still that she could hear the flames rustling in the stove and the sound of her mother's breathing.

She swung her toes to the ground as the noise that must have disturbed her came again, jarring up through the soles of her feet as though the earth had moved. Guns, far off. She heard them every night; every night a little closer.

She stole to the window to tend the lamp. Something swooped towards her, she caught the movement from the corner of her eye. A grey bird? No, an animal, lunging over the snow - out of sight now. It must be just outside the door. Although she was terrified, her mind worked automatically. Her uncle's axe hung on the wall within reach. She unhooked it and crouched there, waiting.

A faint scratching and scrabbling, then nothing. From the window, leaning so close that she could see all around - nothing.

She slept with the axe on the chair beside her.

In the morning it had snowed again, the air, softer and warmer when she unbolted the door. The crock was empty.

By nightfall, her uncle had not returned. After lighting the lamp on the sill she made potato cakes and set one aside for the domovoi.

She was in bed when it came. She did not see it but she heard it rattle the plate. The guns went on, intermittently, for hours. They scared her mother, who cried and wet the bed.

The next day was the same; silent, grey. The sheets froze to her fingers as she pinned them out on the line and hung there like cardboard, so she took them in again as the snow began to fall out of

A Share For The Domovoi

the white sky, blowing in gusts across the ranks of the black trees. She spent an hour shovelling the yard clear, and then there was the milch cow, stalled in the byre adjoining the room they lived in, to feed, along with the fowls.

Leaning on her spade to draw breath, she thought - our house is like Noah's ark on a frozen sea and the pines sticking out of the snow are the spars of drowned ships.

Dusk fell quickly after a phantom sunset, its fires banked down low and crimson. The moon rose on a landscape sheathed in ice.

Prodigally, she put out dark bread and the rest of the salt-fish pie they had had for supper, although no-one knew how long their stores would have to last; priests never starved. Then she turned down the lamp and watched, sidelong, from behind the curtains.

Wolf! What else could move so fast across the ground? Shadow moving among shadows, slipping forward, snatching; ragged, famished; blurred by the sparse drift of flakes.

There was no need to clear the path in the morning. The ice held the prints of the domovoi as precisely as sealing wax.

All that day the guns crumped, nearer and nearer, like a herd of huge animals browsing their way inexorably through the forest towards her.

Some distance from the house, the priest before her uncle had built himself a hut, rough but solid, a lair he withdrew to for longer and longer periods as the silence grew over his soul. She had dared herself to go inside once and it repelled her, as though some vestige of his spiritual rigours lingered like stale incense within. It was there that her uncle had hidden the holy icons which he had rescued from the church at the beginning of this war, so that the enemy should not disfigure them or scratch out their terrible eyes.

She had wandered beyond the clearing, her gaze intently searching the path that led to the hut. Now she stood staring up at it. There was a bare patch on the roof where the snow had melted and above it the air was faintly smudged. She sniffed, then she turned and fled back to the house.

That night, while her mother slept, she searched through her brother's things. A patched coat, a scarf, a pair of old boots went out to the domovoi with the heel of a loaf and some black sausage.

*

The men filled the room with their grey uniforms and their clattering boots, their shiny, stubbled faces; red hands tearing bread, starveling

Katharine Hill

mouths champing the slaughtered chickens. They had hauled the cow out into the feather-strewn yard and one of them held the beast's head while another raised the priest's axe. She cried out then, and the young officer who had been circling the house, came back to find out what was going on and stopped them.

Do they live alone here, she and the old woman?

Peasant child of peasant stock, she nods in artless terror.

"My uncle, he went away to a sick friend."

"Who is this? And this?" Family photographs thrust under her nose. "Father? Brothers? Where are they?" Her head jerks.

Can't she speak? Has she lost her tongue? In the army? She nods again. "Ah! Which army?" She shrugs, frowning.

They have found the way to the cellar, wrenching up the trap door beneath the rag rug. One goes down, hooting and laughing as he hands up stored vegetables, pickles and jams, plum brandy - even the cough cure she made to last until spring; tasting and spilling, spitting out horse liniment, gobbling dried fruit, until again the officer stops them when he comes in from the yard. He wears glasses, a sullen crop of pimples crusts his neck and chin; his adam's apple jerks up and down as he speaks in a voice high and husky with a head-cold.

"You have a dog? Then what is this bowl doing outside the door?"

Before she can think she has shaken her head.

"What is this bowl for?" He is holding it accusingly towards her.

She turns to her mother who has been sitting up, watching everything that goes on with a gracious expression, as though she entertained guests. Now she smiles and nods.

"Doi. Doi."

One of the boys - they are only boys, copies her, head wagging.

"Doi doi, what's doi doi, Mrs.?" He guffaws, looking round for approbation.

The child's face flushes, her small, stolid body stiffens. She whispers, "She makes me put it out to feed the domovoi."

Except for the officer, they all roar with laughter. The woman in the bed laughs too. Her daughter looks at the trail of flour trodden into the floorboards.

They explain it to their officer. He is not amused. He puts his face, his gaunt, pimply face, so near the girl's that she has to meet his eyes, magnified by their wire-framed glasses.

"So, tell me, does the domovoi take the food you give him, eh?"

A Share For The Domovoi

Her eyes are round and dark and foolish, gazing hypnotized into his as the men shuffle and snigger. She can smell the stale sweat, the grease and the thawing dampness on their uniforms, can hear them murmuring behind his high-pitched tones "... bully the poor brat ... thinks he's onto the deserter ... long gone or dead by now..."

"Well, does he? Answer me please. Speak up."

"I said, she thinks he does, sir. But really, it's just the wild things. And once - once I saw a wolf."

"So no-one else has been here today?"

"No, sir, not that I know of."

He is smiling now. It is all right, he believed her.

He swallows, mouth tightening.

"All the same, I think we shall see if we can catch your domovoi."

*

The house is silent, only the sighing of the stove. One of the boys lit his cigarette from the icon taper, then drowned the flame in its oil, so the room is dark except for the snow-glimmer seeping through the half-drawn curtains.

The men squat on the floor with their backs to the wall. Their officer sits in the chair, his glasses glinting, cat's eyes in the gloom. The best marksmen are by the door, one standing, one kneeling. They made the girl fill the bowl with hot potatoes and push it out onto the step, the boy nearest the door mouthing "Puss, puss, puss" as she did so.

She sits on the bed with her knees drawn up under her skirt, her hands clenched in her apron. She can see, like a picture, the still oblong framed by the curtains; sky at the top, then forest, then the flat, white expanse of the yard covered in new-fallen snow glittering in the frosty starlight.

Nothing moves.

A shape has detached itself from the mass of the trees. No, her eyes, too wide-stretched for too long, are playing tricks. Someone snuffles and yawns. Her mother gulps on a snore, stirs, and sleeps again.

There is something out there, coming from the direction of the hut. It stops as though to listen, lopes forward a few paces, halts, outline distorted against the dazzling drifts.

The soldier at the window beckons the officer, who goes round to stand beside him, then, as the child hurtles screaming to her feet, he shouts

"Out!"

The door is wrenched open and the red bullets rip across the night. Another cry that is snapped off; a mad, frantic dance, a body turning and turning on itself in a wild agony of black blood and scuffed snow, and they are all out, like the men on the small grey screen that has become reality; running stooped, fanning in tightly disciplined order towards the trees.

When they come back the child has shrunk down under the blankets, only a grubby hand visible, clenched on the cover.

"We'll look again in daylight. He can't get far," they tell one another, unslinging equipment, posting guards while the rest prepare to sleep on the floor. And sleep they do, like shrouded corpses stacked about the room.

*

The priest returned at noon; it had been a slow, hard death. When he saw what the soldiers had done he bent down and raised the girl's face to his. The beard rippled over his black cloak, sleek and curling with melted ice.

"Did they touch you, little one?"

"No, uncle."

"Nor mama?"

"No, uncle. She liked them, she cried when they went away."

"What did they want, eh?"

He was striding away from her across the yard. "What happened here?"

Blood spattered brown on trampled snow, footsteps spreading out and disappearing into the wood. Then he disappeared too.

She stood with her hands thrust into her armpits, waiting.

The horse shied away, stamping and rolling its eyes when he laid the emaciated body down.

"He'd holed up in the thicket, no wonder they didn't find him. Sometimes the cold will make a wound congeal and save a life, but he didn't stand a chance, just look at him. I'm surprised he managed to crawl so far."

Eyes half closed, lips drawn back, stiff in death, the grey wolf lay at her feet. She knelt and stroked his frozen pelt wordlessly, then helped her uncle to unharness the horse and feed and water it while the broth she had made on the chicken carcasses heated.

When she had told him all about the soldiers, he said,

A Share For The Domovoi

"You're a good, brave girl. And you remembered to light the lamp every night?"

She stood there, smiling, short for her age in the baggy jumper and skirt that hid her figure and it was hard to remember that she was sixteen.

"Good girl," he said again, yawning, his head already tilting to one side, spectacles slipping down his nose.

After she had settled her mother for the night and built up the stove, she scraped the remainder of their meal into a bag and set it outside in the crock. Then she closed the door on the night.

She was up and out first in the morning. The sky was grey as lead. Snow gusted against her face, prickling and blinding. As she lifted the crock to carry it indoors she could hear the mutter of the guns below the voice of the wind.

When the slush in the bottom began to melt under the jet of warm water from the kettle, she saw that the bowl was not quite empty. A leaf - no, a scrap of coarse fabric rose to the surface. It was anchored by something that felt hard and smooth.

She went out again, to make quite sure, as she had done for the past few days, that the domovoi's tracks had been obliterated by the fresh fall; slipped the button with its military crest into her pocket and closed the door against the wind.

Nick Pemberton

Truckstop

It was about two thirty in the morning, still fifty kilometres or so from Almeria, when the clown pulled off the coast road at a bar and filling station. I peered out of the caravan window and saw petrol pumps and rows of trucks parked in the darkness.

The clown had asked me to travel in his caravan because he wanted someone to look after Hannah, a Belgian speedfreak who travels with the circus. She gets her drugs from the clown or the cowboy, and in return she does just about anything they want her to. She washes their clothes and twice nightly lets the cowboy shoot cigarettes from her mouth or strap her to a revolving wheel and throw knives at her. What she does for the clown I'm not certain, although I know she spends a couple of hours in his caravan each night after the circus has closed down. The rest of the time she wanders aimlessly around the circus hawking her wares in irritable, machine gun Spanish. If she has none she sits alone, dabbing a tissue at rheumy, bulbous eyes, holding her knees up under her chin, and talking to herself in what I take to be Walloon. She is in the terminal grip of something terrible yet seems not to have noticed. Strangely, she seems to regard the clown and cowboy as the exploited figures in this relationship.

"Why are we stopping," I asked the clown as he opened the door.

"I have to meet someone," he said. "How's Hannah?"

"Asleep," I said. "She was sick earlier."

"How d'you make her do that?" he asked.

"Be sick?" I asked.

"No. Fall asleep," he replied.

"I didn't. She fell and banged her head."

The clown bent to where she was lying on the floor, then got up, beckoned me outside and locked the door of the caravan. With another key on the same bunch he unlocked his petrol cap and began to fill the gas tank. A fat man appeared momentarily in the lighted doorway to the bar. A shout and harsh quack of laughter came from inside. I asked the clown who he was going to meet.

"Ramon," he said, hanging the nozzle back on the pump. Ramon is the cowboy. When he's in the circus ring in his black boots and stetson, he's Billy the Kid. The rest of the time, dealing dope, giving the circus hands a hard time, or, if the clown's not doing it, fucking

Truckstop

Hannah, he's plain Ramon.

As I walked with the clown along a row of trucks towards the light of the bar I saw Ramon's caravanette parked between two of them. A Michelin man loomed out at us from a chrome bumper in the shadows.

The bar's harsh, bright interior was crowded with rowdy drivers. Posters of women, trucks, and soccer teams covered the walls. Hams hung on hooks above. On a TV screen high up in a corner sex from a satellite flickered silent and largely ignored. Loud, unfettered conversation frequently broke down into laughter. The clown asked me what I wanted. I asked for a coffee and a brandy. The clown shouted the order down to the fatman who was pulling levers amongst the hissing steam of the espresso machine. The fatman set down glasses and cups, made a chalk mark on the edge of the bar, and then, with a blade curved and worn thin through use, began to slice one of the hams.

"You're going to end up like Hannah, Norman," said the clown. The fat man banged down a saucer of olives, some ham and bread on a plate, then chalked on the bar again.

"There are worse ways to be," I said. "She was telling me she wants to go home. Are you going to let her?"

The clown shrugged. "It's nothing to do with me," he said. "Hannah is a free agent. She can do as she likes. Just like you."

The clown took out a pocketknife and cut bread and meat into pieces. He picked up a piece of each between thumb and knifeblade and ate. He gestured that I should eat too. I tipped the rest of the brandy into my coffee cup and chewed a few olives, putting the stones back in the saucer. The clown frowned and spat an olive stone amongst the sugar wrappers, cigarette stubs, and shellfish heads at his feet.

"Oyga, Roberto! Acqui! Venga!" shouted a voice. The fat man was beckoning the clown to join him at the far end of the bar. He was leaning talking to a man in a black t-shirt. With him was Ramon. The clown told me he'd be back in a minute and walked down the length of the bar toward them. I watched them talk together and then the clown handed them his keys. Ramon and the man in the t-shirt went out together.

"What was that all about?" I asked the clown when he had crossed back across the bar.

"Is that any of your business?" he asked.

"Look, Roberto..."

"How d'you know my name is Roberto, Norman?" he asked me.

"How d'you know my name's Norman?" I asked back.

"I have heard people talking. Is it your given or your family name."

"Both," I said.

"Norman Norman. Perhaps your father thinks you might forget your name. So he names you twice," said the clown.

"Actually, he's dead," I said.

"Who?" asked the clown.

"My father."

"Do you remember him?" His question surprised me. Suddenly, an argument flared halfway down the bar. The fat man began shouting at both parties involved and banged what looked like a broom handle down on the bar top. There was a sudden silence, then laughter.

"It's good to remember," the clown said, ordering two brandies and turning his attention back to me. "This is how I keep my parents alive. I talk to them still. People say it is best to forget but they are wrong. Forgetting is dying. Forgotten things are dead things. People, skills, crafts, languages. They are alive because people remember them."

He stopped and looked at me then shrugged, as if he had spoken out of turn.

"No," I said. "Go on."

"Look," he said and his voice had a kind of weary urgency to it, as if he were trying to convince someone, maybe himself, maybe me, that what he was saying was true, "the past is only what we remember. But however we put our memories together we can never make the past come back. It is a kind of lying. Do you understand?" His words had lost me. For a moment we both stood at the bar in silence. Then he said, "Once, when I was young, my father gave me a puzzle. A polished block of wood, a cube made up of many smaller, different shaped pieces, each a different kind of wood. The puzzle was to put the pieces back in their original shape after they had been taken apart. My father took them apart and held a piece of paper in his hand. On it was..." He paused, looking for the word he wanted, muttering to himself. "The words that explain what you must do," he said.

"The solution."

Truckstop

"Yes, the solution," he said. The clown knocked back what was left in his glass. "He waved this paper at me. He said I could make a thousand different shapes with the pieces but without the paper I would never be able to put things back as they were before. But I took the pieces and it was as if a spirit was making my hands move. Without a mistake I assembled the pieces until the six sides were square once more."

"What did your father do?" I asked him.

"He was a circus clown - like me," said the clown.

"I mean what did he do when you solved his puzzle?"

"He took it from me and burnt it. It had taken him months to make," said the clown, grinning at the memory. "Now, tell me, what is it you do all day?" I looked at him blankly. "All the time now, you are writing," he said. "First in the circus whilst it is disappearing all around you. Then in the Bar Hollywood and the caravan you are doing the same. What is it that you are setting down that makes your face so serious? Is it a diary? A story? Or perhaps a..." Once again he fished for the word he wanted. He seemed to be getting a bit drunk. "The thing that says what is to be done after you die."

"A will," I said and looked at him. His smile was as bland and newly minted as ever.

"What have you been writing?" he asked me again.

"I don't know," I said after a long pause; I had to think about it. He continued to stare, expecting more. "A journal, I suppose. A kind of diary."

For some reason this seemed to put him into a good humour. He laughed and told me that he had once kept a diary. "It was when I was a child," he said, "and when my father was still a clown. Each day I would write, but always, when I read what I had written, though it was true, it seemed like pretending. It was not what I wanted to say. It was always about the outside of things and not how they are. So I began to tell lies about things. Small lies at first; about the people I loved and the people I hated. And in those days I did hate people. You see, my mother was having an affair with a conjuror. Whilst my father was in the circus ring he would come to our caravan. My mother would send me out. I would lie beneath the caravan and listen to them - laughing, fucking, fooling around - and I would write in my diary. Does this surprise you?"

I shook my head. His sudden intimacy convinced me he was

drunk. I watched him pause and light a cigarette.

"I was a king of a secret kingdom. Some of the subjects of this kingdom I would punish. Humiliation after humiliation I piled upon them. When I became bored with this I would kill them. Their cars would crash from high cliffs, poisonous spiders would fall into their snoring mouths. Those that I loved I would reward - yachts, fast cars, aeroplanes, diamonds, servants, fine clothes. Everything a nine year-old finds sophisticated I gave to them, for I was still young and foolish enough to find sophistication an admirable quality."

The clown was laughing as he told me this. Now he stopped and pressed the palms of his hands to his eyes then ran them backwards through his hair, his nails scratching at his scalp. The gesture surprised me. His eyes were unfocused, as if seeking something lost or forgotten, something hidden in the words he had been speaking.

"You were playing at being God," I said to him.

This seemed to restore his high spirits. He gave a hoot of good humoured laughter before speaking again.

"No, no, Norman; I told you. I was only nine years old. My diary was like a cave painting." I looked at him blankly. "When they were going out hunting," he said by way of explanation. I continued to look blank. "Hunters painted pictures of the beasts they hoped to catch on the walls of their caves. I wrote down things in my diary to make them happen."

"Did it work?" I asked him.

"Did what work?" he asked me.

"What you wrote in your diary. Did it ever come true?"

"Sometimes. On my father's birthday the conjuror was killed in a hotel fire. I had already written this."

"You must have felt terrible," I said.

"Not really," he said. "It happened thirty years later. In Melbourne. His brother wrote and told me. My mother and father were already dead."

"Why would he do that?" I asked.

"Why would who do what?" he replied.

"The conjuror's brother. Why would he write to you to say his brother had died."

"Because for a while the conjuror was my stepfather," said the clown. He seemed on the verge of tears, weighed down by the burden of memory. He turned and looked out of the door. Then suddenly and briskly he said, "I am sorry, Norman. I was forgetting myself. If I am not in Almeria in time for the show tomorrow, Circus Luxemburg will get a new clown. We must go."

He called towards the fat man who began to examine the last half hour's accumulation of chalk marks on the bar. The clown added it up for him and paid for the drinks and the petrol. Then we went back outside. Ramon was standing beside the clown's Studebaker counting some money. The man in the black t-shirt was with him. As we approached, he left. Ramon gave Roberto some of the money and clown and cowboy talked quietly together. I looked inside the caravan. Hannah was sitting up now. Her face was wet and she had a bruise over an eye. She shrugged when she saw me then looked away. I understood now why the clown had stopped there.

CONTRIBUTORS

FIRST PUBLISHED STORY

Richard Beard born in 1967 is doing the East Anglia Writing MA and was formerly private secretary to the Duchess of Argyll. He has published in French as Marcel Barbon. **Susan Davis** lives in Shropshire and is 43. **Katharine Hill** born 1935 published a novel called *Ladies' Chain* in 1987 and lives in Dorset. **Frederick Lightfoot** worked on *Panurge* in the mid eighties. Born 1960 he teaches drama at West Cumbria College. **Mary Maher** is a Devon writer with three poetry collections published. **Nick Pemberton** is 48 and lives in Westmoreland. A comic strip specialist he has also stripped furniture and worked in a circus. **Jen Waldo** is an American from Aberdeen who won the 1993 story competition in *The European*.

OTHERS

Jack Debney teaches in Germany and has had stories in *Passport* and *Panurge*. **Freeda Fitzgerald** is a Co. Kildare writer whose stories have been in the *Irish Press* and on RTE. She has had multiple sclerosis since 1971 and has just finished a self-help book about the same condition. **John Gower** has had stories in *Stand* and *Panurge*. He is 42 and lives in London. **Paul Lenehan** is a Dublin writer who won first prize in the 1993 Sunk Island story competition. **Dick McBride** lives in Herefordshire and had a story in the last *Panurge*. **T.M. Merremont** lives in San Francisco and has been in *Lost Creek Letters*. **Alfred Nadin** is 46, from Todmorden, and has had fiction in *Critical Quarterly, London Magazine* and *Panurge*. **Kathy Page** lives in London. Her novels and stories are published by Methuen and she has done numerous residencies. Her first published story was printed in *Panurge*. **Dorothy Schwarz** is an Essex writer born 1937. Her stories have been in *Iron* and *Tees Valley Writer*. **Peter Slater** is a London teacher born 1956. He has a collection scheduled to appear with Iron Press. **Jonathan Steffen** teaches at Heidelberg University and has had stories in *P.E.N.* and *Firebird* anthologies, *London Magazine* and elsewhere. **Edward E. Stonelight** is in his fifties, lives in California and has had work in many small press magazines. He has been in and out of Vietnam, Iran and Los Angeles. **Philip Wolmuth** was working in the West Indies last year. **Richard C. Zimler** won First Prize in last year's Panurge Story Competition. He lives and works in Portugal.